RELIGION AND RACE

Religion & Race

SOUTHERN PRESBYTERIANS, 1946–1983

JOEL L. ALVIS, Jr.

The University of Alabama Press
Tuscaloosa & London

The paper on which this book is printed meets the minimum requirements
of American National Standard for Information Science-Permanence of
Paper for Printed Library Materials, ANSI Z39.48-1984.

Library of Congress Cataloging-in-Publication Data

Alvis, Joel L.
Religion and race : Southern Presbyterians,
1946–1983 / Joel L. Alvis, Jr.
p.   cm.
Includes bibliographical references and index.
ISBN 0-8173-0701-X (alk. paper)
1. Presbyterian Church in the U.S.—History—20th century.
2. Race relations—Religious aspects—Presbyterian
Church in the U.S.   3. Southern States—Race relations.
4. Southern States—Church history.   5. Presbyterian
Church—Southern States—History—20th century.   I. Title.
BX8962.A685   1994
285'.133—dc20
93-23923

British Library Cataloguing-in-Publication Data available

CONTENTS

ILLUSTRATIONS AND TABLES

PREFACE

The PRESENT book is an institutional history. It explores how one institution, the Presbyterian Church in the United States (PCUS), shaped and was shaped by its culture. It explores the denomination's own culture as it struggled to determine what role racial issues would have in the definition of being a Presbyterian.

This book should not be read as a chronicle of the black experience within Presbyterianism. There are others more capable of telling that story. Nor is it only an account of civil rights activity by a group of white religious liberals. Rather, this is an account of how one denomination bounded by its tradition and geography and controlled by white men moved from paternalism toward a more inclusive posture. The journey was not fully completed, but significant events occurred along the way. I hope this work is a legacy for the present, not a polemic from the past. This is not the full story of race relations in the Presbyterian denominations nor among Southerners, black and white. But it is a part of that story that deserves to be heard.

I would like to thank Michelle Francis of the Presbyterian Church (U.S.A.) Department of History, Montreat, North Carolina; William Peterson, executive director of the Mountain Retreat Association; the session of the First Presbyterian Church in Auburn, Alabama; the Southern Historical Collection, Library of the University of North Carolina; and the Library and Archives of the Martin Luther King, Jr., Center for Non-Violent Social Change for the use of records in their organizations and/or collections.

I must express my thanks to Margaret Calhoun, who has permitted the photograph of Martin Luther King, Jr., to be used. She has provided welcomed encouragement and support.

Other individuals have also encouraged and shepherded me along my journey. Special thanks are due to my colleagues from 1982 to 1986 at the Historical Foundation of the Presbyterian and Reformed Churches in Montreat, North Carolina, now a component of the Presbyterian Church (U.S.A.) Department of History. These included the late Jerrold

Lee Brooks, Ruth D. See, Mary G. Lane, Jane P. Britton, William Bynum, and John M. Walker III.

I owe a deep debt to Wayne Flynt of Auburn University. Not only did he direct the initial research and writing of this project, but while I was an undergraduate at Samford University he was a source of encouragement and support.

John M. Mulder read a draft of the manuscript and encouraged me to continue and also offered a useful critique.

Vicki Welch Alvis has supported me at every stage of this work, even during a time of vocational redirection and family changes. Without her love and the support of Joe and Martha Jean Alvis, the study would never have started.

A special thanks goes to Malcolm MacDonald, director of The University of Alabama Press, and his staff. His persistent correspondence brought faithful reminders of the task yet remaining.

Finally, I want to thank those who allowed me to share a part of their stories and to have the privilege of coming to know them. Some I know only through their records, writings, and correspondence. Others I have been privileged to meet. A few have given me the honor of their friendship. In particular, I wish to honor the memory and give thanks for the ministries of Robert H. Walkup and Malcolm Calhoun. Each in his own way and place was a model of integrity and faithfulness in ministry.

Joel L. Alvis, Jr.
St. Pauls, North Carolina

RELIGION AND RACE

I

"AN AGONY" FOR THE PRESBYTERIAN CHURCH, U.S.

THE COMMITTEE on Thanks always offered sincere but predictable resolutions of appreciation to the hosts of the General Assemblies. It was never a source of controversy. Things changed, however, in 1942. At this General Assembly of the Presbyterian Church in the United States, sometimes called the Southern Presbyterian Church, meeting in Montreat, North Carolina, William Bouchelion of Central Louisiana Presbytery was appointed to chair the committee. The appointment of Bouchelion was significant, for he was the first black to chair a General Assembly committee. Although this committee had only a perfunctory task to perform, some members thought that Bouchelion's race made it inappropriate for him to present the report to the gathering. In his place, the stated clerk of the assembly read the report. The black commissioners protested by boycotting the final meeting of the assembly when the thank yous were said, but their absence was noticed only in retrospect.[1] Such was the situation for Presbyterians of African descent who remained communicants in the predominantly white Presbyterian Church in the United States (PCUS).

The segregated order of which this incident is indicative developed over many years. Race relations were seriously affected by the transformation of black Americans from slaves to freedmen. The religious order of the Southern United States as well as the political, social, and economic structures were profoundly affected by this transformation. Segregation developed to counteract some of these changes. Blacks were denied the civil rights to which their new status supposedly entitled them. American churches cooperated with the segregated system—indeed they contributed to its rationalization. Different segments of the Christian community, however, have always been able to view the same issue from several perspectives simultaneously, and periods of crisis and transition tend to emphasize and exacerbate these

I

differences.[2] The era of the civil rights movement in post–World War II America was such a period.

The PCUS, known also for its geographic identity as the Southern Presbyterian Church, was peculiarly susceptible to such internal conflicts in the 1950s and 1960s as it struggled to understand the "bounds of its habitation." St. Paul's sermon in Athens recorded in Acts 17 contains only one of several texts used to justify segregation: "And [God] hath made of one blood all nations of men for to dwell on all the face of the earth, and hath determined the times before appointed, and the bounds of their habitation; That they should seek the Lord, if haply they might feel after him, and find him, though he be not far from every one of us" (Acts 17:26–27 KJV).

This proof text is suggestive for the current task. The PCUS had to face a peculiar set of relationships dealing with racial attitudes and actions. These "boundaries" are the history, polity, and theology of the denomination, the racial history of the South as it emerged in the era of the civil rights movement, and the changes that transformed the South and the nation after World War II.

Presbyterian church government is predicated on a system of church court connections. These connections allow for the flow of action and information from the local court, the session, to the highest court, the General Assembly. Ministers of churches and representatives of the sessions, called elders, compose the presbytery. Three or more presbyteries unite to form a synod. The General Assembly is the only court above the various synods. Each court has its own grounds of original jurisdiction, but the actions of a lower court may be passed to a higher court for review and control, reference, appeal, or complaint. Church court jurisdictions cannot impinge on civil jurisdictions, nor can they bind the conscience of a member. The General Assembly and each synod are required to meet at least in regular annual session, but the presbyteries and sessions must meet at least quarterly. Each court has two officers—a moderator and a clerk. The moderator of the session is the minister; those of the other courts may be clergy or laity and are elected for specific terms, as are the clerks. The moderator is responsible for the manner in which the court conducts its business and rules on parliamentary procedures. The rulings may be appealed and overruled by the court.[3] This system has remained essentially the same since the first General Assembly in 1789. Understanding the relations of church courts is critical to gaining an appropriate understanding of Presbyterians and their dealing with race as an issue of church polity and ideology.

Presbyterians experienced both theological and sectional schism in the antebellum period. Theological schism racked the Presbyterian Church in the United States of America in 1837 with the Old School–New School controversy. This debate centered on the New School's advocacy of revivalistic practices and cooperative efforts with Congregationalists. Sectional schism affected the Baptists and Methodists in 1845–46, but sectionalism was not as significant an issue for the Presbyterian division in 1837. Both of the Presbyterian denominations retained the same name—the Presbyterian Church in the U.S.A.—causing some confusion, but most Presbyterians in the South remained in the Old School, opposing New School revivalism and Congregationalist cooperation. Yet some pockets of New School adherents persisted in the South past the Civil War. Sectional schism came to the New School in 1857 and to the Old School in 1861. It is from this latter group that the Southern Presbyterian Church emerged. The schism resulted from debate over whether or not the Old School General Assembly would support the Union, and this led to the formation of the Presbyterian Church in the United States.[4] The PCUS was not the only Presbyterian denomination in the region, but it was the largest and the one whose origins and history were most intimately identified with the sectional conflict.

One of the notable aspects of Old School Calvinism above and below the Mason-Dixon line was its dependence on Scottish common-sense realism. "Realism was not so much a set of conclusions," Brooks Holifield has written, "as it was a way of thinking that would commend itself to a variety of thinkers."[5] Indeed, many nineteenth-century Americans were influenced by this approach.

This philosophical method developed in the eighteenth century in response to the writings of John Locke and especially David Hume. Bishop George Berkeley also developed this philosophy, giving it a religious form. Together, such thinkers took an empirical approach to understanding human experience that many have called skepticism. Human knowledge may be gained only through sensory data, which cannot be uniform. Such a conclusion raises questions of the reliability, and even the reality, of human experience.

Thomas Reid of Glasgow in the eighteenth century, followed by

Dugald Stewart in the early nineteenth century, confronted the skeptics, making critiques of their views with questions of the validity common to human experience (hence the name "common sense"). Stewart elaborated on Reid's work and introduced the inductive scientific method of Francis Bacon. Later, in the mid-nineteenth century, Sir William Hamilton of Edinburgh synthesized this work with Kantian philosophy, which led to his statement, "A learned ignorance is ... the end of philosophy, as it is the beginning of theology."[6]

Scottish commonsense realism migrated to the North American continent with John Witherspoon, president of the College of New Jersey (later Princeton University) and a signer of the Declaration of Independence. Through Witherspoon's teaching and influence this approach to knowledge spread throughout the colonies and new nation. Commonsense realism was the dominant method in the 1800s at Harvard, Yale, and Andover seminaries, despite the rather disparate views of Harvard's Unitarianism, Nathaniel William Taylor's effort to maintain the covenant, and Andover's more traditional orthodoxy. Later in the century Charles Hodge of Princeton based his systematic theology, often referred to as "the Princeton theology," on commonsense assumptions.[7]

Southerners of several denominations warmed to commonsense realism. Nowhere was it more fully integrated, however, than in the writings of antebellum Southern Presbyterians such as Robert J. Breckenridge of Kentucky, Robert Lewis Dabney of Virginia, and especially James Henley Thornwell of South Carolina.

God could be experienced in nature, and that experience could be relied on as true. Yet Old School Calvinism also was concerned with the proper relationship of humankind and God. Experience could not answer all questions about the classic Protestant doctrine of "justification by faith"—only revelation could do that.[8] For Thornwell and others, the Bible provided the revelation of God's word. In it were to be found the answers that the empirical data acquired by the senses could not supply. Since the biblical data could be trusted as true and valid, the authority of Scripture became a linchpin of this orthodoxy.[9]

The PCUS came to be marked by its own distinctive doctrine, the "spirituality of the church," in measure due to the commitment to this theological tradition. As much of Southern history was marked by the controversies over slavery, so too was the church. Southern Presbyterian ministers led in the defense of slavery. From this defense a sensitivity to social criticism arose and with it a doctrine as peculiar to post–Civil War Southern Presbyterianism as the defense of slavery was peculiar to antebellum Presbyterianism in the South.

In the wake of defeat as a nation and as a church, Southern Presbyterians needed to have their theology gauge the new realities. The division between Old School and New School groups was healed in the North in 1869. By that time defense of the Union and disparagement of the Confederacy had become so intense that numerous Presbyterians in border states were expelled and joined the PCUS. This development added to the intense animosity between the Presbyterian denominations.

Given this deep feeling, the spirituality of the church came to be a primary defense of the PCUS in every aspect of its operation. Simply put, this doctrine affirmed a dualism between affairs of the world and affairs of the spirit. A Christian could engage in contemporary events as a citizen informed by Christian convictions, but the church could not act solely on the grounds of being a group of Christians. This distinction came to be a fine point, and much if not all of the denomination's history can be written in reference to it.[10]

Policy decisions in the denomination were made by the church courts, but each court had a supporting system of committees (agencies or divisions) that helped implement the policies. The PCUS General Assembly was initially organized with executive committees. This system existed with four major executive committees and a variety of other committees until 1947, when boards were introduced. Divisions then became the operating subunits of the boards. For example, the Executive Committee on Home Missions became the Board of Church Extension, and the Committee on Negro Work became a division of the board. Another major reorganization took place in 1972. At that time the Board of National Ministries (a name adopted for the Board of Church Extension in 1967) became a division of the new General Executive Board (later known as the General Assembly Mission Board).[11] Middle and lower courts did not have similar bureaucracies but usually had a committee structure with corresponding areas of concern and interest.

As the PCUS modified its church government, the other dominant Southern Protestant denominations moved to expand their geographic limits. The Southern Baptist Convention expanded to become a national denomination, and the Methodist Church reunited. Assisted by population migration, the Baptists adopted other areas of the nation for home mission work. The Methodist Episcopal Church, South, reunited with its Northern counterpart in 1939. The PCUS did not merge with the "Northern" Presbyterian Church until 1983, after several previous efforts to do so. Thus at the time when the civil rights of black Americans became a major political and ideological issue, the PCUS was the only major religious body that retained its approximate Civil War boundaries. No other major denomination could claim such regional identity.[12]

Southern whites, who composed 98 percent of the PCUS membership, were ambivalent about the plight of black Presbyterians, and this attitude arose in large part from simple indifference. Some tried to establish a separate black Presbyterian Church, but those efforts failed. Black Presbyterians were eventually included in a segregated system of church government. This black remnant perplexed church leaders and formed yet another boundary.

Despite its lack of a national constituency, the PCUS struggled to become part of mainline Protestantism. This trend was countered at numerous junctures by strong opposition that thwarted these efforts in the 1930s. The struggle between larger ecumenical commitments and regional identity was present throughout most of the twentieth century. Being part of the region, however, did not mean that Presbyterians were always identified with the stereotype of poverty. Southern Presbyterians were noted for their collective wealth and privilege and for the power these benefits provided.[13]

Within the PCUS there remained a small group of black Presbyterians. What was the role of these Christians in their denomination? What was their relationship to others of their own race? Gayraud Wilmore has identified divergent desires of black Presbyterians throughout this century. "The prevailing attitude among black members of the Presbyterian Church toward this predominantly white, middle class denomination has been deep and persistent ambivalence." The "desire for African-American cultural identity" was placed over against "a desire for racial integration as an indispensable characteristic of any church that is truly Christian and visibly united."[14] One aspect to note in the development of these events is the playing out of ambivalent feelings and desires by both black and white Presbyterians.

Southern Presbyterian action and ideas toward the civil rights movement traced back to the years before the Civil War. Black slaves were introduced to and frequently adopted Christianity in the antebellum period. Although the races were segregated in worship services, they attended the same churches and listened to the same ministers. After the Civil War, organized religion had to deal with a new set of race relations. Some whites wished to keep relationships as they had been before the war, with former slaves sitting in the galleries. Freedmen thought differently and left their former masters' churches in large numbers. One motivation for this exodus was the desire to develop black institutions and leadership, which in fact happened. But further examination reveals that many whites encouraged this exodus because of racial prejudice. Virtually all black Baptists and Methodists left churches controlled by Southern whites. Presbyterians, Episcopalians, and Lutherans retained a remnant of black communicants but did not allow them to hold significant leadership positions. Black and white church contacts became less frequent, and relationships were established through ministers, representatives of institutions seeking funds, and white curiosity seekers attending black church services.[15]

By the 1890s segregation was not only a fact of church life, it was the law as well. The Mississippi Constitutional Convention of 1890 was the first in a series of such conventions that swept through the South and legally disfranchised blacks. Once segregation was legal, state and local legislative bodies wasted no time enacting further restrictions. In the 1910s the *Progressive Farmer* even called for segregated landholdings. Faced with many unpleasant realities, large numbers of blacks began a great migration from the South during World War I. Times were hard for blacks, and "Judge Lynch's" frequent administration of justice was swift and undeliberative.[16]

The movement for interracial goodwill began amid these conditions. Initially its concerns were both progressive and paternalistic. Several regional organizations such as the Southern Sociological Congress and the Young Men's Christian Association organized local chapters. Other groups such as the Commission on Interracial Cooperation (CIC) and the Association of Southern Women for the Prevention of Lynching (ASWPL) were organized. Several of these groups received support from the National Association for the Advancement of Colored People (NAACP) for their opposition to lynching and the Ku Klux Klan.[17]

The CIC was formed in Atlanta in 1919 with a Presbyterian layman, John Eagan, as its first president. Rather than attacking segregation, the CIC worked to improve public facilities, promote favorable publicity for blacks, and oppose lynching. The PCUS and the Methodist Episcopal Church, South, officially endorsed the cause of interracial cooperation in 1921 and 1922. Women of these two denominations and others took especially active roles in the CIC. The Federal Council of Churches (FCC), a group of Protestant denominations organized in 1908, began Race Relations Sunday in 1922. The day was intended to foster better race relations through pulpit exchanges and interracial worship events. Although mass participation was never achieved, it remained a symbolic effort for the betterment of race relations.[18]

Claims for interracial work before World War II should not be exaggerated, but neither should they be ignored. Such efforts involved many church people and crossed denominational lines. Churches were concerned not with the issue of segregation but with the education and evangelization of blacks. Although the interracial meetings were contrived to defy segregation laws, the groups tried to separate legal and social equality, which failed to satisfy the spirit of interracial work.[19]

World War II and its aftermath brought heightened awareness of racial problems. The appearance of Gunnar Myrdal's *American Dilemma* represented a major attack on the system of segregation at the time that Hitler's talk about a master race was easily linked to American white supremacy. Denominations felt a need to respond. After the conflict, pressure for racial change did not abate, and Communists began using segregation in propaganda against America around the world. The United Nations received representatives from more and more new nations, many populated by dark-skinned peoples. Racial injustice was a foreign policy problem for the U.S. State Department and an ethical problem for American missionaries.[20]

Numerous changes took place in Southern life after 1945. Urbanization increased at a substantial rate, and racial ideology was well entrenched. The *Brown v. Board of Education* decision in 1954 is frequently used to mark the beginnings of the civil rights movement. This case was several years in the making, and discontent had been building for a considerable period of time prior to the decision. There were numerous points of conflict between white and black communities, including education and public transportation. Blacks were frequently treated rudely by bus drivers, who sometimes drove off before all riders were seated or even before all riders had boarded. Discontent in Baton Rouge, Louisiana, flared into a bus boycott during June 1953.

The boycott was successful, as numerous demands were met by the city authorities. The *Brown* decision, however, served as a catalyst for white reaction. After an initial period of disbelief, whites mobilized a massive resistance. Gradually the South was overwhelmed with court orders, executive orders, and the pronouncements of labor unions, churches, educators, and businessmen, as well as civil rights groups. Potential areas of conflict over segregation were everywhere.[21]

The civil rights movement in the 1950s and 1960s was dominated by the philosophy of nonviolence. Martin Luther King, Jr., was the major exponent of this philosophy, which also attracted some Southern whites. Others, perhaps most, were confused by the expressions of patience and submission which the movement used to confront the authorities who administered segregation. This confusion resulted in numerous cases of violence, such as the murder of three civil rights workers in Neshoba County, Mississippi, as they participated in the Freedom Summer Project of 1964.[22]

A fundamental shift developed in the movement's emphasis during the mid-1960s. The struggle against segregation and inequality began to have ramifications on both sides of the Mason-Dixon line. Large black populations in the urban areas of the West and North became restive. White paternalism came under fire from within the movement as the nation was reminded that racial discontent was not exclusively a Southern phenomenon.[23]

Significant changes in opinion began to occur among Southern whites, particularly in regard to federal legislation guaranteeing civil rights. In 1964 several leading Southern urban newspapers endorsed such legislation. Just as white opinions began to support measures such as the Civil Rights Act of 1964, Martin Luther King, Jr., and others began advocating policies and programs that highlighted the economic relationship between the races. After the 1965 Selma march King spoke of the need for other marches to bring attention to and mobilize action against poverty, segregated school systems, and race-baiting politicians.[24]

The movement's leadership was also changing from those rooted in the church to those who questioned or even rejected the Christian faith. The church was an important training ground for leaders. Black church leadership was frequently coterminous with local NAACP chapter leadership. Black church services allowed the release of "social emotions" across denominational and geographic lines. Yet King and others recognized that a "New Negro," one who had rejected Christianity, frequently because of its practice by whites, was participating in civil rights activities. These people and their concerns had to be accommodated by the movement.[25]

The civil rights movement did not occur in a vacuum, as many changes were affecting society as well as religion. Scholars have often used World War II as the demarcation line in describing these events and trends. Robert Wuthnow in *The Restructuring of American Religion* maintains that during this period a fissure was growing in American religion. There were many fault lines, but surely one of the most important was the division between conservatives and liberals in the churches. This occurred within the mainline churches as they began to take part in civil rights activities. One of the results was to highlight the differences between those who believed that actions flowed from faith and those who favored a faith beginning with action. It is a gross oversimplification to say that this was the crux of a split between the pulpit and the pew. Clergy participation in various civil rights activities, however, did highlight the conflict. Other factors, such as the antiwar movement and the new religious movements, also challenged the foundation of American religion in the 1960s.[26] In the South, where race had been so entwined in the fabric of life, many people and churches saw the fabric of society being cut apart and resewn in unfamiliar patterns.

Local interdenominational efforts to improve race relations and meet the civil rights movement developed along with those of regional and national agencies. The "long, hot summer" of 1964 was a period of significant interracial violence in Mississippi. A group of ministers, Christian and Jewish, banded together in response to the bombings of black churches throughout the state. The Mississippi Committee of Concern sought contributions to provide an assistance fund for rebuilding churches. These acts of benevolence happened in a milieu of racial crisis.[27]

This local effort was fundamentally different from those at the national level such as the work of the National Council of Churches (NCC). The NCC was formed in 1950 when several ecumenical agencies, chief among them the Federal Council of Churches, merged. The NCC continued to advocate better race relations as its predecessors had earlier. In the 1950s it frequently urged its constituent members to abolish the practice of segregation.[28] The concerns of the NCC were translated to political activism in the 1960s after many years of merely passing resolutions on racial issues.

Several reasons account for the transformation. A number of penetrating studies of American religion appeared during the early 1960s, including Peter Berger's *Noise of Solemn Assemblies* and Martin Marty's *New Face of American Religion*. NCC officials were also affected by the civil rights movement. Martin Luther King, Jr.'s *Letter from Birmingham Jail* riveted their attention and demanded a response. The leadership of the NCC acquired a degree of latitude in acting on civil rights issues, as the organization offered services to its members which they frequently could not provide for themselves. This organizational freedom translated into a measure of protection when elements within constituent denominations attacked the ecumenical organization for its involvement in the civil rights movement. Such criticism was quite frequent in the PCUS, which was one of the council's most conservative members. There were frequent requests in the PCUS General Assembly to withdraw from the council, but these were always rebuffed.[29]

The differences between local ecumenical and benevolent groups, such as the Committee of Concern and the NCC, were significant. The local effort was a more traditional response to physical crises and tragedy. The latter involved what some believed was the church crossing the wall of separation of church and state, a position that engendered debate throughout society. Many clergy, like those involved with the NCC, were perceived as racial liberals, and others were likewise characterized, even if they only participated in the more benevolent ecumenical efforts, and such charges transcended denominational bounds. Much of the interracial work noted previously was undertaken at the impetus of clergy and was one of the results of the Social Gospel in the South.[30]

The mainline churches consistently attacked segregation. Their preliminary attack in the 1940s coincided with a number of critical events such as the proposed march on Washington, the appearance of Gunnar Myrdal's *American Dilemma*, and the Truman Commission on Civil Rights. The leadership of most major Protestant denominations supported civil rights legislation. This stance led to trouble and caused tensions when clergy representing denominational offices were refused "Southern hospitality" because their trip to a locality dealt with a civil rights issue.[31]

The effect of ecumenical support of civil rights legislation was considerable. The National Interreligious Conference, which met on April 28, 1964, at Georgetown University, was addressed by President Lyndon B. Johnson. He told the delegates: "It is your job, as men of God, to awaken the conscience of America" on civil rights issues. They did not ignore this task; Senator Richard B. Russell from Georgia, for example, noticed the effectiveness of the religious lobbyists in this effort.[32]

Such rhetoric and organization came into conflict in denominations where the question of civil rights had not been resolved. Differences between pulpit and pew were frequently highlighted in the crucible of the civil rights issues. Generally speaking, clergy had broader contact with individuals who caused them concern about these issues. One study even argued that churches' activities on behalf of civil rights began and ended with clerical involvement.[33]

All churches had to deal with the ethical implications raised by the civil rights movement, but many people within the churches were reluctant to deal with contemporary experiences, preferring to cling to the paternalism of an earlier day.[34] The practice of segregation pricked the conscience of the churches. Concern in white Protestant churches for black Americans had developed over a long period. This concern was not totally independent of others, and many observers believed that this constellation of issues would pose significant challenges to American religion.[35]

As the *Christian Century* observed in 1962, "What is merely a dilemma for the rest of the nation is an agony for the Church."[36] Nowhere was the agony as specific as it was in the PCUS. The boundaries of Southern history seemed to fix white Southerners as white supremacists. Yet the testimony and actions of many within the denomination proved that such an absolute characterization was inadequate. Presbyterians had to encounter their own history, theology, and polity. Along with the sovereignty of God, they had to consider the spirituality of the church. Considering all of the conditions of the time in the Presbyterian Church, U.S. gives us a unique opportunity to explore the "bounds of the PCUS habitation."

2

JIM CROW, JACOB'S LADDER, AND THE NEGRO WORK PROGRAM

BEFORE THE Civil War, Presbyterians were very interested in evangelizing slaves, and several notable divines, such as Charles Colcock Jones, John B. Adger, and John L. Girardeau, worked particularly to that end. Presbyterian efforts, however, were not as successful as those of Baptists and Methodists.[1] Despite their efforts, Presbyterians after the Civil War were unable and unwilling to allow blacks anything more than nominal ecclesiastical self-government. This desire to exercise control over black Presbyterian church life was a part of the basic racial prejudice pervading all Southern denominations.[2]

Racial prejudice and the refusal to accommodate black leadership frustrated the attempts of the PCUS to maintain freedmen as communicants. In 1869 the General Assembly adopted a measure that anticipated the establishment of a separate black denomination. In the interim, however, black ministers were allowed to hold membership in white presbyteries. This seemed rather inconsequential at the time, as the total number of affected ministers was very small. The status quo of de facto segregation was not challenged until 1881, when a minister was asked to cast his vote on a critical issue before Memphis Presbytery. He had never before been asked to vote (and had not voted) on any issue, and the exercise of his ecclesiastical franchise was appealed to the synod and ultimately to the General Assembly. There it was decided that the 1869 action, in its amended form, allowed all ministers, regardless of race, *all* the privileges and responsibilities of the office.[3]

Presbyterians have always required an educated ministry, and this was a primary concern when white Presbyterians contemplated the evangelization of the freedmen. Charles A. Stillman, pastor of the Presbyterian Church in Tuscaloosa, Alabama, was the first minister to express interest in such work. He succeeded in having the 1874

General Assembly approve the establishment of "an institute for the training of a colored ministry." He served as superintendent of the institute that the PCUS established, working with one or two other instructors while he remained pastor of the Tuscaloosa church. The institute was planned as a two-year school and was expanded to a four-year curriculum in 1884. Enrollment that year reached thirty-one, the highest before 1900. Stillman remained superintendent until 1893, but during the 1920s the school, which by that time had come to bear the founder's name, reverted to a two-year training institute.[4]

Concurrently, a number of independent presbyteries were established for black ministers and churches in the 1870s and 1880s. The Presbytery of North and South Carolina, the first of these, was formed in 1876. Four others followed: Texas (1888), Central Alabama (1890), Ethel (in Mississippi, 1891), and Zion (in Louisiana, 1891). Fifty-six churches with 1,600 communicants were in these judicatories, with thirty-nine ministers, candidates, and licentiates to serve the church population. All but six of the ministers received some form of financial support from the Executive Committee on Home Missions. A few black ministers continued to hold membership in geographic presbyteries. Two of the five segregated presbyteries merged with two others to form a separate denomination in 1898. This body, known as the Afro-American Presbyterian Church, still received much of its support from the PCUS General Assembly.[5]

This denomination was an outgrowth of the Executive Committee on Colored Evangelization, formed in 1891. The Reverend A. L. Phillips of Birmingham was the first secretary, and he was largely responsible for the creation of the new and segregated church. James G. Snedecor and Oscar B. Wilson also worked in this effort, which was merged into the Executive Committee on Home Missions in 1910.[6]

The viability of the "separate but equal" denomination was always in question. While Wilson was attending a meeting of the Afro-American Presbyterian Church in Chester, South Carolina, in 1899, he wrote, "I took the most charitable view possible, but," he concluded, "[I] failed to see its [the new denomination's] *raison d'etre*—as a separate body."[7]

The Afro-American Presbyterian Church was an obvious failure by 1915, when the Executive Committee on Home Missions recommended the inclusion of the churches of this denomination in a segregated synod of the PCUS General Assembly. The assembly agreed and created a constituent synod of the PCUS from the presbyteries of North and South Carolina, Central Alabama, and Ethel. Another presbytery, Central Louisiana, was organized in 1916. The synod's name, Snedecor Memorial, honored the last executive secretary of colored evangelization; two years after it was organized it claimed 1,492 communicant members.[8] The establishment of a segregated synod committed the denomination, perhaps unwittingly, to maintaining a black constituency within the limits of Presbyterian polity. This relationship grew to demand more and more attention and action from the church.

Presbyterian segregation of minority groups was not confined to blacks. The PCUS had numerous Spanish-speaking congregations in the Southwest. The idea of a Mexican-American Presbytery was first broached in 1892. Its advocates argued that a separate judicatory would foster contacts among Spanish-speaking congregations, allowing benevolence money to be spent on other projects. The presbytery was constituted by the Synod of Texas in 1892.[9]

Neither was Presbyterian segregation only a Southern practice. In 1904 the Presbyterian Church in the United States of America adopted a policy of segregation based on race. This position reversed a 1873 stand of their General Assembly which provided only for geographic presbyteries. The 1904 policy came in response to pressure for the merger of a sizable portion of the Cumberland Presbyterian Church, much of which was in the South.[10]

Evangelization of blacks was the key concept of PCUS work from the Civil War through World War II. The 1921 report of the Executive Committee on Home Missions pointed out that the success of this work depended on evangelization, but it added that such work would not occur without regard to social conditions faced by blacks, particularly that of lynching. The best way to have good race relations, and thus to improve the environment for evangelization, the report said, was through the application of the Golden Rule. This entailed above all else the right to live without fear of unjust accusations or threatening mobs, for all Southern Christians had to face the reality of Judge Lynch's justice. "Is it not a mockery," asked the committee in 1923, "to send missionaries to Africa and burn Negroes in America?"[11]

The executive committee's work in the 1920s and 1930s involved three operations: evangelism, the Stillman Institute, and urban missions. Frequently evaluation of evangelistic work was done simply by noting how many pupils were enrolled in Presbyterian Sunday school stations. Thirty-eight schools had 2,795 enrollees in 1938. Stillman Institute operated as a high school and two-year training institute with special courses in theology and nursing. Urban mission stations were the last type of work to develop. By the 1930s four such stations existed in Atlanta, Richmond, Louisville, and New Orleans. These places offered a variety of organized activities, and they were frequently staffed by students from nearby seminaries in Louisville, Richmond, and Decatur, Georgia. This working relationship had a significant impact on the students and their institutions, as urban missions recognized and attempted to deal with the issues raised by the migration of black populations to the cities.

Occasionally the work of the urban missions was given publicity in one of the denominational periodicals. Benjamin Lynt, a student at Union Theological Seminary in Richmond, recorded his impressions of the Seventeenth Street Missions in the *Presbyterian Outlook* in February 1945. "I began to see firsthand the commodities with which the staff of the mission work so long and tirelessly—for the most part, personalities starved and pinched by circumstance and the distinction of race—living in abject poverty; ill-housed, ill-clothed, ill-fed, illiterate—subjected until their outlook is warped, their hope is all but dead, and their souls forgotten." Despite the great odds that they faced, needy children and young people found the mission a place for spiritual as well as physical and emotional sustenance. The seminarian concluded that without the mission, "there would be no agency in the area bringing the full message of the gospel, and there would be little hope for any good coming out of that neighborhood. Much has been done and much more remains to be accomplished."[12]

During World War II a new emphasis on establishing black congregations emerged. The denomination adopted an evangelism program in 1943 with a separate emphasis on black churches. This renewed emphasis brought attention to many of the inadequacies at Stillman Institute. Many church leaders believed that more black churches should be established and that a new strategy was called for to fulfill this need.[13]

The 1945 General Assembly confronted these changing conditions. The assembly appointed a committee to investigate the manner in which the Executive Committee on Home Missions handled black Presbyterian church work. The investigation revealed that all phases of the operation were disappointing and suggested that a special committee of the General Assembly be established with the exclusive responsibility for black church work. This recommendation was sweeping in scope, calling for a separate department for "Negro Work" and for reorganizing and upgrading the Stillman Institute. Despite the magnitude of the indictment and the scope of the proposed change, the General Assembly gave the Executive Committee on Home Missions a standing ovation when it finally relinquished its responsibilities for this area in 1947.[14]

Presbyterians knew the statistical aspects of social inequality in the South. Members of the Synod of Mississippi in 1948 knew that their state spent $30 per student for the education of white children but only $9.70 per black student, and that there were 1,360 white medical doctors in the state but only 37 black medical doctors. Within this context the synod made a commitment to help sponsor more local Sunday school outposts and preaching points in black communities.[15] Though these commitments may have been needed, the more serious problems of deficient educational and medical opportunities indicated in their report were left unattended by the synod.

The social conditions were more fully comprehended by white Presbyterians when they experienced the inequality firsthand. Alexander R. Batchelor, a white Presbyterian minister and the first head of the Negro Work Program, recounted a trip he made with two black Presbyterians, Lawrence W. Bottoms and Dean B. B. Hardy of Stillman Institute. Traveling to a meeting in Florida, they were unable to find a place where they could eat together. Upon their arrival at the home of a black Presbyterian minister in Thomasville, Georgia, they finally ate. "He knew," Batchelor wrote, "what I had never realized, that these men could find no restaurant along the way so he had a meal ready for them." Batchelor asserted that white Presbyterians did not truly understand the hopes and aspirations of Southern blacks, much less their legacy of travail. The Florida trip as well as exposure to such works as Gunnar Myrdal's *American Dilemma* changed Batchelor's mind about the aspirations of black Americans. He saw clearly, as Myrdal suggested, that what whites attributed to blacks as their goals, namely, amalgamation and intermarriage, were the least important issues to them.[16]

Despite this comprehension of the implications of segregation, the debate to establish a separate Negro Work agency in the 1946 General Assembly was very lively. Opponents objected to the idea of a separate church agency to deal with church issues for one race. Dr. W. H. Mc-Intosh of Hattiesburg, Mississippi, articulated the opposition: "Negroes are just lost, guilty persons like the rest of us until they are redeemed, and here we are proposing a new department. . . . The report has much to do with social and political aims. . . . It involves the complete repudiation of the work of Home Missions we've been trying to do all these years. It involves the attention of the church in things that have heretofore been considered outside the church's work." McIntosh's arguments did not convince the General Assembly, who approved the program by a comfortable margin.[17]

Immediately after the General Assembly endorsed this new program, it adopted a set of suggestions for the new assembly's committee to examine. They included studying the possibility of a separate Presbyterian Church for blacks by combining the constituencies from several denominations, abandonment of the postsecondary program at Stillman College, a program of sending black Presbyterian college students to colleges operated by the Northern Presbyterians, and the desegregation of denominational seminaries.

William Crowe, Jr., set forth these proposals and reasoned that a separate church would give black Presbyterians more autonomy over their affairs. The lack of autonomy had been thought to be one reason for the decline in black membership through the years. He advocated the abandonment of Stillman's junior college program because it was dying a slow death. And if black seminarians were able to attend PCUS seminaries, there would be less chance of losing these future ministers to other denominations.[18]

The proposals engendered significant debate over the beginning course of the Negro Work Program. The Snedecor Memorial Synod meeting of September 1946 debated the proposal and responded that the idea of a segregated Presbyterian Church was ill advised. Other opponents thought that the idea of creating another Presbyterian body during negotiations for the reunion of the two major branches of American Presbyterianism was not wise. A third reason for opposition of a separate church arose from the conviction of some in the denomination that segregation itself was wrong. Yet sentiment persisted in the PCUS that a separate black denomination would serve everyone's best interest. As for the other proposals of the Crowe resolution, there was a wider spectrum of opinion regarding the function of Stillman and the desegregation of the seminaries.[19]

The Assembly's Committee on Negro Work took up the suggestions as three recommendations: (1) establishment of a separate black denomination, (2) disestablishment of Stillman Institute, and (3) the education of black ministers in PCUS seminaries. The committee recommended that the first two ideas be dismissed because sentiment in Snedecor Synod opposed a separate church and the committee still saw hope for Stillman, but it retained the third suggestion for future reference. The General Assembly adopted these suggestions, elected new trustees for Stillman College, and requested that synods and presbyteries establish Negro Work committees.[20]

The response of Snedecor Synod to this new program reminds us of Gayraud Wilmore's observation on the tensions between identity and integration among black Presbyterians. The synod sought to seek the maintenance of a separate identity that was different from the segregated reality of the 1940s. Yet this church body wanted to maintain that identity within a denomination where they were a tiny minority.[21]

The establishment of the Assembly's Committee on Negro Work represented something new in the denomination's life. There were hopes that this would become a fraternal rather than a benevolent enterprise. As a proponent in the 1946 General Assembly debate put it: "Men keep talking about keeping the Negro in his place. What is his place? It's anyplace he by his own work and effort can achieve. We've had enough rope in the South. We've had too much paternalism." Paternalism indeed was one of the major characteristics of previous efforts.[22]

Reconciling the two differences in attitude fell the lot of Alexander R. Batchelor. (See fig. 1.) Before taking this position, he served in pastorates in South Carolina and North Carolina and had extensive administrative experience in denominational agencies. Batchelor had to develop the confidence of both black and white Presbyterians and convince them that the task of establishing black congregations was viable. But it was difficult in the 1940s and 1950s for whites to work with blacks in the establishment of churches, as a variety of segregation customs and laws had to be observed and diffused so that opposition to the plans would not destroy the program. Events outside the church, however, such as the 1954 *Brown v. Board of Education* decision had all-pervasive effects on Southern society. The committee chose to maintain segregated operations, an approach which had only limited viability.[23]

1. Alexander R. Batchelor (Courtesy
of Presbyterian Church [U.S.A.], Department
of History, Montreat, North Carolina)

Ensuring adequate funding for the new agency was a major concern. From 1890 until 1915 the denomination had tried a separate church agency responsible for the work of "Colored Evangelization," but it had proved to be an unpopular cause before the denomination instituted systematic benevolence offerings. The 1946 General Assembly sought to eliminate this problem for the new committee by allocating $100,000 of the denominational budget for its first year's work. The budget reflected anticipated revenue for the coming year; unfortunately, contributions which were necessary for this budget did not materialize, and the committee ultimately received only about two-thirds of its projected budget.[24]

The Assembly's Committee on Negro Work established three areas of concentration: evangelism, Christian education, and higher education. The evangelistic effort consisted of financial support of ministers in Snedecor Synod, the establishment of missions, encouragement to geographic presbyteries to establish Negro Work committees, the making of loans and grants to congregations through the denomination's

Church and Manse Erection Fund, and cooperation with the General Assembly Committee on Evangelism. Christian education efforts centered on the recruitment of potential black ministers and financial aid to them, the promotion of Presbyterian literature in black churches, and the development of new literature where appropriate. Stillman Institute was the primary focus of higher education efforts. The Negro Work Program worked to have the institute upgraded to an accredited four-year degree-granting college and encouraged black graduates to seek postgraduate training.[25]

Criticism of the new program was noticeable from the start, and the most stinging barbs came from those who wanted to do more. After reviewing the proposal before the 1946 General Assembly, the *Presbyterian Outlook* charged: "We are not daring to be Christian; certainly not Christian enough." As the Negro Work Program developed, others found fault because it maintained segregation. A 1953 General Assembly debate considered whether or not race should be the basis of judgment in the operation of PCUS institutions. The Division of Negro Work, as the assembly's committee was called after 1949, was the most extensive effort to develop black Presbyterianism, but "it is still working within the framework of our cultural pattern and it means we will simply have more segregated churches." The 1953 General Assembly referred the issue to the Council on Christian Relations, which made a significant report to the 1954 General Assembly on the race problem.[26]

The 1954 action of the General Assembly came shortly after the Supreme Court decision in the *Brown* case. The church's position paper, "A Statement to Southern Christians," had a significant impact in the life of the church, and people engaged in the Negro Work Program welcomed it. Alexander Batchelor cast the issue in religious terms:

> The question before us, my friends, at this time is not whether or not some of our well-established traditions may be upset. The question is what does God's word say about the souls of men. If you study the action of the General Assembly, you will find that its emphasis is there. The ground at the foot of the cross is level. All men stand before Him equally in need of redemption purchased by our Lord on the cross and equally justified by its powers.

Yet Batchelor warned this truth should not give license to foolhardiness. Deliberate steps were in order: "Most of the mistakes I have made in my service to the Church in Negro Work," Batchelor wrote, "have been made because I have gone too fast."[27] This new program did not break the segregated pattern established in 1916, but it was in marked contrast in leadership and direction to the previous operations. A desegregated church was years away from being realized. (Some would argue today that even in the 1990s it has not been realized.)

The Division of Negro Work did not promote the cause of the civil rights movement per se. Batchelor and Lawrence Bottoms, his assistant, both approved of the 1954 General Assembly condemnation of segregation. But they were more concerned with church construction, not direct action. The division left the problems created by issues of segregation and direct action to be addressed by the Division of Christian Relations.[28]

The PCUS addressed race relations after the Civil War by establishing a segregated system of church courts. Segregation was maintained with the establishment of the Snedecor Memorial Synod in 1917. At the same time a new set of requirements was placed on the geographic church courts. As a constituent court in the denomination, the synod, its presbyteries, ministers, and churches all enjoyed equally the privileges of other courts and members. This equality arose out of the demands on polity, not from a conviction that the Gospel was egalitarian. Demands for more equitable treatment of black Presbyterians arose to help redress the imbalance between the demands of Presbyterian polity and Christian action, and the first move to abolish Snedecor Synod came in 1946.[29]

In 1950 Walter Lingle proposed that the synod be abolished. Lingle's career spanned positions as pastor of First Presbyterian Church in Atlanta, professor at Union Theological Seminary, president at the assembly's Training School (later the Presbyterian School of Christian Education), and president at Davidson College. Perhaps better than anyone of his generation he represented the Social Gospel among Presbyterians in his denomination and region. Taking his cue from Charles M. Sheldon's Social Gospel novel *In His Steps; or, What Would Jesus Do?* Lingle analyzed treatment of blacks within the PCUS and found it lacking. He noted that at one time blacks attending Montreat as official representatives of a church court at the General Assembly were accorded the treatment of servants. Though some conditions had changed, Montreat and other church institutions still practiced segregation. The time had come, said Lingle, to abolish such practices.[30]

An overture to that effect was presented to the 1950 General Assembly, which provoked a very lively debate. Proponents argued that several geographic or mainly white presbyteries already had black congregations as members. This involved eleven churches and six ministers. However, one of these presbyteries, Mecklenburg, centered in Charlotte, North Carolina, had stipulated that the black congregation could remain a member only if the minister sought his membership in a segregated presbytery.[31] This restriction had the effect of denying representation to the church at presbytery meetings.

Lingle's original suggestion encompassed all segregated church courts. As church boards and agencies studied the issue, the proposal was modified. Many were concerned that without some form of representation in their own separate church court, black Presbyterians would disappear from the PCUS. Without segregation black representation at the General Assembly would drop from eight commissioners to two. To prevent such a drastic measure, the Board of Church Extension proposed the reduction of the four existing segregated presbyteries to three and the transfer of these bodies to selected geographic synods which had bounds with close proximity to the black presbyteries. The logical step beyond this action would be the reception of black churches into geographic presbyteries at some appropriate time in the future.[32]

This path to desegregation was adopted when the 1951 General Assembly approved this proposal after some debate. Several individuals again proposed establishing a segregated black denomination by transferring the new church programs and church courts to a new entity, while others argued that more time was necessary before taking action. Voice votes defeated both suggestions. Even after the General Assembly acted, some questioned whether the responsible synods would accept the black presbyteries. These fears were not realized as the Synods of Louisiana, Alabama, and Georgia received the Presbyteries of Louisiana-Mississippi, Central Alabama, and Georgia-Carolina, respectively. In all three cases the synods received the presbyteries that had member churches outside of the synods' bounds. But accept them they did, and the Synod of Georgia even sang the Doxology after the vote of acceptance.[33]

Despite the segregationist opposition to the abolition of Snedecor Memorial Synod, a major policy concern was for the maintenance and identity of the small population of black Presbyterians. To fill the vacuum created by the disappearance of the synod, the Division of Negro Work planned programs and institutes for ministers and other black church leaders. The idea of a Snedecor Region emerged as the vehicle for this. The region was not a church court but an administrative vehicle for implementing the programs of the Division of Negro Work. It theoretically included all black Presbyterian churches, regardless of their geographic location or presbytery membership. However, the Negro Work Program placed most of the emphasis on work in the three segregated presbyteries. Each area of church work—women's work, youth and student work, Sunday school, ministerial conferences, and other activities—had a Snedecor Region Council that helped the Region Planning Committee in devising and executing programs.[34]

The Division of Negro Work used the Snedecor Region Plan as a method of advertising the activity of the division to the larger church. Black Presbyterians noted that the region served a fellowship function and offered leadership development opportunities. The division also produced material for all churches in the denomination for use on Race Relations Sunday.[35]

With the dissolution of Snedecor Synod and the establishment of Snedecor Region, little changed in day-to-day program operations. The Board of Women's Work acknowledged this fact when it considered the implications of abolishing the synod. Of all the boards of the church, the Board of Women's Work had the most active program among black Presbyterians. The abolition of the segregated synod could be achieved only with the retention of a segregated church program. The trade-off was an emphasis on black leadership development, which church leaders had heretofore thought of as a conservative effort because it allowed for the maintenance of segregated groups within the denomination.[36]

From the beginning, critics perceived the implications of this plan. A *Presbyterian Outlook* editorial caustically noted that "except in attendance at Synod meetings, there is no change at all." Following Snedecor's abolition, administrative problems began to arise. The segregated presbyteries were very weak, and any attempt by them to gain the necessary strength to become viable church courts met resistance from the geographic presbyteries assisting in the development of new congregations. Thus by complying with efforts to establish black churches, the black presbyteries were faced with problems of identity and morale. Moreover, Snedecor Region failed to develop a separate sense of identity for black Presbyterians. Some of the churches in the geographic presbyteries did not want to be lumped into such a region. Eventually the Snedecor Regional Plan was dismantled because of these problems. The Board of Church Extension opted in November 1957 to establish an Advisory Council to help coordinate efforts for black Presbyterians with the other denominational agencies and boards.[37]

The abandonment of the Snedecor Regional Plan also occurred during a time when the Board of Christian Education was reevaluating the Negro Work Program. As a result, the committee which met to study the Snedecor situation recommended that the denomination take another step to develop stronger ties with the geographic presbyteries. It proposed that presbytery-level activity be continued, whenever possible, by the segregated presbyteries themselves and that the Boards of Women's Work, Christian Education, and Church Extension deliver assistance as needed.[38] The step did not mean that closer relations between the black and white presbyteries within the geographic synods developed immediately, but it removed another level of the segregated church system.

The General Assembly separated the denomination's Negro Work Program from other church programs in 1946 because of unsatisfactory progress under the former arrangement. When the PCUS underwent a major reorganization in 1948–49, the Assembly's Committee on Negro Work became a division of the Board of Church Extension.[39] This board had many of the same responsibilities as the former Executive Committee on Home Missions. Alexander Batchelor continued to direct the Division of Negro Work in the new board.

Batchelor utilized the talents of Lawrence W. Bottoms, a black Presbyterian minister from Louisville, Kentucky, as a resource person for the Snedecor Synod before its dissolution. (See fig. 2.) When it became apparent that Batchelor needed more than part-time assistance in his work, Bottoms was the logical candidate for a full-time assistant position. He assumed his duties on January 1, 1953, and was responsible for helping to interpret the work of the division to the church at large. During this period, Batchelor developed a terminal illness, and when he died in 1955, it fell to Bottoms to continue the division's work.[40]

The board was moving toward another, albeit smaller, reorganization. It appointed a committee at the November 1955 meeting to investigate possible reorganizational strategies. The committee's report

2. Lawrence W. Bottoms (Courtesy of Presbyterian
Church [U.S.A.], Department of History, Montreat,
North Carolina)

noted that there were several problems with the administrative position of the Division of Negro Work. The division's existence called
attention to racial distinctions and created confusion in the administration of programs. Should a black church in a geographic presbytery
apply for financial assistance from the board through the Division of
Negro Work or through the Division of Home Missions? The committee also noted that if it combined Negro Work with another division,
the emphasis of the Negro Work Program would be on people and not
on racial issues such as segregation. The board ordered the incorporation of the Negro Work Division into the Division of Home Missions
in 1956 after considering these questions. There Lawrence Bottoms
was the assistant secretary assigned to work with black congregations
and James J. Alexander was the other assistant secretary, both with
equal status in the division's administration.[41]

There was hesitancy in some quarters to make this move, for it
seemed to be a reversal of the 1946 General Assembly action. The
Presbyterian Outlook noted that whenever the church had incorpo-

rated such a program into another program in the past, it had been to the detriment of black Presbyterians. Such fears did not materialize, as Bottoms remained on the staff of the Division of Home Missions as a consultant to black congregations in the 1960s. By then the board again thought a change was necessary and discontinued the position of the home mission program designated as Negro Work in 1963. Bottoms and Alexander continued to serve as assistant secretaries, with Alexander responsible for chaplains, military personnel, and loans, while Bottoms "shall have responsibility for promoting our denominational program among Negro people, serving as an ambassador of goodwill between the races," and performing such tasks as the executive secretary of the division assigned him.[42]

Under its various names, the Division of Negro Work was responsible for coordinating the denomination's program for black Presbyterians. This entailed coordinating operations with the Presbyterian Church in the U.S.A., interpreting the denominational program to local churches and other groups, conducting surveys to determine the feasibility of establishing churches, working with geographic presbyteries to this end, and promoting the cause and interests of black Presbyterians, including the work of Stillman College, coordinating conferences, and raising funds. The division had to maintain these operations within the context of a region and a denomination increasingly concerned with the implications of the civil rights movement.

Because the PCUSA began an active missionary effort among the freedmen in the Reconstruction period, PCUS efforts often have been overlooked. Although there were numerous black Presbyterians in the South who were associated with the PCUSA and although it might have seemed logical to coordinate Presbyterian efforts, the General Assembly program of 1946 did not specify any cooperation in this area. No significant cooperative efforts developed between Batchelor and the PCUSA's Board of National Ministries during the 1950s. In fact, some instances of denominational competition occurred that required the PCUS's Board of Church Extension to request a top-level consultation to deal with the issues.[43]

The division was considerably more successful in presenting its case to the denominational constituency. Both Batchelor and Bottoms kept busy speaking schedules, and both men addressed many church courts. They sometimes made presentations in response to specific requests from a presbytery or synod, and sometimes only for the purpose of providing information; groups often pledged a donation to the Negro Work Program after such presentations. Bottoms more frequently spoke to women's and youth groups, though Batchelor also spoke to such audiences.[44]

Speaking was only one avenue of interpretation open to division personnel. Printed promotional materials distributed through the churches were also a very important outlet for information. The Negro Work Program distributed such materials, which often appeared in nonofficial periodicals for Presbyterians. In addition, the Board of Church Extension approved the idea of preparing materials for the Negro Work Program in conjunction with the Boards of Christian Education and Women's Work. The 1953 General Assembly commended to local churches a study book by Batchelor, *Jacob's Ladder: Negro Work in the Presbyterian Church in the United States.*[45]

The division applied its program by working for the establishment of black congregations. The process began with a survey of residential areas to determine whether or not there was sufficient interest among residents for a Presbyterian church. The requests for the survey originated in the local community and usually came from the presbytery's Church Extension committee, though a church or group of churches could also request a survey. The division would not initiate a survey without this kind of local support. Both Bottoms and Batchelor were involved extensively in the administration of surveys. Some situations required more than one survey before any plans came to reality. In Richmond, Virginia, for example, surveys were conducted in 1947 and 1952.[46] (See table 1.)

The survey procedure required a team consisting of two ministers, one black and one white. This arrangement facilitated contacts for the team that neither could do individually. Originally they were employees of the Division of Negro Work, but volunteer teams were also employed. The surveyors would take a map of the city or town and mark certain landmarks in the residential areas, such as schools, colleges, playgrounds, and churches. They would also mark the locations where new schools, playgrounds, streets, and other services were planned. Next, the surveyors would contact local leaders, such as school principals, teachers, college presidents, professors, and professionals. The major factors considered in the compilation of this data were the unchurched areas, population trends of the area, and possible location sites for a new church. The team would make a tentative report to its local contacts before leaving the area and then would provide a final report incorporating these comments for the sponsoring group. This survey procedure did not attempt house-to-house canvases; rather, it focused on demographic trends and opinions of community leaders.[47]

The establishment of the Assembly's Negro Work Committee in 1946 spurred the creation of similar organizations in the denomination's synods and presbyteries. The lower court committees were the vehicles to implement the Negro Work Program in local situations. Such committees were also an acknowledgment of the race relations problem and of the institutional efforts to solve it. The initial response to the General Assembly program was encouraging, as fifty-one presbyteries and seven synods organized Negro Work committees by 1949. The denominational reorganization of 1948–49 had an effect on these committees, and their work was most often transferred to the jurisdiction of the presbyteries' Church Extension Committee.[48]

There was some opposition to implementing the Negro Work Program at the local level. The Church Extension Committee of Harmony Presbytery (in South Carolina) stressed that the program was that of the General Assembly. "As far as we know," the committee reported in April 1951, "very little work is being done among the Negroes in our Presbytery." Even where presbyteries and synods assigned committees the responsibility of Negro Work, they often did little at the local level, or the committee's responsibility took on significance only in relation to a local problem.[49]

Throughout the 1950s the participation of presbyteries in the Negro Work Program was spasmodic. Significant work did develop, however, particularly in the establishment of new churches, and the existence of the committees did keep the program before the church courts. Sometimes all that could be said, as Red River Presbytery heard at its fall 1958 meeting, was that "there was nothing to report on Negro Work." In several instances references to Negro Work disappeared from presbytery Church Extension Committee reports in the late 1950s. Increasingly, the responsible committees in presbyteries dropped racial distinctions in reporting their activities.[50]

Many blacks settled in cities across the South after World War II. Their relocation was often occasioned by new economic opportunities, which resulted in an emerging black middle class. It was widely thought that this group would desire a less emotional form of worship.

Table 1. Black Churches Established in the PCUS, 1946–1962

Date organized	Church name	Location	Presbytery[a]
?, 1946	Westminster	Birmingham, Ala.	Central Alabama (S)
Oct. 31, 1946	John Calvin	Nashville, Tenn.	Nashville (G)
Mar. 9, 1947	Bethel	Florence, S.C.	N. and S. Carolina (S)
Apr. 21, 1948	Faith Chapel	Jackson, Miss.	Ethel (S)
May 29, 1949	Bethany	Washington, D.C.	Potomac (G)
Feb. 19, 1950	Pioneer	Beaumont, Tex.	Brazos (G)
?, 1952	Westside	Elberton, Ga.	Georgia-Carolina (S)
Feb. 17, 1952	Eastminster	Richmond, Va.	East Hanover (G)
Nov. 30, 1952	Calvary	Greenville, Miss.	Louisiana-Mississippi (S)
Nov. 30, 1952	Parkway Gardens	Memphis, Tenn.	Memphis (G)
Dec. 14, 1952	All Souls	Richmond, Va.	East Hanover (G)
Jan. 31, 1954	Trinity	Tallahassee, Fla.	Central Alabama (S)
Apr. 11, 1954	Fairview	Chattanooga, Tenn.	Knoxville (G)
May 23, 1954	Covenant	Norfolk, Va.	Norfolk (G)
May 30, 1954	Hope	Dallas, Tex.	Dallas (G)

Oct. 10, 1954	Harrison Street	Longview, Tex.	Paris (G)
Jan. 23, 1955	Westminster	Tuskegee, Ala.	Central Alabama (S)
Mar. 27, 1955	Westhills	Atlanta, Ga.	Georgia-Carolina (S)
July 10, 1955	College Heights	Fayetteville, N.C.	Fayetteville (G)
Oct. 14, 1956	Dellabrook	Winston-Salem, N.C.	Winston-Salem (G)
Nov. 18, 1956	Washington Street	Dublin, Ga.	Augusta-Macon (G)[b]
Sept. 30, 1957	Hollywood Heights	Shreveport, La.	Louisiana-Mississippi (G)
Nov. 10, 1957	Washington Shores	Orlando, Fla.	St. Johns (G)
Apr. 6, 1958	Carver Heights	Columbus, Ga.	Georgia-Carolina (G)
June 1, 1958	Woodville	Richmond, Va.	Hanover (G)
July 13, 1961	Community	Itta Bena, Miss.	Louisiana-Mississippi (S)
July 30, 1961	Nicholtown	Greenville, S.C.	Georgia-Carolina (S)
Apr. 29, 1962	Peabody Heights	Eastman, Ga.	Georgia-Carolina (S)

Source: Compiled from statistics in the PCUS General Assembly *Minutes.*

[a] In this column, (G) denotes a geographic presbytery (i.e., one that is predominantly white); (S) denotes a segregated presbytery (i.e., one composed exclusively of black churches).

[b] This church was organized by Augusta-Macon Presbytery (G) but immediately transferred to Georgia-Carolina Presbytery.

To capitalize on these factors the division tried to establish black congregations within new residential areas of Southern towns and cities. Such locations would help attract professionals and other local citizens. A significant number of new churches began in close proximity to black colleges, such as Texas Southern University in Houston, Florida A&M College in Tallahassee, Tuskegee Institute in Alabama, Arkansas AM&N College in Pine Bluff, and Fayetteville State Teacher's College in North Carolina. The division also gave attention to residential areas not associated with colleges. Mid-Texas Presbytery received something like a religious monopoly by accepting "exclusive rights for the development of religious work in this area known as Carver Heights."[51]

Such efforts by the Division of Negro Work required close cooperation with the various presbyteries. Before it would spend any money on the development of a new congregation, there had to be appropriate understandings between the division, the concerned presbytery, and the potential congregation members. Once these relations were in order, the division would proceed to carry out the agreed-upon plans. Funding new church development and supporting ministers were coordinated through the presbyteries. The expenditure of these monies frequently amounted to totals in the tens of thousands of dollars for a single congregation. These efforts were dependent on the cooperation of the geographic presbyteries with the division, but the churches founded as a result of the cooperation were not always allowed to become members of the presbyteries responsible for their organization. This was particularly true in the Deep South, in the synods of South Carolina, Georgia, Alabama, Mississippi, and Louisiana. In the long run, this exclusion had an adverse effect on the morale of black ministers and contributed to an atmosphere that stifled the development of black presbyteries as church courts of equal significance.[52]

Several examples illustrate how the Negro Work Program operated in the establishment of new churches. The Seventeenth Street Mission in Richmond, Virginia, served as the initial nucleus for what became All Souls Presbyterian Church. All Souls Church was different in a number of ways from usual church development projects. In the 1950s some Richmond Presbyterian leaders hoped that All Souls could serve as a prototype for an integrated congregation. It drew its white minority from the faculty and student body at Union Theological Seminary in Virginia, located in Richmond. East Hanover Presbytery made a survey of the area in 1947 and authorized its Negro Work Committee to investigate the purchase of property in 1949. It soon became evident that two black congregations could be formed and served by one minister. The presbytery then organized the Eastminster Presbyterian Church in April 1952 at the Seventeenth Street Mission, and the All Souls Church was organized in December 1952.[53]

All Souls Church did not have its own building until 1955. To the dissatisfaction both of church members and of some white Presbyterians, the congregation used a public school building in the interim. In the early 1950s the white congregation of the Overbrook Presbyterian Church moved out of the area All Souls served. The new church eventually acquired the Overbrook facilities, first using them on January 15, 1956. The church grew rapidly and became a self-supporting congregation on October 1, 1957.[54]

The Eastminster and All Souls churches called the Reverend Irvin Elligan as pastor of both congregations. Elligan was the first black minister to become a member of East Hanover Presbytery. He came from Knoxville College in Tennessee, largely at the instigation of Dr. Ernest Trice Thompson of the Union Seminary faculty. Elligan found that a dual rationale for the black churches existed within the mind of the presbytery. Some favored it as a means to build toward an inclusive church, while others simply wanted to keep black Presbyterians out of white churches. Elligan himself was initially on the periphery of presbytery life but gradually became more deeply involved.[55]

The students at Union Seminary and the Assembly's Training School instituted additional projects where Christian Education opportunities existed. They began holding Sunday school and worship services in the Creighton Heights area of Richmond in late 1953. The presbytery was initially reluctant to take on additional work and instructed the students that if they wished to take further action, they should do so through the Presbytery's Negro Work Committee. However, the presbytery soon allowed a minister to conduct preaching services in the area. A commission of Hanover Presbytery organized the Woodville Presbytery Church out of this effort on June 1, 1958.[56]

Brazos Presbytery in Texas, encompassing the Houston area, was another locale where black churches existed prior to the Negro Work Program, but several initiatives developed out of the new program. The

Pioneer Presbyterian Church in Beaumont, Texas, originated out of the desires of some black leaders and a group of young people in the Westminster Presbyterian Church in Beaumont. The presbytery called and received a black minister, the Reverend Hosea Rasberry, who began to organize the work. Growth was not spectacular, but money available from the Board of Church Extension allowed for construction of a building. Gradually the size of the congregation increased. Unfortunately, the congregation was not able to meet the presbytery's expectations as to how quickly it should become self-supporting, although it made some progress toward that goal by 1960.[57]

Memphis had had very little PCUS black Presbyterian work prior to the 1950s. In 1949 the young people's group at Buntyn Memorial Presbyterian Church began to work for the establishment of a black Presbyterian church in the city. The Youth Project Council of Memphis designated $1,000 toward the building of this church. Memphis Presbytery established a chapel in 1952 using the preaching services of the Reverend J. A. McDaniel, a PCUSA minister. The presbytery organized the Parkway Gardens Church on November 30, 1952, with thirty-seven members. The congregation soon purchased a lot and, with funds from the Board of Church Extension, began construction. The membership grew to 104 by the fall of 1954, with increased contributions matching the increased size. Between 1963 and 1964 the church increased its budget from $15,000 to $20,000.[58] (See fig. 3.)

Geographic presbyteries also developed black churches which became members of one of the segregated presbyteries. These churches were begun with the overt understanding that they were to be exclusively for blacks. The efforts often grew out of clergy concern over the lack of church opportunities in certain black communities. For white ministers to be involved with the organization of black churches at the height of the massive resistance movement could place their careers in jeopardy if involvement were not undertaken with traditional paternalistic notions.[59]

The Henry Memorial Presbyterian Church in Dublin, Georgia, supported the organization of the Washington Presbyterian Church in Dublin from its inception as a chapel for the black community. The Washington Chapel requested to be organized as a member of Augusta-Macon Presbytery at the September 1956 meeting, and presbytery officials sent the request to the Church Extension Committee for study. The chapel was later organized as a church by the presbytery,

3. Parkway Gardens Presbyterian Church, Memphis, Tennessee, 1960 (Courtesy of Presbyterian Church [U.S.A.], Department of History, Montreat, North Carolina)

but then it was "reluctantly" dismissed to Georgia-Carolina Presbytery in order "to promote the peace, unity and purity of the Church."[60]

Some black congregations started more from the determination of the members than from the concern of any presbytery. Faith Presbyterian Church in Jackson, Mississippi, was one such case. The church held its first services on December 28, 1947, although the support of the Jackson Presbyterian Council had been evident since 1944. The council was an ad hoc group within the Presbytery of Central Mississippi, which expressed no interest in such endeavors. The council did all-black church development in Jackson and received no support from the presbytery for its work.[61]

Straining geographic boundaries was required whenever churches were organized by geographic presbyteries and dismissed to the segregated presbyteries. Florida Presbytery helped found Trinity Presbyterian Church in Tallahassee to serve the students and faculty at Florida A&M College, but the church became a member of Central Alabama Presbytery. Another example was the Westminster Presbyterian Church in Birmingham, Alabama, which was founded originally as a mission effort of Birmingham Presbytery. This church also became a member of Central Alabama Presbytery after its organization. It soon became a stable congregation and offered a day-care nursery to working women. By 1957 the church was self-supporting, and Birmingham Presbytery turned over all property it held for the church to the congregation.[62]

The church development plans resulted in a significant increase in the number of black PCUS communicants. When the Negro Work Program began, there were approximately 3,000 black church members. The number rose to 5,000 by 1955 and then to 7,000 in the early 1960s. This growth was welcomed, but there simply were not enough black ministers to serve these new churches. The General Assembly, synods, and presbyteries encouraged qualified young black men to pursue ministerial careers, but Stillman College was the only black institution of higher learning in the denomination. A ministerial candidate then had to further his education at one of the previously segregated Southern Presbyterian seminaries.[63]

One of Lawrence Bottoms's jobs was to help recruit ministers from other denominations to help provide the necessary black ministerial leadership that was not always present in the PCUS. He himself had grown up in the Reformed tradition but not in the PCUS. Irvin Elligan, who served the All Souls Church in Richmond, came from the United Presbyterian Church in North America's Knoxville College; before his attendance there, he had been a Baptist. Neither case was unusual. Bottoms began his searches within the Reformed communions, primarily the PCUSA. Many of the ministers came from Johnson C. Smith University in Charlotte, North Carolina. When Bottoms failed to find enough ministers there, he looked to the Methodist and Baptist denominations but without total satisfaction, though some Baptist and Methodist ministers did very good jobs as Presbyterians. A major problem in accepting these ministers came in the method of receiving them into a presbytery. This was of more significance for the segregated presbyteries than for the geographic ones. Bottoms tried to determine what were adequate requirements for such acceptance and resolved that the membership requirements should be no different for a black Baptist or Methodist seeking admission to a presbytery than for a white Baptist or Methodist seeking similar admission.[64]

The recruitment of ministers from outside the denomination did cause some problems. On some occasions, geographic presbyteries perceived ministers from outside the denomination as troublemakers. For example, in Tallahassee, Florida, the Reverend Metz Rollins came into the denomination in 1952 from the PCUSA and was active in the city's 1957 bus boycott. The direct action approach, modeled on the Montgomery bus boycott, troubled local white sponsors of the work. The Division of Negro Work had to broker several meetings between the sessions of the First Presbyterian Church and the Trinity Presbyterian Church. The result was a situation that stifled the denomination's program in Florida Presbytery.[65]

Other problems arose when white churchmen overlooked the requirements of the Presbyterian system. In this system local churches issue calls to their ministers, but the minister becomes a member of the presbytery. In some cases, white churches supporting a mission project called ministers for black churches without consulting the congregation. And at times the nature of ministerial leadership was a problem. Many of the older ministers were products of Stillman, and they resented the influx of new people into "their" church. The new system of church development posed a direct threat to many who had been supported by the pattern of home mission prior to 1946.[66]

The Negro Work Program and church agencies encouraged new churches to establish local programs for their members. The participation of black communicants in these churchwide efforts became a point of contention between various factions in the denomination as black women and youth tried to attend denominationally planned leadership training meetings. Segregated opportunities were sponsored by the Division of Negro Work in conjunction with the Board of Women's Work and the Men's Council of the Board of Christian Education.

The Board of Women's Work had long been interested in developing opportunities with or for black women. After World War II, the board implemented a Field Work Plan to help establish more Woman's Auxiliaries in all areas. The board approved the idea of a black field worker in theory in July 1946, although a white woman already was doing some of this work. Beginning in late 1946, Arena Devarieste worked with Louise Miller, a former missionary to Korea who was preparing to return to that country. Devarieste assumed total responsibility for field work for churches in Snedecor Synod in November 1947 and continued to work for the board in conjunction with the Division of Negro Work until her retirement in January 1960. In addition to employing this one worker for all black churches, the board supported the work of women within certain presbyteries who were doing similar organization.[67]

The Board of Women's Work tried to adjust to the changes in church polity that occurred with the abolition of Snedecor Synod and the establishment of the Snedecor Regional Plan. Initially the transfer of black presbyteries to the geographic synods did not apply to black Presbyterials (i.e., women's organizations associated with a presbytery). The board appointed a representative to work with the Snedecor Regional Council and help coordinate women's efforts. When the Board of Church Extension abolished the region, the Board of Women's Work tried several actions to ensure the continuity of the program. This involved having programs at the level of the segregated presbytery, offering educational opportunities at a district (or sublevel) of the presbytery and developing ways to coordinate better the work of the Synodicals of Alabama, Georgia, and Louisiana with the black Presbyterials. Some of these opportunities were Tri-Board (Women's Work, Christian Education, and Church Extension) presentations.[68]

Official concern for race relations among Southern Presbyterian women was evident from the 1920s. It continued in the postwar period, although modified by social context. A group of Presbyterian women in Jacksonville, Florida, began to seek better race relations in the

1940s. Their efforts led to interracial conversations, and some white Presbyterians attended meetings of black organizations, such as the Parent-Teacher Association and Urban League. An interracial prayer group stimulated concern for housing and led to a Federal Housing Office survey of conditions in one black section of the city. In the 1940s some Presbyterian women's groups even advocated antilynching laws.[69]

PCUS women supported the Negro Work Program in a variety of endeavors. The women of the First Presbyterian Church, Tallahassee, Florida, gave $400 and a communion service set to help establish a black church in that city. Norfolk Presbyterial pledged $10,000 toward the building of a black Presbyterian church in the area. Local organizations and Presbyterials also conducted surveys to help determine the religious needs of the black community. Presbyterial organizations sponsored short-term workers to organize Vacation Bible schools or Sunday schools. (See fig. 4.) Fayetteville (N.C.) Presbytery's Home Mission Committee responded to their Presbyterial's efforts and underwrote the expenses of a worker, which helped lead to the organization of a church near Fayetteville State Teachers College. The women's organizations also were interested in seeing that these new churches founded corresponding women's programs. Arena Devarieste and the Board of Women's Work helped the geographic Presbyterials in this task.[70]

The most frequent reaction to the concern of PCUS women for improved race relations was sponsorship of Presbyterial and Synodical conferences similar to those begun in the 1910s. The number of these conferences dropped during the depression and World War II, but their popularity increased again with the emergence of the Negro Work Program. The Board of Women's Work foresaw that these would be popular conferences and set out in 1946 to set up guidelines for them by holding planning sessions for directors. Eight conferences were sponsored by the board and various synodicals in 1952.[71]

Presbyterian women were quite proud of the conferences. Several different denominations sponsored the meetings, with Presbyterians taking a conspicuously prominent role in their planning. Moreover, the women who attended were from several denominations. For a period these conferences were well attended, and participants took courses for credits and after a prescribed number received a certificate. The conferences always featured Bible study as well as courses and discus-

4. Vacation Bible school, Calvary Presbyterian Church, Greenville, Mississippi, June 1954 (Courtesy of Presbyterian Church [U.S.A.], Department of History, Montreat, North Carolina)

sion sessions such as "Police Responsibility in Community Relations" or "Accidents, Their Causes and Prevention." The list of speakers at any given conference was always biracial and on occasion included prominent leaders such as Benjamin E. Mays.[72]

The popularity of the conferences waned in the 1960s, although many white women wanted them to continue, as they represented tangible evidence of their own racial concern. The date of discontinuance varied significantly between 1959 for the Georgia conference to 1969 for the one supported by the North Carolina Synodical.[73]

The capstone of the system was a conference sponsored by the Board of Women's Work at Stillman College every summer. Hallie Paxson Winnsborough founded it in 1916, and it continued until 1965. (See fig. 5.) After the implementation of the Negro Work Program, the conference took on added significance, as it was a model for the other conferences. Local women's organizations and Presbyterials sent delegates to Tuscaloosa, and the various organizations also helped underwrite the operation of the conference. There black women were exposed to the black version of the Board of Women's Work program for white women. The board tried to open the conference's planning process to black women although the conference had to operate in a segregated system.[74]

The Negro Work Program encouraged the organization of youth groups along with that of women's organizations. Alexander Batchelor and Lawrence Bottoms requested and received the backing of the Men's Council of the General Assembly to sponsor a series of youth conferences for black Presbyterian youth. The various men's councils of the synods in turn did the actual local support work, with planning left in large part to the Division of Negro Work staff. Conferences took place in a number of states, including Georgia, North Carolina, Virginia, Alabama, Florida, Louisiana, and Arkansas, though they were never as widespread as the women's conferences. In addition to youth conferences, the division attempted to coordinate college student work. Several workers served college campuses such as Florida A&M College and Tuskegee Institute, but this was not one of the more active areas of the division's program.[75]

Stillman College was a historically important part of the PCUS program for black Presbyterians. The Negro Work Program resulted in a total revamping of the institution and the upgrading of the institute to a four-year degree-granting college. New leadership was necessary

5. Louisiana-Mississippi Presbyterial group attending Snedecor Region Woman's Training School, Stillman College, Tuscaloosa, Alabama, 1954 (Courtesy of Presbyterian Church [U.S.A.], Department of History, Montreat, North Carolina)

for this development, and Dr. Samuel Burney Hay, pastor of the First Presbyterian Church in Auburn, Alabama, answered the call to lead the new effort. Hay helped Stillman gain accreditation by recruiting faculty and securing money needed to improve the campus.[76]

Initially Stillman College worked closely with the Division of Negro Work, and the General Assembly considered it a part of the new work. Gradually the interest of the college and division diverged, though Stillman still remained an important symbol of the Negro Work Program as the denomination's only black college and its only internal source of leadership development; furthermore, Tuscaloosa was a convenient location to hold conferences and other meetings.[77]

Stillman always had a close relationship with the women's organization in the PCUS. Six times in its history the college was the recipient of the women's Birthday Offering (1928, 1939, 1942, 1952, 1960, 1972). This offering originated as a way to commemorate the founding in 1912 of the original Woman's Auxiliary of the General Assembly and always went to a denominational agency or program. Twice during the existence of the Negro Work Program (1952, 1960) and once afterward (1972), Stillman received the gift. The 1952 offering endowed a chair of Bible, and the Alexander Batchelor Building for administration and classes was completed with the 1960 gift. The offering in 1972 helped endow a chair of business and provided additional scholarships. President Hay credited much of Stillman's success to the long-term support of the women of the church. He even declared that "without the Women of the Church there would be no Stillman!" This sentiment might be hyperbole, but the financial support the women's organization gave to the college, at both the national and local level, was very important.[78]

A common problem for both the Division of Negro Work and Stillman College was a lack of sufficient funds. Though the General Assembly promised ample funding when the program began, it soon became obvious that much more financial assistance was needed. The 1952 General Assembly adopted a plan to raise two million dollars, and the Board of Church Extension intended that the funds generated by this campaign be split between the division and Stillman College. The board carefully outlined how it would spend money that was received by establishing criteria that included close cooperation with geographic presbyteries in the development of new congregations. Thus a challenge was added to the fund-raising effort.[79]

Support for the campaign was widespread. The two denomination-ally oriented independent periodicals, the *Presbyterian Outlook* and the *Southern Presbyterian Journal*, which had very different ap-proaches to many theological and sociological issues, both endorsed the campaign. The goal of two million dollars was broken down by a quota system to the various synods, presbyteries, and local churches. Some presbyteries reported that they quickly had their quota pledged and that black churches were well ahead of the quotas assigned to them. Other churches and presbyteries were more reluctant to fill their quotas.[80]

The results of the campaign were generally good. Early in the pro-cess the Board of Church Extension received a $100,000 challenge grant it used to encourage the completion of the campaign. By 1954 the various church courts had pledged over $2,223,000. However, the funds were slow to arrive, and the last push to complete the campaign occurred only in 1956–57.[81]

The events of the times delayed the completion of the campaign from 1952 to 1957 as the emerging civil rights movement was defined by *Brown v. Board of Education* and the Montgomery bus boycott. More specifically, the delay followed the statement of the 1954 General Assembly on segregation. The action declared that segregation was incompatible with the profession of Christianity and caused much dis-cussion in church circles, as it came within several weeks of the Su-preme Court's decision in the *Brown* case. The Division of Negro Work began to receive questions about funds being diverted from the campaign to support civil rights causes. The division never used any of the money in such causes, but suspicions remained. Numerous peo-ple expressed suspicion as a pretext for canceling their pledges, though the General Assembly remained committed to the campaign.[82]

The PCUS Negro Work Program originated out of concern which had been present in the denomination for many years. Albert C. Winn observed that the presence of a small minority of black members, never more than about 1 percent of the total communicants, caused the church to be sensitive to issues of race. The program was an effort to address those issues in a constructive way. Prior to the *Brown* deci-sion there was even the possibility that some new congregations would be interracial, but reactions to the events of the 1954 Supreme Court decision and the General Assembly declaration on desegregation effec-tively ended those hopes.[83]

One goal of the Negro Work Program was to help change the manner in which white Presbyterians thought about and worked with their black brothers and sisters. Whether this goal was achieved is still debatable,[84] for the theology and ideology of Presbyterians were deeply embedded in denominational lore. The work of Batchelor, Bottoms, and the host of others at all levels in the PCUS did increase the modest number of black Presbyterians; more important, it made their presence known and felt. The issues involved in the incorporation of black and white Presbyterians into one church were frequently the issues all Southerners faced, regardless of their religious label.

3

ECCLESIASTICAL EQUIVALENTS FOR LIBERALS AND CONSERVATIVES

T HE ORIGINS of the Presbyterian Church in the United States are found in the history of intradenominational schism (Old School vs. New School) and in the outbreak of sectional conflict. A peculiarly Southern denomination emerged during the Reconstruction and post-Reconstruction periods, and the theological justification of this separation was elaborated and enhanced as reason for not rejoining the Northern Presbyterians. Appealing to the theology of James Henley Thornwell, advocates of the continued existence of the so-called Southern Presbyterian Church argued that it should be an institution concerned only with "spiritual" affairs. The way to ensure this focus was to remain a separate entity. This doctrine came to be called the spirituality of the church.[1]

Adherence to the doctrine was most ironclad in the 1890s and 1900s. Benjamin Morgan Palmer of New Orleans argued that ministers could participate in secular affairs only as citizens, not as clergymen. Palmer was an avid secessionist in 1861 and an outspoken critic of the Louisiana lottery in the 1890s. In each case he claimed to maintain the clergy-citizen dualism. Such spirituality, however, became increasingly difficult to maintain, particularly as advocates for such causes as prohibition and Sabbath observance grew in the church.[2]

Conflict over the application of this doctrine began to emerge in the early years of the twentieth century. One of the leaders calling for a new understanding of this doctrine was Walter Lee Lingle, longtime professor at Davidson College and later its president. When he gave the Sprunt Lectures at Union Theological Seminary in Virginia in 1929, he addressed the issue of the Bible and social problems. Others began to question the parameters of the spirituality of the church. Opponents of the doctrine argued that it permitted church people to absolve themselves from involvement in contemporary issues and restricted application of the faith to their private lives. The controversy was highlighted by the denomination's decision to participate in the Federal Council of Churches, a Protestant cooperative body formed in 1908. The PCUS joined the council in 1912, and complaints emerged when the FCC adopted its "Social Creed" that same year. Critics charged that this document deviated from the denomination's understanding of the spirituality of the church, particularly in regard to its proper relationship with the state, and the denomination temporarily withdrew from the FCC. The PCUS rejoined the council after reconsidering the issues and adopting a statement that the church's proper role was to encourage laypeople to effect social change by individually joining voluntary associations. The advocates of continued participation thwarted numerous withdrawal attempts throughout the 1920s. In the early 1930s, however, opponents of ecumenical activity succeeded in withdrawing the PCUS for a second time.[3]

These activities coincided with the fundamentalist-modernist controversy that was occurring in several Protestant denominations, including a prominent battle in the Presbyterian Church in the U.S.A. A period of tremendous intellectual and social turmoil followed the Civil War, during which time the emphasis on commonsense realism waned. The scientific method came to be defined by deductive reasoning, as opposed to the Baconian inductive process. Charles Darwin's theory of evolution presented a challenge not only to what people believed and thought but also to how they believed and thought. In the debates of this time "liberal" came to be associated with those who adapted their thought to the new scientific method. "Conservatives" were still rooted in commonsense realism, which stood over against the deductive-critical method.[4]

The PCUS used the doctrine of the spirituality of the church to help distinguish "liberals" from "conservatives." Those who favored the traditional interpretation of this doctrine separating spheres of life were conservative, while those seeking to disregard it were liberal. But unlike the liberal-conservative and fundamentalist-modernist debate in other denominations, the dispute within the PCUS did not include the issue of dispensationalism, a theological movement that was often connected to fundamentalist actions. Nonetheless the controversy within the denomination was bitter and acrimonious. Robert H.

Walkup revealed the depth, breadth, and length of the feelings when he noted that in the 1960s, "Liberal was the ecclesiastical equivalent of S.O.B."[5]

In the 1930s the Social Gospel movement found expression in the ecclesiastical structure of the PCUS. The General Assembly organized a Permanent Committee on Moral and Social Welfare in 1934. The committee, instigated largely through the efforts of Ernest Trice Thompson, was responsible for studying important social issues and bringing them before the General Assembly. This approach conflicted with the earlier understanding of the spirituality of the church, and the challenge was based on new theological perspectives derived from a more critical approach to the Bible and to religion in general.[6]

Race relations were an important part of the committee's mandate, although other issues also came within its purview. During the depression, many church people concluded that "the church must teach men to love in accord with the teachings of Jesus, to practice the Golden Rule in all relations of life, to work as well as to pray that God's will may be done on earth as well as it is in heaven." The committee first included race relations in its 1936 report, when it discussed disfranchisement, inequitable funding for public schools, and lynching. This report, adopted by the General Assembly, called for organizations within the denomination to be concerned with race relations and for all citizens to be treated fairly. There was some favorable response in the denominational press, but ministers still did not broach the subject in Sunday morning sermons. Other issues the committee studied and addressed were war, alcohol, venereal disease, pornography, and divorce.[7]

Not all appreciated the efforts of the committee. The year after it was established, there were attempts to dismantle it, and criticism persisted in later years. The General Assembly refused to abolish the committee and occasionally commended its efforts. Critics and advocates of the committee agree that 1935 was the watershed year. The PCUS turned away from its previous understanding of spirituality. Even though the work of the Permanent Committee on Moral and Social Welfare did not engage the denomination in anything more than a study of social ills, this process opened the way for the development of a church that was arguably less concerned about the distinctions between the civil and ecclesiastical spheres.[8]

During World War II, the denomination came to grips with the issue of racial prejudice in the context of worldwide conflict. Nazism formed the mirror by which Presbyterians could examine their attitudes and beliefs concerning racial superiority. Not only Presbyterians but all "Christian citizens" were called upon to "combat with all earnestness and power, racial superiority against Negroes, anti-Semitism and unsympathetic treatment of Japanese in internment areas." The implications of these words were not lost on the General Assembly. Numerous blacks were cited as having risen above the conditions of poverty and illiteracy common for so many of their race. Booker T. Washington, George Washington Carver, Paul Robeson, and Marian Anderson were all held up to white Southern Presbyterians as examples of the achievements possible by blacks.[9]

Historians, however, have not found much to commend in the treatment of black America by white churches.[10] Their criticism is justified. At the same time it must be acknowledged that the PCUS and other mainline denominations were struggling to respond from within a segregated system which they helped establish and perpetuate.

The words of the Committee on Moral and Social Welfare reinforced for a number of Presbyterians the idea that some things were wrong in race relations. Ministers, presbyteries, and the church press began to call upon fellow church people to be concerned about these relations. Segregation enforced a system of legal discrimination that thwarted the economic aspirations of black Americans. "Discrimination is ultimately a question of power," Ansley C. Moore noted, and white Southerners should do what they could to assist blacks. Church members found support for such ideas in a variety of sources. In 1944 Gunnar Myrdal's seminal work *An American Dilemma* had an important impact on many Presbyterian readers. The effects of World War II and events in the Truman administration made others sensitive to racial issues. Many in the PCUS believed that if their Christian profession of belief was to have any meaning, action was required.[11]

Growing official concern for race relations did not change individual attitudes. A commissioner to the 1953 General Assembly told a "Negro story" in the course of debating the report of the Christian Relations committee, and a black minister, the Reverend Casper Glenn, objected. The chair concurred in the objection, and the commissioner apologized: "Did I say that? I didn't know I said it." This "Who? Me?" unconscious racism remained in the institutional church. Opposition to black advancement continued, much of it coming from people who claimed to have the interest of blacks in mind but who refused to accept changes on a variety of grounds.[12]

Change was occurring in Southern society, however, and it had implications for the churches. Blacks within the PCUS had remarkable tenacity, and they were encouraged by whites like Ernest Trice Thompson to hope that a better day would come. Thompson was a witness to changes of attitudes in the church. In the 1930s he was charged with heresy for using the critical and historical approach to study of the Bible. Eventually he was absolved of any irregularities. Throughout the controversy he received the steadfast support of his teaching colleagues, the Union Seminary president, and his presbytery. His social views were constantly challenged by conservatives. Yet his leadership helped the denomination create a means to address social issues, and his unfailing support for the ecumenical activities aided in keeping the PCUS involved in the movement for church unity.[13]

The debate over the pros and cons of segregation, integration, and the civil rights movement took place within a liberal-to-conservative spectrum. The term "liberal" is one of relative application. Liberalism in the South has nuanced meanings not readily evident in other regions. Southern Presbyterian liberals did have an appreciation for the trademarks of religious liberalism such as higher criticism and the Social Gospel. One student of the denomination has used the labels "reformers" and "preservers" to refer to liberals and conservatives respectively. He further identifies an independent periodical with each group: the *Presbyterian Outlook* and the *Southern Presbyterian Journal*.[14]

The *Presbyterian Outlook* was organized in 1944 and continued the traditions of ten independent American Presbyterian periodicals from the South. In 1954 the *Presbyterian Tribune* merged with it, giving the *Outlook* added distribution in the Presbyterian Church in the U.S.A. and later the United Presbyterian Church U.S.A. (UPCUSA). The *Outlook* could be counted on to support ecumenical activities such as church union and to argue for the use of biblical criticism in the PCUS.[15]

An obvious way in which the *Presbyterian Outlook* attempted to help educate its readers was by printing articles by authors from outside their communion. The writings of H. Shelton Smith, professor of church history at Duke Divinity School, Martin Luther King, Jr., Benjamin Mays, and Ralph McGill all appeared in the periodical at one time or another. Though usually reprints, these columns did present the writers' ideas to a Presbyterian audience. The *Outlook* also printed materials prepared by the National Council of Churches and the World Council of Churches on the race issue, a law journal article on segregation, and excerpts from the 1967 report of the President's Commission on Civil Rights.[16]

Not all readers approved of such wide diversity. An elder of the Peachtree Presbyterian Church in Atlanta was particularly incensed after an article appeared by Benjamin Mays in 1950. "I consider Mays' views a lot of rot," Carl F. Hutcheson wrote, "and beneath and back of the lines is his ambition to become the white man's equal, socially and otherwise." A reader from Yazoo City, Mississippi, was upset when a legal treatise on the unconstitutionality of segregation was printed. "Keep on bud," he wrote, "until you drive all the Southern Presbyterian churches out of the General Assembly, then you and the N.A.A.C.P. can be happy." Other readers, however, approved of the editorial policy and wrote to say so by ordering reprints of articles.[17]

The *Southern Presbyterian Journal* presented an opposing point of view. This periodical was begun in 1942 in an attempt to counteract the liberal movement within the denomination. Ever since the 1920s conservatives lacked an independent periodical, and many had high hopes for this new effort launched in Weaverville, North Carolina. The first issue's lead editorial stated: "The civilization of which we are a part is perched precariously on the edge of an abyss. . . . The tragedy is that, in part, the Christian Church is to blame." The core issue was the "integrity of the scriptures," and the *Journal* intended to help restore right thinking to the church. The PCUS was headed in an ecumenical direction which it should reconsider, and the editor particularly condemned participation in the Federal Council of Churches and the idea of union with the Presbyterian Church in the U.S.A.[18]

The founder of the *Southern Presbyterian Journal* was L. Nelson Bell, a former Southern Presbyterian medical missionary to China who practiced in Asheville, North Carolina. (See fig. 6.) The *Journal* advocated fundamentalist theology and endorsed segregation, supporting its case with biblical references. Bell and the other writers used arguments from an earlier day to support their theological positions. They believed that personal salvation was the preeminent concern of the church and that liberalism was a destructive force based on theological dishonesty which confused generosity with the Gospel. Their racial

6. L. Nelson Bell (Courtesy of Presbyterian
Church [U.S.A.], Department of History,
Montreat, North Carolina)

position was largely cultural, and little consideration was given to an-
thropological evidence which liberals used.[19]

The editorial defense of segregation began early in the periodical's
life. It constantly referred to the need to improve race relations and
implored its readers to assist in this task, but this paternalistic goodwill could not be represented as an endorsement of social equality.
Segregation was necessary not only because it was outlined in the Bible
but because it was sound social policy in the South. The true danger
was one of intermarriage, which Bell and other *Journal* writers believed
would occur if social intermingling between black and white Presbyterians, especially youth, occurred. Articles and editorials relentlessly
called attention to this danger in the hopes of preventing miscegenation.[20]

The *Southern Presbyterian Journal* not only defended segregation
but sought to discredit the liberal position on race and all other sub-
jects. Every year a group of *Journal* supporters met in Weaverville,

North Carolina. The 1957 meeting adopted a statement approving "voluntary segregation" as a means of maintaining "racial integrity." The *Presbyterian Outlook* immediately attacked the statement, helping to make the position of the denomination increasingly obvious even to the staunchest segregationist. The November 23, 1966, issue of the *Presbyterian Journal* carried the statement of the World Congress on Evangelism held earlier that month, "One Race, One Gospel, One Task." The paper flatly rejected any doctrine of racial superiority. The *Journal's* decision to carry the text reflected an editorial policy of associating with evangelical organizations and their changes in the thoughts of such groups about race.[21]

Also available to the church's communicants was the official periodical of the denomination, the *Presbyterian Survey*. This magazine was founded in 1910 with the primary purpose of educating church members about foreign and home missions. Throughout the 1960s the *Presbyterian Survey* produced material that was congruent with the various denominational stands. This magazine tried not to be drawn into the pointed and antagonistic debates that were carried on between the other two periodicals. However, since General Assembly policies were contrary to policies the *Journal* editors advocated, the positions of the two magazines often clashed. The editor of the *Presbyterian Survey* was frequently subjected to the criticism "Why don't you print the other side?" Editor Ben Hartley responded by citing the various statements of the General Assembly. Beyond these statements, he continued, the editorial policy must have the integrity to be guided by truth. Though no one had a monopoly on the truth, discerning it was to be part of the religious enterprise. Large numbers of Southerners had come to know and believe that segregation was wrong. This was a separate issue from the behavior of individual blacks or various direct action groups. Christian actions and decisions in the context of civil rights could be irrelevant to who and what people are.[22]

Presbyterians, both conservative and liberal, marshaled scriptural references to support their case. The Bible served all Christians as the source of doctrine, but doctrine was embellished and enhanced. The function of biblical texts in the PCUS's theological and ideological debate over race needs careful examination.

The biblical case for segregation rested upon several common texts, including the curse of Ham (Gen. 9:18–27), the Tower of Babel (Gen. 11:1–9), calls for the nation Israel to "segregate" itself from the other tribes (Gen. 27:46–28:4; Deut. 7:2–3), and the teachings of Paul (Acts 17:22–31). Defenders of segregation who used these texts argued that they gave ample warrant against the intermingling of races. Granting that blacks were fellow human beings, Presbyterian segregationists nonetheless maintained that racial separation was divinely instituted for the benefit of humankind.[23]

G. T. Gillespie, a Mississippi clergyman and president of Belhaven College, defended segregation after the 1954 Supreme Court decision, relying heavily on such texts. Gillespie's comments were first made on the floor of the 1954 meeting of the Synod of Mississippi. Local supporters received them so favorably that they appeared in pamphlet form as *A Christian View on Segregation*, printed by the White Citizens' Council. They were later reprinted in both the *Southern Presbyterian Journal* and the *Presbyterian Outlook*.

Gillespie began by arguing that there was no absolutely clear mandate for or against segregation to be found in the Bible. He maintained, however, that the weight of Christian practice and scholarship supported the biblical interpretation of a segregationist. He cited numerous passages to support his conclusion. Moreover, argued Gillespie, American leaders such as Thomas Jefferson, Abraham Lincoln, and Booker T. Washington supported racial segregation in one form or another.[24]

These arguments and those of some Southern Presbyterian academics struck a responsive chord within the denomination. The *Presbyterian Outlook* printed Gillespie's piece to serve as a foil for antisegregationist writers. Response was mixed. One reader wrote to order six additional copies just to have Gillespie's article. "God segregated the races when he brought them into existence," she wrote. "Since he segregated them, I don't think it well that we try to put them together." Her emphatic postscript left nothing unresolved: "P.S.—Between the 'H' bomb and integration, give us the 'H' bomb."[25]

But this segregationist point of view was countered by those who found no justification for segregation in the Bible. Gillespie's arguments were closely scrutinized and attacked. In the issue of the *Presbyterian Outlook* that included Gillespie's comments, Donald G. Miller, a professor at Union Theological Seminary in Virginia, noted that if Gillespie's critical method was the only acceptable one for biblical interpretation, "then we might as well seek guidance in *Alice in*

Wonderland!" Miller thought that the biblical scholarship which Gillespie cited was inadequate to defend segregation.[26]

Whether the Bible could be used to defend segregation concerned several church courts in the 1950s. East Alabama Presbytery appointed a special committee to study the matter. It reported that when analyzing the Bible alone, "we find no scriptural basis for racial segregation in the Church." In reaching this conclusion, the report debunked some of the popular arguments using biblical notions. For instance, it noted that the curse of Ham was placed on his son Canaan, not on Africans. Old Testament injunctions for the Israelites to segregate themselves from other tribal groups arose for religious, not social, reasons.

The committee used other references to support its report. Isaiah 2:2–4 and Micah 4:1–4 asserted that all who worshiped God in Jerusalem would have universal peace. Jesus himself talked to Samaritans, an ethnically despised group. Peter's vision of the unclean foods helped open up the proclamation of the Gospel to Gentiles, whereas it had previously been confined to the Jewish community. The committee found no support for racial segregation as a policy of the church in Paul's epistles. After serious consideration, the presbytery adopted this report.[27]

The dispute over popularly held beliefs about the Bible was a long-standing source of conflict. The *Presbyterian Outlook* and E. T. Thompson, whose weekly Bible study column appeared in the *Outlook*, tried to debunk segregationists' interpretations. Thompson was not alone in his writings on the subject. Ben Lacy Rose, his colleague on the seminary faculty in Richmond, wrote *Racial Segregation in the Church* in 1957. He concluded that racial segregation had absolutely no place within the Presbyterian Church in the United States. The *Presbyterian Outlook* published numerous sermons and articles which challenged the belief that the Bible supported racial segregation.[28] The widespread geographic distribution of the authors suggests the significance of the debate over the Bible and segregation.

The actions of church courts or governing bodies were, next to the Bible, the most important occasions for denominational controversy and debate. Ideally the actions of the sessions, presbyteries, synods, and the General Assembly were reflective of biblical concerns. This connectional system allowed for vigorous debates throughout the denomination. The actions of the General Assembly frequently served as the focus of such debates. This was true also in regard to matters of racial policy and ideology, where the Permanent Committee on Moral and Social Welfare gave way to a Department of Christian Relations. The General Assembly instructed the new department not only to identify and study issues of importance to the church but also to make recommendations for action.[29]

The department brought to the 1949 General Assembly a position paper entitled "States' Rights and Human Rights." It identified civil rights as basic in an American society which also recognized special prerogatives for the various states. Though progress had been made, the paper argued, there was room for the substantial extension of civil rights to black Americans. Southern churches were called upon to help provide the kind of education necessary for this extension. The report was important also in that it challenged the prevalent Southern historiography of the Lost Cause; it argued also for the humanity of blacks.[30]

No sooner had the report been released for preassembly consideration than it was attacked. Two ministers in Virginia wrote the *Richmond Times-Dispatch* to say that the church was not disavowing the time-honored position of states' rights. "This is merely the report of a committee," wrote Willis Thompson and W. E. Davis, "that will in a few weeks be presented to the general assembly of our church, and should never have been published as representing the position of our church on civil rights." The General Assembly, however, did adopt the report and sent it down to the other church courts for study and recommendation.[31] At least this action indicated that the one major Southern religious body still living exclusively within its Confederate boundaries no longer defended segregation.

The synods and presbyteries of the denomination were beginning to recognize that Presbyterians would have to deal with questions of justice. Red River Presbytery in Louisiana commmended the 1949 statement "States' Rights and Human Rights" for study by local congregations. Aside from the 1949 General Assembly resolution, the most far-reaching statement of a church court on race prior to 1954 came from the Synod of Alabama. In 1950 it prepared a report recounting statistical information as to the poverty which blacks faced in that state and noted that the federal government was moving toward the elimination of segregation. It called on the church to support black ministers and congregations and the institutions which prepared and nurtured them. It denied that Christians could freely defend segregation. Not all within the synod agreed with this reasoning. The Reverend Robert McNeill, chairman of the committee which drafted the report, noted the intensity of opposition, when numerous dissents were registered in writing. But the statement did pass, and the *Presbyterian Outlook* noted that it placed God firmly on the "right" side.[32]

Then came 1954. In *Brown v. Board of Education* the Supreme Court ruled that the "separate but equal" doctrine used to justify Jim Crow was unconstitutional. It did in fact mark a new period in American history. But the response of the PCUS to the *Brown* decision did not arise de novo. The 1953 General Assembly had discussed issues bearing on segregation in the church, though a move to take a definite stand on the subject was referred to committee for further discussion. The result was "A Statement to Southern Christians," a position paper adopted by the 1954 General Assembly. This report was predicated on a number of contemporary theological concepts, such as the derivation of human dignity from Christ's incarnation. Because there was an essential oneness of humankind, love could bridge barriers such as race. From this theological point of view there was no justification for racial segregation as practiced in the PCUS or in the United States.[33]

This condemnation of segregation passed the General Assembly by a vote of 239 to 169. The 1954 assembly had the distinction of being the first major church body to meet after the *Brown* decision, and many portrayed the paper as an immediate response to the current situation. It was not. The 1954 General Assembly did not reach its decision in reaction to the Supreme Court and based it on theological rather than legal grounds. Criticism that the Assembly was responding to particular pressure, however, continued to persist among those who disagreed with the action.[34] As 1954 was a watershed year in the history of the civil rights movement, so it was for the PCUS. The reasons were related but distinct.

Reaction to the General Assembly's action came swiftly. A lay commissioner from Memphis Presbytery, John R. Wallace, expressed confusion and shock at the report. Several former moderators voiced general approval but emphasized the necessity of moving gradually. Many sessions, presbyteries, and synods expressed their opinions during subsequent meetings. South Highland Presbyterian Church in Birmingham, Alabama, Tuscaloosa Presbytery, and the Synod of Alabama all

expressed disagreement with the General Assembly action. The resolution of the South Highland Church and those of several other sessions across the assembly were unanimous. Others such as that of the
Synod of Alabama, which had just a few years previously issued its
own statement, carried by a handful of votes. Some church courts
counseled caution and suggested that nothing be said until the action
had been "carefully and prayerfully" studied. Other governing bodies
wholeheartedly endorsed the 1954 statement. One observer believed
that the black presbyteries were caught unprepared for the changes
which the General Assembly implied would happen. But the assembly's statement, in and of itself, did not remove the racial barriers
within the denomination.[35]

After a year of debate and ferment, many presbyteries presented
overtures to the General Assembly to repeal the 1954 condemnation
of segregation. The assembly reaffirmed its decision, however, by an
even larger vote. Segregationists continued to hope that they could
change the course of the church and suggested that a poll be taken
among all presbyteries on whether or not the denomination favored
segregation, but the request was refused.[36] The direction of General
Assembly statements was irrevocably cast. Segregation was officially
incompatible with Christianity as interpreted by the Presbyterian
Church in the United States.

The application of this doctrine to daily church life and, at a more
profound level, to the lives of individual church members was another
matter. On hearing a speaker give what they suspected was an endorsement of the 1954 General Assembly statement, one church men's
group in South Carolina sought to control what future speakers said
to them. Other localities, however, accepted the spirit of that document. A locally sponsored ecumenical gathering scheduled in the summer of 1957 in Auburn, Alabama, was canceled when the host church
(which was not Presbyterian) realized that students from nearby
Tuskegee Institute would be involved. The Session of the First Presbyterian Church, Auburn, was dismayed, and the minister, John H.
Leith, circulated a statement lamenting the action. Later that year the
session offered the use of its facility for future community-type services without restriction on the race of participants.[37]

Additional insight into the function of race as an issue within the
PCUS comes from the experience of a churchman within the larger
civil rights movement. James McBride Dabbs served as an elder in his

family church, the Salem–Black River Presbyterian Church near Mayesville, South Carolina, near his family's plantation of Rip Raps for much of his life. He began his career as an English professor at Coker College in South Carolina but gave that up in the 1930s to manage the family plantation. He turned his hand to writing, and his articles were first published in such periodicals as the *Presbyterian Outlook* and the *Christian Century*. His first two contributions to the *Outlook* addressed the issues of revivalism and race.[38]

Convinced that "how a man makes his living determines how he relates to the universe," Dabbs lived the life of a planter and writer committed to the people with whom he shared his corner of the world. His writing is instructive, for he was in the forefront of those calling for equal rights for blacks. Yet, one scholar argues that aside from this issue, Dabbs would have been comfortable among the Vanderbilt agrarians of the 1920s. His first book, *The Southern Heritage*, addressed the race issue in a forthright manner in 1957. But in 1956 he had published an essay in Louis D. Rubin, Jr., and James J. Kilpatrick's *Lasting South*, along with some noted Southern conservatives and iconoclasts. This occurred just prior to Dabbs's becoming president of the liberal Southern Regional Council.[39]

Perhaps no one other than Dabbs would have hanging on his mantel a set of Confederate firearms, the seal of the state of South Carolina, and a commendation from the NAACP for "wise and dedicated efforts to unify the American people in their quest of the democratic ideal." This unique collection of memorabilia was made possible only after Dabb's encounter with personal tragedy in the death of his wife in 1937. That experience led him to consider the losses and injustices that others also experience, and it moved him to involvement in behalf of others.[40]

The irony of the Southern Presbyterian position on race may be illustrated by juxtaposing Dabbs and a minister living in nearby Clarendon County, the Reverend L. B. McCord. Dabbs was welcomed as a church leader in General Assembly agencies. Harmony Presbytery, however, never elected him as a commissioner to a General Assembly meeting. McCord served for several years as superintendent of education for the county and was responsible for administering a separate but unequal school system. The black community became increasingly intolerant of this situation and filed a lawsuit, *Briggs v. Elliott*, one of the four cases decided under the name *Brown v. Board of Edu-*

cation. Undoubtedly McCord and Dabbs disagreed profoundly on the issue of segregation. Yet churchmen, even those who openly disagreed with Dabbs, readily admitted that the PCUS record on race relations contained "appalling deficiencies."[41]

The effect of race as an issue was very important in a number of instances in Southern Presbyterian life, as it was one of the real dividing issues for defining liberalism and conservatism within the denomination. As the debates between these groups heated up, racial issues increasingly became the subject of the debates, which focused on a range of issues affecting the program and direction of the denomination. This was true in the debate over church union with the Presbyterian Church in the U.S.A., in several cases of ministerial discipline, and in the development and implementation of church programs and statements.

Perhaps none of the issues on which Presbyterians disagreed was more important than that of church union. The divisions caused by the Civil War were not finally resolved until 1983. Prior to World War II several attempts at union had been rejected. The *Southern Presbyterian Journal* had already been formed to oppose such efforts in the 1940s. But proponents of reunification succeeded in persuading the 1954 PCUS General Assembly to adopt a plan of union. Church polity required that three-fourths of the denomination's presbyteries approve the action. The reunion plan fell one presbytery short of a simple majority between the 1954 and 1955 General Assemblies, so the measure died. Although the correlation between race and union cannot be proven in absolute terms, David Reimers notes that the 1954 General Assembly approval of the "Statement to Southern Christians" and that of the plan of union were by equal margins.[42]

Such a coincidence may suggest that a causal relationship existed between those favoring desegregation as a social policy and those favoring union with other denominations. The opposite may also be argued from this relationship. Since there are no records of who voted for or against these proposals, however, there must remain an element of caution in assessing this evidence until it is illuminated by other events. There can be little doubt, though, that the issues of segregation and union were the most prominent of the 1954 General Assembly.

Since 1955, Presbyterians have debated the role of race in the defeat of union. Some scholars and church people argue that the race issue was the real cause of that defeat. The most sophisticated form of this argument appeared in the *American Journal of Sociology*. There a brief study based on a content analysis of anti-union printed materials and an analysis of the votes for and against union, emphasizing demographic racial patterns, appeared in 1959. The review of the contemporary Presbyterian literature by Sanford M. Dornbusch and Roger D. Irle indicated that race was less frequently mentioned in print than issues such as theological liberalism, the ownership of church property, and the loss of regional identity. The sociological explanation juxtaposed what was written against union with the proportion of rural residents and blacks in given geographic areas. This was the same criteria which had been used to analyze the Dixiecrat movement in the 1948 presidential election. The authors concluded that religious ideology was often used to rationalize behavior. They found it difficult to believe that people acted solely on the basis of dogma. Dornbusch and Irle corroborated their conclusions with selected interviews.[43]

This analysis created controversy within the PCUS. The *Presbyterian Outlook* reprinted the entire article along with editorial criticism. Acknowledging that race was an issue in the reunion debate, it noted that a few key votes in several presbyteries would have substantially changed the presbytery-by-presbytery count. Moreover, Dornbusch and Irle misquoted the prime creedal document of PCUSA "liberalism," namely, the Auburn Affirmation of 1924, which conservatives relentlessly attacked. Finally, notice was taken of those PCUSA Presbyterians living in the South who voted for union but had the same racial prejudices as white members of the PCUS.[44]

The defeat of the church union movement in 1954–55 and a residual anti-union sentiment in some parts of the church resulted from many years of struggle. Race was one of several issues in this debate. A committee to oppose reunion organized in 1945 had promulgated ten arguments to oppose reunion: (1) inadequacy of the plan under consideration; (2) doctrinal differences; (3) the plan's changes in the status of ruling elders; (4) the possible ordination of women; (5) regional synods; (6) creation of a powerful General Council; (7) changes in church property arrangements; (8) different stands on "social, political, and racial problems," which would lead to controversy; (9) a belief that unity among Christians was not necessarily a matter of denominational structures; and (10) a strong faith in the regional identity of the denomination. These objections, listed in the order initially argued, indicated a wide variety of factors. Each bore some relation to the others, but none should be lifted out of context. The ambiguity of the position of anti-union forces was pointed out in an anonymous letter from "A Loyal Southern Presbyterian" to the *Presbyterian Outlook* in 1957. The writer knew of a PCUS congregation which forced a PCUS minister favoring reunion to resign. After accepting his resignation, the church then called a non-PCUS minister who opposed reunification.[45]

Both the pro-union and anti-union forces organized during the 1954–55 campaign. The pro-union forces chose Francis Pickens Miller of Virginia as their executive secretary. Miller was from the valley of Virginia and the child of a Presbyterian minister. He worked with the YMCA in Europe after World War I and later with the Student Volunteer Movement. In the 1940s he entered public life when he ran for the governorship of Virginia against a candidate of the well-entrenched Byrd machine. He then challenged Harry Byrd directly in 1948 when he ran for the Senate seat which Byrd occupied.

An active Presbyterian, Miller served as a commissioner to four general assemblies. The pro-union forces indeed had a knowledgeable political strategist and dedicated Presbyterian as their organizer. Miller engaged in a series of debates with anti-union speakers. He was floored to hear them telling the "Big Lie" about various leaders in the PCUSA, including John Mackay, the moderator. The opposition alleged that Mackay was a Communist and cited a *New York Times* editorial as proof. When Miller researched the charge and produced the editorial cited, which did not say what was purported, the accuser refused to admit an error had been made and persisted in the charge. Unfortunately, many chose to believe the lie.

In analyzing the defeat of church union in 1954–55, Miller spent time talking to a variety of pro-union activists. One conversation epitomized the problem. Miller's contact indicated that anti-union forces found elders in a Deep South presbytery from churches that had not been active for years. Transportation was arranged for them to the presbytery meeting voting on the issue, and they delivered the votes. "What in the world could have caused them to work so hard?" Miller asked his friend. Though hesitant to reply, the answer came, "You know perfectly well . . . Niggers and damn Yankees." As much as he hated to admit it, Miller concluded, "I knew he was right."[46]

Race was an important item in the conservative critique of supposed PCUSA liberalism. Church agencies of the PCUSA sponsored interracial community visits in the 1940s, worked to dismantle racially segregated church courts, and permitted the stated clerk of the General Assembly to appear before Congress in favor of the Fair Employment Practices Commission.[47]

Black Presbyterians, Northern and Southern, were not of one mind on the reunion issue. In the PCUSA General Assembly, blacks largely opposed the plan, while Southern blacks generally endorsed it. All three segregated presbyteries in the PCUS voted for the union plan. At least one black minister joined the PCUS hoping that the proposed three-way union of the two larger Presbyterian bodies with the smaller United Presbyterian Church in North America would become a reality. When the plan failed in the 1950s, he and other proponents of union decided to wait for another day.[48]

Conservative opposition to the reunion movement persisted throughout the 1960s and into the 1970s in particular areas. In Central Mississippi Presbytery, which was notoriously conservative, clerical leadership mixed a conservative approach to ecclesiastical matters with the race issue to sustain ecclesiastical control. After that control was broken in the late 1960s, the presbytery remained staunchly opposed to reunion efforts until 1983. The 1969 General Assembly approved the establishment of a joint reunion committee with the United Presbyterian Church in the U.S.A. Central Mississippi Presbytery responded in 1971 with a scathing attack on attempts to adulterate the Westminster Confession of Faith, in reunion talks rejected ecumenical efforts such as the Consultation on Church Union, and then upheld congregational control over property.[49] The persistence of such anti-union sentiment had important consequences in the 1970s.

Another consequence of the debate over race was the reinterpretation of the idea of the spirituality of the church. This resulted in a number of cases where ministers jeopardized their pulpits and even their careers by taking stands favoring desegregation. Because race was so rarely broached as a sermon topic prior to 1954, congregations often reacted with confusion or anger when they heard it discussed from the pulpit in the post-*Brown* period. Some congregations became restive when ministers began to suggest in earnest that black Americans deserved equal access to all facilities and the respect of white Americans, not only because this was the law of the land, but because it was Christian. Reprisals took various forms. Some churches would query prospective ministers to ensure that they were racially orthodox. This meant that all ministers had to take a position regarding racial issues. Marion Boggs, a pastor in Little Rock and a moderator of the PCUS General Assembly, noted to a group of seminary students that parishioners would react in a wide variety of ways. Some verbally expressed their hatred, others left the church, while others stopped making contributions. Furthermore, Boggs noted that the official positions of the denomination supported desegregation and could not be used to uphold segregation.[50]

Some ministers looked back on their experiences with humor; others found them harrowing. During the 1950s one minister in Orlando, Florida, offended a significant contributor with a reference to race. The church member ceased attending services and stopped payment on his pledge. When the minister asked the man if he was withholding his pledge to buy the minister's conscience, the man announced that he would neither change his mind nor return to the church while the pastor was there. (He did return after the offending clergyman left.) After blacks appeared in two worship services in Birmingham, Alabama, pressure began to mount on the minister of the First Presbyterian Church to take some action to ensure that such visits did not become a permanent pattern. He began to receive anonymous phone calls at night, and his tires were slashed.

The ultimate retaliation was expulsion from the pulpit, a development the Presbyterian system was designed to prevent from happening arbitrarily. The system was intended to protect the integrity of the minister's conscience. The dominant polity among Southern Protestants was congregational, and some of these notions spread into PCUS congregations. In some cases, the system of church courts in fact did not protect the minister's position.[51] Several of these instances deserve discussion, for collectively they illustrate how Presbyterian polity and theology dealt with the effects of race.

Charles Jones served the Presbyterian Church of Chapel Hill, North Carolina, for a number of years beginning in the late 1940s. Both the church and Jones were thought of as liberal, not only from a theological viewpoint, but also for their stands on social issues. When Jones allowed several officers to serve in the church without proper training or installation, Orange Presbytery appointed a Judicial Commission to investigate. The commission had authority to act in the interest of the presbytery. It brought no charges against Jones but dissolved his pastoral relation with the church in 1953. The congregation was very upset with this development, which also involved the dissolution of the session. The church protested to the Synod of North Carolina, to no avail.[52]

Jones's views were unpopular with many of his fellow churchmen, and race was advanced as the explanation for this action. Supporters of the action of Orange Presbytery bristled at such an accusation. They charged that Jones had been derelict in the ministerial duties required by Presbyterians. The ecclesiastical irregularities which had developed over a period of years were well documented; however, the circumstances suggest that other factors also operated in the case.[53] Jones's dismissal was widely discussed in the denomination. It illustrates how race was connected to a host of other issues for Southern Presbyterians.

An even more celebrated case developed during the pastorate of Robert McNeill at the First Presbyterian Church, Columbus, Georgia, from 1952 to 1959. McNeill went to Columbus with high hopes and much praise, but several events soured relations with his church members. McNeill supported the church union plan of 1953–54, despite a congregational straw poll which indicated that over 60 percent of his Columbus congregation opposed it. In 1957 Chester Morrison, editor for *Look* magazine, was searching for a Southern moderate to write an article on race relations which would counteract negative Ku Klux Klan publicity. Morrison's contacts in Atlanta indicated that McNeill was the proper person for the task, and the article McNeill produced was mild and conciliatory in tone. McNeill intended to inform the church of the article before it was printed, but before he had a chance, word of publication was leaked in Columbus, causing rumors to circulate. Many of the people in the church and city believed the worst of the rumors. McNeill read the article to a joint meeting of elders and deacons to help defuse the issue, and they agreed that there was nothing radical in their minister's word, but local segregationists pilloried the Presbyterian minister.[54]

McNeill's position within the congregation went from bad to worse in 1958–59. Church members and the local segregation press assailed him when he tried to help the League of Women Voters arrange a meeting place for Ralph McGill, editor of the *Atlanta Constitution*, who was widely known for his moderate racial stands. Then McNeill tried to assist Clarence Jordan of Koinonia Farms near Americus, Georgia, to purchase supplies. Koinonia was boycotted by local merchants because it practiced racial equality based on Christian principles. Both of these modest attempts to assist other groups failed. In addition, staff dissension in the church was used to embarrass McNeill. When the situation appeared to be improving, a young reporter for the *Columbus Ledger* wanted to write a follow-up article for *Look*. The article was a premature embarrassment and was never printed.[55]

During this time a Judicial Commission of Southwest Georgia Presbytery was at work. McNeill welcomed what he thought was help from the presbytery. The commission dissolved the session of the church in what was generally thought to be an action favorable to the minister. Gradually, however, commission members distanced themselves from McNeill. The commission was aware of a history of congregational discord in the church and realized that much opposition existed to McNeill's *Look* article. In the spring of 1959, a commission representative reported that the pastoral relation was dissolved. The tragedy of the situation was compounded the following week, when McNeill suffered a heart attack. After his recovery, he went to Charleston, West Virginia, to serve the Bream Memorial Presbyterian Church.[56]

McNeill's plight received regionwide attention, principally through the efforts of Ralph McGill. The Atlanta newspaperman lamented the situation and blamed racial prejudice for it. McGill was right in believing race was a major issue in McNeill's eviction. Equally important and overlooked, however, was the deteriorating relations between McNeill, his congregation, and the presbytery. The *Presbyterian Outlook* lamented that a system designed to provide integrity could be abused in such a way. If the same spirit was manifested by other presbyteries in maintaining Presbyterian order, the *Outlook* commented, "it will not be worth keeping."[57]

The third and final case involved not only a minister and presbytery but ultimately the General Assembly. Early in 1962 the Trinity Presbyterian Church in Meridian, Mississippi, issued a call to the Reverend Abel McIver "Mac" Hart, then serving a church in Wynne, Arkansas. Hart appeared before the Presbytery of Central Mississippi to be admitted as a member. After examining Hart in the standard areas of experiential religion, theology and sacraments, and church government, the presbytery found him unqualified and refused to receive him as a member and permanent pastor. However, he was allowed to serve the Trinity Church temporarily.[58]

The Meridian congregation pursued the matter, and its leadership, along with a minority of ministers in the presbytery, sought to have the Synod of Mississippi take corrective action. The synod appointed a Special Judicial Commission to investigate the situation. It found acrimonious relations among members of the presbytery, a very divisive atmosphere, and a mentality which tolerated only legalistic interpretations "inconsistent with the spirit of governmental processes of the Presbyterian Church, U.S." The synod then instructed Central Mississippi Presbytery to reexamine Hart, though it noted both Hart and the Trinity Church had "acted imprudently" in the call and its acceptance.[59]

Hart's reexamination took place in July 1964. As with the first examination, the theological section was crucial. Questioning focused on the historicity of Adam and the inerrancy of the Bible. Hart refused to be identified as a fundamentalist and to link the infallibility of the Bible, "the only rule of faith and practice," as Presbyterians called it, with inerrancy, the belief in God's literal verbal inspiration of the Scriptures. The presbytery again ruled that Hart had failed the examination, and another complaint was filed with the synod, which ruled that the questions were "improper, arbitrary and oppressive in that bias and prejudice was manifest in both form and content." The Trinity Church Session appealed in the interim to the 1964 General Assembly, requesting that it make Hart a member of the presbytery. There was moral support for his case there, but this extraordinary request was refused. Soon thereafter, Hart left to answer a call from the Second Presbyterian Church in Little Rock, Arkansas. The presbytery was warned that future examinations should not be conducted with similar intensity and malice.[60]

After Hart's rejection in the first examination, a group of ministers representing a variety of churches in the presbytery sent a "Memorial" to the Synod of Mississippi about the oppressive manner in which the Presbytery of Central Mississippi conducted its business. They charged that decisions were not made at presbytery meetings, but in prearranged closed meetings. The presbytery leadership was most distressed at such a complaint and appointed a committee which seriously contemplated prosecution of the eleven signers of the memorial and even prepared indictments. Eventually the presbytery's charges were dismissed in return for the "withdrawing" of signatures from the memorial. Gradually, most of the signatories left Mississippi.[61]

Hart's racial views were thought to be the cause of his failing the examinations and partly the cause of the memorial sent to the synod. Those closely associated with the presbytery's case said that race was not an issue at all. Race, however, was indeed a litmus test for the archconservative theology of the presbytery, and as such race was an issue as in the ecclesiastical power struggle.[62] Though the issues in the Hart case and racial attitudes may never have been officially connected, they were interrelated by the political groupings in the presbytery.

Racial ideology cannot be pointed to as the only issue in the cases of Charles Jones, Robert McNeill, and "Mac" Hart. Important clues, however, point to it as a factor of varying degrees of strength. Presbyterian polity in the twentieth century has developed the fine art of procedure. In each of these cases there were procedural issues at stake. But the procedure must be informed by the content and context. The views of Jones and the Chapel Hill congregation, the article in *Look*, and the social and theological reactionary conservatism in Mississippi suggest the strong causality of social ideology in these cases.

In a similar way, there is no apparent reason to connect marriage with race. However, fear of intermarriage was a very powerful topic for white Southerners. After World War II, there were indications in PCUS circles that fear of racial intermarriage would no longer be the red herring of race relations. Such a hope had scarcely been entertained before a controversy involving the subject at a youth mission conference emerged in the denominational press. A Presbyterian minister heard that a leader at the denominationally sponsored Nashville Youth and Mission Conference had called intermarriage of the races legitimate. This sentiment enraged many in the PCUS. Convention officials responded that no platform speaker had argued for this position and that the charges were hearsay. They defended the right to consider race relations at such a convention because "you can't discuss the responsibility of Anglo-Saxons going to other races today with the gospel and not discuss race. But race amalgamation is another thing."[63]

Presbyterian segregationists were not satisfied with such an answer, and they argued that segregation allowed for the maintenance of racial integrity. "Nonsegregation" would inevitably mean the increase in incidences of miscegenation. G. T. Gillespie of Mississippi asserted in 1954 that racial separation was a time-honored Anglo-Saxon tradition. The only available alternative was "the Communist goal of amalgamation." Morton Smith, a professor at Belhaven College and conservative critic of church events, argued that intermarriage would be the probable result of the 1960s social revolution. Such a turn in events would destroy the divinely created diversity of humankind and help establish Communist domination.[64]

Liberals in the PCUS disapproved of the facileness with which segregationists connected integration and intermarriage. These were scare tactics to divert attention from the real issues. The matter at issue was whether treatment of black Americans was just. Questions about intermarriage should be answered as Jesus answered the Pharisees about Sabbath observance, said one *Presbyterian Outlook* reader: "Is it lawful to do good or to do harm, to save life or to kill?"[65]

The civil rights movement also raised questions about the limits of government authority. After the *Brown* decision in 1954, desegregation was the law of the land. The General Assembly and many synods, presbyteries, and sessions endorsed it. When the government moved to enforce the law, official policy of the denomination could be counted on to support the rule of law. Marion Boggs, pastor of the Second Presbyterian Church in Little Rock, Arkansas, called for moderation and cooperation with law enforcement officials in that city's planned school integration of 1957. He addressed the issue of desegregation only once from the pulpit, but his sermon, "The Crucial Test of Christian Citizenship," on July 4, 1957, was an important statement in support of school desegregation. Boggs gave three reasons to eliminate segregation: the system "is in direct contradiction to the Christian doctrine of the dignity of man," it reversed the concept of American freedom, and it harmed the missionary work of the church, particularly in Africa. He had reflected long before saying anything about the school desegregation plan. His words were spoken prior to the violence of that year, and they were anything but radical. Boggs noted that desegregation occurred only after several years' preparation of a modest plan which should have broad support in the white community. His call for Christian citizenship was well received in the denomination but did not prevent violence in Little Rock. Citizenship was a major theme of the PCUS General Assembly for the 1956–57 church year, and many church groups used Bible study materials which focused on the responsibilities of Christian citizenship. Some thought the topic was not biblical, however, and several people strongly objected to the women's Bible study on that grounds.[66]

The racial violence of the 1950s and 1960s put Christian citizenship to the test. The Southern Presbyterian call for support of the law was the denominational means of supporting equal rights guaranteed by the government. It had definite theological implications. These were clearly indicated in a collection of sermons published in 1965, *The Unsilent South: Prophetic Preaching in Racial Crisis*. These sermons were collected by Donald W. Shriver, Jr., then professor of religion at North Carolina State University in Raleigh and a Presbyterian minister. Together they represented a new understanding of the major Southern Presbyterian doctrine, the "spirituality of the church." A major part of this reevaluation centered on the role of church-state relations.[67]

The legal enforcement of desegregation came from the federal government. Resistance to the integration of the University of Mississippi in the fall of 1962 greatly disturbed Robert Walkup, pastor of the First Presbyterian Church in Starkville, Mississippi. Starkville was the home of the state's land grant university, Mississippi State University. Had James Meredith wanted to be a farmer or engineer rather than a lawyer, Starkville might have become as infamous as Oxford did in the September 1962 news reports.

In the tension-packed days when a great debate raged in Mississippi over segregation and state sovereignty, Walkup declared to his people: "All this talk about the United States government being sovereign is *foolishness*! And all this talk about the State of Mississippi being sovereign is *foolishness*! Sovereign means: 'one who has power that is not diminished by anything anywhere.' There is only one type of sovereignty and that's absolute sovereignty, *and that belongs to God*! And that's the *only* place it belongs."[68] The Mississippi minister attempted to have his congregation recognize that there were larger issues at stake than whether the federal government was at fault in the Oxford riot. Southerners daily confronted the legacy of segregation. The corrective step would be to adhere to laws which righted past wrongs, even though such adherence would not remove the cumulative judgment of the sins of slavery and segregation. Walkup's declaration gave notice that if laws were wrong, Christians had an obligation to rectify them.

The civil rights movement confronted white America with people who practiced civil disobedience. Many whites were confused by this strategy; some were enraged. Presbyterians were caught between supporting legal authorities and condemning unjust laws. This conflict encouraged some to engage in activities of the civil rights movement. The faculty at Richmond's Union Theological Seminary adopted a resolution urging Congress to pass the 1964 Civil Rights Act. Other Presbyterians argued that such laws helped alleviate inequities and that the 1964 law had a moral purpose. Christian principles coincided with the needs of American democracy in this case.[69]

The increasing use of civil disobedience made other Southern Presbyterians uneasy. What limits were there to such behavior? Liberals pointed out that civil disobedience was not new. There were prominent biblical examples in Daniel and Acts. John S. Brown cited American history for other examples of resistance to authority which was later glorified: the American Revolution and (at least for white Southerners) the Civil War. Others urged that critics of civil disobedience remember how much pain and suffering had been endured by black Americans. Blacks' civil disobedience derived from the experiences of being either ignored or abused by legal authorities. Such a legacy had to produce some movement for justice.[70]

The General Assembly formally stated its opinion on civil disobedience in 1965 and again in 1968. Its statement entitled "The Civil Rights Movement in the Light of Christian Teachings" placed the denomination in support of the use of civil disobedience when "Higher Law" had been violated. The church should be concerned with "a more truly redemptive society." It should also tolerate civil disobedience as a legitimate expression of social protest. However, participants should bear the responsibility of their actions. This statement created much contention within the denomination, but attempts to rescind the statement failed. By 1968 violence had to be added to the range of issues involved in civil disobedience. The General Assembly moved to respond in its paper "Toward an Understanding of Racial Disorder." Violence was wrong, but the proper response to rioting was justice, not vengeance. Proper justice should take into account the conditions spawning violence.[71]

Conservative critics were offended by these statements, which, they argued, moved the church into the realm of activities properly left to the state. They interpreted the Bible and the various confessions of the church, especially the Westminster Confession, to support the authority of the state. With these statements, as well as those regarding other social issues, conservatives argued that the denomination had moved away from the historic position of Southern Presbyterians, "which in its 'Opening Address' (of 1861) declared the realm of Church and state to be distinctive and separate."[72]

No matter how much explanation was given, nothing could satisfy these critics. A correspondent to the denominational periodical *Presbyterian Survey* was upset at the inclusion of a photograph of Eugene Carson Blake, stated clerk of the United Presbyterian Church, as he participated in a march at a Baltimore amusement park. "To obey a law you disagree with is one thing," he wrote; "to violate it because you deem it unjust is contrary to the New Testament teaching, especially Romans 13." In such an analysis civil disobedience could not be tolerated. In this order of things the church supported the government in things nonspiritual, as the government left the church to deal with spiritual matters.[73]

During the years of the civil rights movement, the Presbyterian Church in the United States did reevaluate its position regarding appropriate acts of protest. It regarded segregationist protest as unacceptable, for no justification could be made for the maintenance of segregation, but as civil disobedience became a tool increasingly utilized to achieve the goals of desegregation, the denomination began to approve activities which involved violations of the law.

All Presbyterians in the South, white and black, lived with segregation as law and custom since the late nineteenth century. The denomination, however, never abandoned its impulse to pursue mission work with dark-skinned peoples, and the PCUS was active in sending black missionaries to Africa. Some of their work was quite significant. Although the missionaries were not always egalitarians, African missions continued to be of importance to the church. Mission activities were frequent topics of young people's meetings in the late 1940s and 1950s, which considered both the physical and spiritual needs of Africans.[74]

Church people recognized that in the postwar world it would be increasingly difficult to combine adherence to Christianity and to segregation. Such a contradiction could result in anti-American attitudes. This realization came to one woman while in Sunday school with a group of Mexican Presbyterians studying Romans, where God is declared to be "no respecter of persons." If that is so, one participant asked, why were there signs in the United States barring blacks and Mexicans from businesses and public places? The denominational leadership also took up this cry, and missionaries reported that their efforts were adversely affected by the continued practice of segregation in the United States. The effectiveness of such an argument on the church membership is difficult, if not impossible, to document. Impressionistic evidence indicates that it did little to change the mind of the firmly convinced Presbyterian segregationist. If opinions changed, they changed for other reasons.[75]

The tensions between liberals and conservatives always lay close to the surface among Southern Presbyterians and covered a variety of issues in addition to race. Southern Presbyterian liberalism should not be confused with the modernist movement in theological circles. One minister noted that he had always thought of himself as "moderately liberal" until he did graduate work at the University of Edinburgh. There "he was classed as a dyed-in-the-wool conservative." The theological opinions which these liberals held were distinct from conservative positions, but were not radical. Ecumenicity and "progressive" action were at the heart of their work, although race was *the* question for them to deal with as Southern Presbyterians.[76]

Nonetheless, conservatives within the denomination were horrified at liberal trends. This was their motivation in forming the *Southern Presbyterian Journal*, from which they launched attacks against liberals in the church. A 1962 *Journal* editorial noted that both conservatives and liberals could go to extremes, but the liberal extreme was worse by far. Liberals should not be trusted because they could not be trusted. They were inclined "to falsehood, for liberalism, with its inclination to see truth as relative, is naturally disposed to hold all truth lightly." Ultimately, liberalism "unchecked leads to license and finally to anarchy." Conservatives believed that liberals controlled the denominational structures and that programs aimed at correcting society rather than at individual salvation were the results.[77] These conflicting ideologies and theologies led to a battle for control of the denomination.

Several moderate and liberal Presbyterians banded together to form a support group for ministers who were subjected to intense pressure for failure to support segregation in the 1960s. They organized the Fellowship of Concern (FOC), a group open only to Southern Presbyterians, clergy and laity, who wanted to help bring about racial reconciliation because they thought the General Assembly was not acting quickly enough on the issues. They welcomed non–Southern Presbyterian support, but limited their membership. The FOC wanted to

interpret Presbyterian history and doctrine to show a social conscious-
ness and "to assert moral leadership in the changing patterns of racial
and cultural revolution." They also made efforts to enlarge their aims
and support Presbyterian reunion, ecumenicity, and biblical scholarship. These, however, remained secondary considerations to the primary goal of serving as a moral agent in the racial revolution.[78]

Soon after the creation of FOC, a conservative group organized to
counter its efforts. Concerned Presbyterians was formed in the summer of 1964. They decided to use the *Presbyterian Journal* as the
sounding board for their positions and employed a staff person to dis-
seminate information, promote local organizations, and cooperate
with other groups with similar goals. In the UPCUSA and the PCUS
they saw trends toward identifying "social problems" as the work of
the church. Concerned Presbyterians believed that "the Church must
be returned to an orientation in terms of the Gospel, or God most
surely will give her up."[79]

The competition between the FOC and Concerned Presbyterians,
though not always direct, was acrimonious. The conflict came to a
head in 1967 when a group of influential ministers and laity composed
"An Open Letter to the Church." The letter asserted that two well-
organized groups were concerned with the purity of the church. The
situation was harming church work, especially evangelistic efforts. If
unchecked, it could result in schism. FOC leadership regretted that
they had been compared with Concerned Presbyterians because they
were not well organized and because they lacked the single-minded
concern for uniformity in the church which many alleged to be true
of Concerned Presbyterians. "We categorically deny every one of the
charges and implications" in the "Open Letter," wrote several FOC
leaders. Many readers and the editors of the *Presbyterian Outlook* as
well as several church courts also objected to placing the FOC in the
same category with Concerned Presbyterians. None argued that Concerned Presbyterians had been improperly classified.[80]

By 1968 what had once been considered a healthy debate was ap-
proaching a very divisive point. Marshall Dendy, moderator of the
1967 General Assembly and executive secretary of the Board of Christian Education, was concerned over the harm which might come to
the church from this debate. He sought to alleviate tension by addressing both groups. The FOC, Dendy said, had come to represent a sin-
ister element to some in the church, who thought it was replacing

evangelism with sociology. Much of this perception could be traced to FOC members' participation in the civil rights movement. He encouraged the organization to study the issues further and be ready to "disorganize" in the best interest of the denomination.[81]

The moderator also addressed Concerned Presbyterians and received generally favorable responses from both visits. Dendy then called a meeting of various church leaders to resolve some of the issues. Forty-one of forty-eight invited leaders attended the meeting, held in January 1968. Kenneth Keyes, president of Concerned Presbyterians, was one of that groups' five lay representatives. He presented a conservative critique of the denomination's programs, beginning by identifying the leaders of the PCUS boards and agencies as liberals. They were supporters of civil disobedience and of the National Council of Churches. There were also issues of ecclesiastical politics which determined the liberal position, such as participation in the Consultation on Church Union (COCU); a central treasury; the Board of World Missions participation in Project Equality (a civil rights program in Nashville, Tennessee); procedural changes which closed avenues of protest to Concerned Presbyterians; the editorial policies of the official church magazine, the *Presbyterian Survey*; rotation of elders to presbytery meetings; unicameral local church government; the General Assembly stands on Vietnam, China, and labor issues; and "packing" the General Assembly to misrepresent the church. Furthermore, liberal leaders lacked interest in evangelism. Keyes and Concerned Presbyterians were opposed to the spread of this liberalism, which they claimed characterized FOC.[82]

Soon thereafter FOC voted to disband. The organization believed that it had accomplished its major purpose within the denomination. It had regularly contributed to a variety of causes, including the Board of Christian Education's Division of Social Action and the Southern Christian Leadership Conference. In dissolution, FOC distributed its remaining funds between the Poor People's March, a scholarship for a Brazilian pastor, and the *Presbyterian Outlook*. The dissolution of FOC did not readily decrease tension. That summer Keyes called upon conservatives to mobilize in an effort to wrest control from liberals. If the liberal church leadership would not respond to the conservative critique, conservatives would give to more ideologically compatible causes than denominational benevolences. Church leaders were obviously dissatisfied with this situation.[83]

By 1968 the days of the overt defense of segregation had passed. Though the conservative-liberal continuum which convulsed the denomination in the late 1960s was not tied exclusively to racial ideology, there was a significant relationship between the issues and the groups vying for power. Conservatives continued their criticisms until 1973, when they decided that they could never gain control from the liberal element and probably could not stop another union attempt because of structural changes that had come about after 1955. Many then opted to leave the PCUS and form the Presbyterian Church in America (PCA). Race was not the only issue motivating these conservatives to form this new denomination, but it was part of the larger debate over the scope of authority in the denomination as well as the impact of a larger social conscience. Defenders of the new denomination are quick to claim that racial ideology had nothing to do with the events of 1973, but their case is unconvincing, as they ignore a substantial body of evidence.[84] Those conservatives who made their peace on race and several polity issues found that they could stay. Those who were unable to do so opened yet another door in the denominational household.

4

OPENING CLOSED DOORS

THE PRESENCE of black Presbyterians in church meetings and affairs was a major issue for the PCUS. The confusion that had characterized the denomination's programs before World War II was still evident in the era of the Negro Work Program and the civil rights movement. Tension over how to relate to black Presbyterians plagued their white brethren, while the General Assembly adopted a position that aligned the denomination in support of the goal of desegregation and integration. The profession of this goal and actual church practice did not coincide until the late 1960s because of segregationist recalcitrance and the ambivalence of moderate white Southerners. Even then, black Presbyterians questioned the sincerity of these actions. The sense of equivocation was evident in the action of Mecklenburg Presbytery at a 1948 meeting, when the continued membership of a black church was considered. The presbytery decided that the church could remain a member of the predominantly white geographic presbytery if the minister joined a segregated presbytery. This removed the ministerial representative of the church at presbytery meetings; at the same time, however, Mecklenburg Presbytery adopted a resolution noting the need for equal legal opportunity for blacks.[1]

Youth and women's groups were the two PCUS constituencies in the forefront of calling for integration of church affairs. The interracial concerns of both continued into the 1950s and 1960s. The PCUS was the only regional denomination that received blacks at meetings of governing bodies. Their presence at the General Assembly and after 1952 at synods presented logistic problems because facilities for black commissioners were always segregated. This problem helped keep the reality of segregation before the church, and gradually its courts moved to address the practice of racial separation. The white male power structure of the denomination was the last to incorporate desegregation into the church program.

An important part of the denomination's program was carried on by women's organizations in the church. A denominationwide women's organization was not established until 1912, although its informal organizational structure developed during the previous century. The local Auxiliary was the basic unit, with regional groupings at the levels of presbytery (the Presbyterial) and synod (the Synodical). The denominationwide administration was through the Assembly's Committee on Woman's Work.[2]

The activities of the Auxiliary in interracial work were noticed by leaders in the denomination. Women's participation was significant in a variety of ways. The Woman's Auxiliary sponsored a series of conferences for black women held at Stillman Institute. The first of these was in 1916, and thereafter the conferences became annual events. Fifty-three conferees, drawn from a variety of denominations, attended the first conference. The conference concept spread to the Synodical and Presbyterial organizations and received interdenominational support. The first was jointly sponsored with the Society of Friends at the Christianburg Industrial Institute in Christianburg, Virginia. The number of conferences grew rapidly to eleven in 1923–24. Some claimed that they had a positive effect on race relations by drawing white and black women into closer contact. Before the conferences, the most common contact of Auxiliary women with black women frequently had been as the employers of domestics. Auxiliary leadership heralded the new dimension of this relationship as representing a necessary improvement in racial conditions.[3]

The Auxiliary put much forethought and effort into these conferences. Training sessions for the directors of the Synodical conferences were first offered in 1931 at Montreat, North Carolina, the denomination's then-segregated conference ground. Local Auxiliaries near black Presbyterian churches encouraged the conferences. A field worker was employed to help organize Auxiliaries in black churches during the 1940s, for by that time conferences had been reduced because of financial crisis and transportation problems.[4]

The Auxiliary-sponsored conferences attempted to educate black women on a variety of topics. They always included Bible studies along with instruction in "sewing, home economics, sanitation, community problems and better ways of living." The early programs were planned for black women by white women. This approach implied cultural superiority, though in later years conference leaders incorporated blacks into the planning process.[5]

The structure of the Auxiliary was segregated, as were the church courts. Black Presbyterial organizations faced the additional obstacles of distance and expense, which were not faced in the geographic presbyteries. Just as white ministers were slow to accept the idea of a women's organization, so were their black counterparts. Hallie Paxson Winnsborough, the founder of the Woman's Auxiliary, claimed that the intent of the organization was always to have minority women included. But the time and distance necessary to travel in segregated presbyteries mitigated against the development of such organizations. Slowly, Presbyterials were organized in Snedecor Memorial Synod. The first was founded in 1925, the fourth and last in 1938. A Snedecor Memorial Synodical was not organized until ten years later,[6] only a few years before the dissolution of the synod. The Presbyterials remained segregated until the 1960s.

The Woman's Auxiliary also supported the work at Stillman Institute. Women were first admitted there in 1897, though only as secondary day students. The institute became coeducational in an effort to provide practical training in the domestic sciences and other fields such as nursing. The proponents of the girl's school chose Tuscaloosa because of Stillman's existence. The Auxiliary took a "Special Cause" offering in 1919 to raise money for a building. The Executive Committee on Home Missions already had $25,000 on hand, to which the Woman's Auxiliary added $10,000 and the General Education Board in New York also contributed $20,000. College officials first used the building as a women's dorm with the advent of coeducation in 1922.[7]

The Woman's Auxiliary took part in numerous aspects of the larger interracial work of the period because of its leadership. Winnsborough was always interested in race relations and frequently supported the cause of the underprivileged. In the 1880s she worked for improved conditions in the Italian community of Kansas City, Missouri. For many years she belonged to two nonsectarian organizations concerned with race relations—the Commission of Church and Race Relations and the Commission on Interracial Cooperation (CIC). Largely because of her interest, the Woman's Auxiliary supported the work of the CIC, as did many other denominational women's organizations.[8]

Winnsborough became dissatisfied with the pace at which the CIC was working and threatened to pull Southern Presbyterian women out of the organization. The CIC developed the "Alabama Experiment" after Winnsborough met with Jesse Daniels Ames of the CIC, who was also a major force in the independent Association of Southern Women for the Prevention of Lynching. The Alabama Experiment was designed to involve local church women's groups in surveying community social conditions. Greatest attention was given to the problems of blacks and poor whites such as mill workers and miners. Tuscaloosa Presbyterial was the pilot project area. The survey began in 1929 and enrolled church women from Baptist, Methodist, Episcopal, and Presbyterian congregations, and the participation of black women was encouraged, but no such participation was recorded.[9]

The effect of these programs, both denominational and interdenominational, was to increase many women's awareness of the plight of Southern blacks in the period before World War II. The programs offered some opportunity for Presbyterian women to participate in antilynching groups, although such participation was restricted. This participation was not a sign of singlemindedness on the part of the Auxiliary, for benevolence and racial superiority coexisted in the minds of many Presbyterian women.[10]

Auxiliary participation in the CIC and individual participation in the ASWPL drew criticism. The president of the Women's National Association for the Preservation of the White Race, Mrs. J. E. Andrews of Atlanta, attacked the involvement of the Auxiliary and similar organizations in the antilynching campaign. Andrews believed that the rights of blacks should be respected, but according to her, there were undoubtedly many black men guilty of ravishing Southern white girls who were then defended by the antilynching groups. Someone needed to protect the poor, defenseless, white girls against both rapists and ASWPL supporters.[11]

Not all Auxiliary women supported the work of the CIC, much less the ASWPL, but many did accept the idea that conditions for blacks had to be improved and that whites bore a large measure of responsibility for this work. In this they shared the same opinion as the larger circle of interracial workers during the period. The Auxiliary did move away from working *for* black women to working *with* black women within the parameters of a legally segregated society. The planning committee of an interracial meeting in Birmingham canceled the event in 1947 because local authorities announced their intention of enforcing segregation ordinances. The committee then held an "informal" integrated meeting.[12]

New levels of cooperation resulted from the participation of the Board of Women's Work (the Auxiliary's name after 1948) with the Negro Work Program. Specifically, they followed precedent and worked to establish women's organizations in newly developed black churches. The board participated in the operation of the Snedecor Region by the division. The Presbyterials of the three segregated presbyteries composed the Snedecor Region, Women of the Church. Thus the transfer of black presbyteries to geographic presbyteries in 1952 did not mean that black Presbyterials became part of the geographic Synodicals. In 1958 the Snedecor Region was dissolved, and then the Presbyterials became members of the geographic Synodicals. In addition, several Synodical organizations in Missouri, Texas, Virginia, and Tennessee desegregated. The symbolic gesture of this new relationship occurred in 1958, when for the first time a black woman attended the Montreat Women's Conference.[13]

The new locations of the black Presbyterials in the geographic presbyteries did allow increased opportunities for black women to participate, both individually and corporately, in the PCUS women's program. Tuscaloosa, Mobile, and Birmingham Presbyterials opened their 1961 retreats to "all" women in their bounds. Black women also were allowed access to previously segregated educational events, as in 1963, when the Synodical of North Carolina's Training School was integrated by the presence of two women from the Dellabrook Presbyterian Church in Winston-Salem, a congregation founded through the Negro Work Program.[14]

These gains were not achieved without some sense of loss. As the black women's organizations were absorbed by the previously all-white organizations, a sense of identity among black women was lost. Georgia-Carolina Presbyterial dropped from 19 groups with 250 members in 1963, to 14 groups with 156 members in 1964, as churches were transferred to geographic presbyteries. The last president of the Georgia-Carolina Presbyterial, Mary M. Blue, stated that past relationships had been helpful and that new ways of service would be needed in the future.[15]

The Board of Women's Work continued to try to provide educational events for black women, such as the Stillman Training School, even after the formal discontinuance of Snedecor Region. The pattern was changed with the General Assembly's effort to dissolve the black presbyteries. In 1964 the board opened an interracial workshop at Stillman to help orient white and black Presbyterian women in Alabama. The Central Alabama Presbyterial executive board requested the program, which met with some success, but the white women's leadership did not participate as fully as was hoped. Another program was attempted in 1965. Similar conferences followed for the churches in Mississippi, Louisiana, and Georgia and were paid for out of the funds that had previously supported the conference at Stillman. Similar results were reported, as many white women in responsible positions did not attend. Nonetheless, the board was generally pleased with the results.[16]

Youth organizations were also involved in the desegregation of Presbyterian institutions. Indeed, much of the controversy about desegregation focused on what kind of interracial relationships would be allowed between males and females of both races. Sometimes unarticulated but always present among the critics of interracial youth events was a fear of miscegenation. This framed the terms of much of the controversy. Policy debates often took place without the direct involvement of youth, but on a number of occasions young people were principal actors.

One such case involved the desegregation of Montreat, the denomination's conference ground. Founded in 1897 by a Congregational minister, Montreat became an exclusively Presbyterian enterprise in 1907. It was located about twenty miles east of Asheville, North Carolina, in a region where numerous other religious centers were also developing. The programs of the center reflected the organizational concerns of the various church agencies.

Young people's work was organized in the early 1930s under the auspicies of the Executive Committee on Religious Education and Publication. An annual Leadership School was held at Montreat with representatives of the geographic presbyteries. This program was organized in a structure parallel to the church courts, like the Woman's Auxiliary. Leadership groups at each level were represented at the immediately higher level. The synod councils designated representatives to the Young People's Council of the General Assembly, which met during the Leadership School and at other times when necessary. The council itself had an Executive Committee. Adult advisers and youth workers also attended the Leadership School. They had representation on the Young People's Council and were given voting privileges.[17]

The council became genuinely concerned about the participation of *all* synod groups in the Leadership School. Their conviction that Snedecor Memorial Synod's Young People's Council should be represented at Montreat conflicted with the segregation policy of the Montreat Program Committee. The early council meetings recommended that Young People's work in Snedecor Memorial Synod be established and intended that this work be fully represented at Montreat. It was organized at Stillman Institute in 1935. The adviser was usually the institute's Bible instructor, a position filled by a single, white woman with a background in religious education. The Stillman program largely dictated the program of the synod work. The student body was largely non-Presbyterian, so the work had to address other concerns while maintaining a visible Presbyterian emphasis. Though there were presbytery-level organizations in Snedecor Youth Work, they were never as strong as those in the geographic presbyteries.[18]

A desire for interracial goodwill motivated the working groups of the Young People's Council. Their statements professed this goodwill, and their continued efforts to have a Snedecor Council representative confirmed their convictions. A crack in Montreat's wall of segregation allowed for such representation in 1935 and 1936. Louie Logan, a student at Stillman and a summer worker at Montreat, was the Snedecor Council's president. He attended the council meetings in Montreat, but community officials frowned on this practice and informed the Council's adult advisers that interracial gatherings would have to be eliminated. The 1936 Council canceled several planned events rather than practice the required segregation. There were other attempts to arrange Snedecor representation, but the living arrangements offered were always unsatisfactory to the council's adviser. As a result of the clash with Montreat authorities, the council unanimously approved a letter to the Montreat Program Committee which questioned the wisdom of maintaining segregation in the Youth Leadership School. It was not coincidental that the "Findings" of the Council's Church and Modern Society Study Group proclaimed "that the Church had a definite responsibility for the solution of the race problem," advocated support of antilynching legislation, and encouraged churches to begin their own efforts to solve "the race problem."[19]

The Joint Committee to examine the Young People's Program was created when the council informed the Executive Committee on Religious Education and Publication of its dissatisfaction with the events of 1936. Dr. Edward Grant, the Executive Committee's adviser to the council, explained that the Snedecor Memorial Synod Committee on Religious Education needed to be better organized before its work was represented at the Leadership School. The 1939 council totally rejected this contention, countering that the Young People's work was well enough organized to deserve representation.[20]

The council continued to make the case for Snedecor representation in the 1940s. It informed the Montreat Program Committee that if Snedecor representatives were received, the council would "forgo social intermingling, except in conferences, classes, and addresses and in going to and from these conferences, classes, and addresses." Occasionally the president of the Snedecor Young People's Council was allowed to be present and report on his council's activities, but a totally acceptable arrangement never was worked out.[21]

The 1942 council decided to inform all executive committees of its convictions. It considered and voted down a motion to call Dr. Robert C. Anderson, president of the Mountain Retreat Association, before one of its sessions. The 1943 council adopted and sent to the synod councils for comment a statement expressing the belief that the Leadership School was ineffectual because of the absence of black church representation. Nine synod councils reported unanimous agreement with the statement. One was ambiguous in its support, one refused to endorse the action, and four did not report at all. The Snedecor Council did not take any action on this proposal.[22]

The Montreat Program Committee made some effort to cooperate with the council in 1944 when it agreed to provide black participants accommodations at the 1945 Leadership School. But arrangements broke down, and the dreams of the council went unfulfilled. It would be several more years before the desegregation of Montreat occurred, although the council continued to invite representatives from Snedecor's Synodical.[23]

Throughout this conflict, the Young People's Council supported the work in Snedecor Synod. Sunday worship offerings were frequently designated for the travel funds to Snedecor's own young people's leadership event, held annually at Stillman. The upgrading of religious education opportunities in Snedecor Memorial Synod was also the object of special offerings. These gifts helped secure the services of a synod regional director of religious education.[24]

Finally, in 1949 official representatives were received for the first time, and this was a major step forward in desegregating Montreat. The development was not viewed favorably in all quarters of the church, however, because many feared that "social relations" of black and white young people would lead to more serious matters, especially miscegenation. The Montreat authorities adopted a policy that maintained segregated facilities but approved the desegregation of the conferences. The youth conferences were specifically exempted from this action, and young people protested vigorously. The 1950 Young People's Council met at Warren Wilson School in Swannanoa, North Carolina, a mountain work school of the Presbyterian Church in the U.S.A., which did allow integrated meetings.[25]

The system which gave black Presbyterians segregated church courts explains the demand of the young people that *all* their organizations in the denomination be represented. As long as the Snedecor Memorial Synod existed, the Young People's Council argued that the representation implied by Presbyterian polity was denied. The dismantling of the synod made the point moot. The Young People's Council then asked that the Montreat management allow for representatives of the Snedecor region to attend appropriate conferences,[26] but because the reorganization of black churches into Snedecor Region never achieved the same cohesiveness the synod had, there was no positive effect of this request.

The greatest impact of Montreat's segregation of Youth Council events may not have been on the Stillman students. One observer conjectured that the council's protests of Montreat's segregation had more of an effect on the white participants than anyone else. Many individuals who would later be prominent in denominational life participated in the council and were affected by the issue of desegregation at Montreat.[27]

Other voices in the denomination called for the desegregation of Montreat. Carl Pritchett proposed the idea in the December 23, 1946, issue of *Presbyterian Outlook*. Numerous opponents argued that such a policy would promote a form of social intermingling which would be disasterous. Kenneth Phifer rejoined that the opponents of racial equality at Montreat were inserting the red herring of intermarriage into the debate. Phifer and others argued that it would be best for Presbyterians to allow blacks to use Montreat's facilities.[28] At the time, however, nothing came of Pritchett's suggestion.

The Board of Directors of Montreat decided to act in 1950. It adopted a policy regarding the use of Montreat facilities by blacks which allowed for adult meetings to be desegregated. Black participants were housed in a separate facility, though whites could indicate if they wanted to be in the same living facility with blacks, and the same policy applied to dining facilities. The dorm provided for black participants was named, ironically enough, Fellowship Hall. The action was a compromise which maintained segregation for the protection of youth from possible interracial temptation in return for use of Montreat by black adults.[29]

Reaction from both sides was swift and strong. Leslie F. Patterson, pastor of First Presbyterian Church in Columbia, South Carolina, objected. "I believe in segregation and expect to practice and preach it," he wrote. "I will do so at Montreat no matter what my brethren think." Others saw the action as "playing directly into the hands" of the ecumenical Federal Council of Churches and the Communist party. Wilmington Presbytery, by a narrow majority, deplored Montreat's abolition of segregation. Some opponents of integration believed their position was precarious. Henry Dendy, editor of the *Southern Presbyterian Journal*, argued that everyone would be better off if there were a separate black Presbyterian Church. He believed that the "emphasis on a non-segregated church" would not solve the race relations problems facing the denomination.[30]

Montreat authorities also received commendation for their action. Vernon Broyles conveyed to President Rupert McGregor the Board of Church Extension's approval of Montreat's policy of "non-segregation." Numerous Presbyterians sent letters of appreciation to Montreat authorities in support of their action. Some of those who approved of the new policy for adults were dismayed that young people were excluded. "There is a strong irony in the fact that the young people of our church have been the spearhead in pressing for the admission of Negroes to Montreat," wrote the Youth Council adviser, John McMullen, "and now they are the only ones excluded from the fellowship they have so long desired." As with the previous ad hoc policies of segregation, McMullen found several problems with the new ones in determining just who could and could not attend. Indeed there was controversy over whether or not Lawrence Bottoms should be a faculty member at the Youth Leadership School in 1951. He participated as an employee of a General Assembly agency and not as a faculty member, but McMullen could not see the point in making such a fine distinction, though it was made to satisfy the demands of the "non-segrega-tion" policy.[31]

Despite this policy, there was some question as to whether or not the Montreat management supported the idea of equal access by blacks to all facilities. Anyone who gave the question serious consideration knew that there were very few Southern black Presbyterians. More-over, few of them could afford to come to Montreat. In 1950 only thir-teen black delegates were registered for Montreat programs. One year later the total was only nineteen. J. Rupert McGregor argued that a conference at Stillman would help serve the needs of black Presbyte-rians better than one at Montreat. Indeed, "the white leaders of our church are the ones who really make the trouble" about equal access for blacks to Montreat.[32]

The quasi-segregation policy remained in force until 1954. The Gen-eral Assembly of that year requested all Presbyterian institutions to adopt policies of desegregation. Montreat's Board of Directors refused to change its policy and received a thorough scolding from the *Pres-byterian Outlook*'s editorial writers, but they were supported by the *Southern Presbyterian Journal*. Though segregating black youths from Montreat was the policy, many black young people were employed in Montreat during the summer. Efforts were made to bring together these college-age youth with white college students and possibly other black college students. The proposed rules for this exchange prohibited any semblance of impropriety such as "folkgames" (i.e., dancing), and allowed only sexually segregated team sports. The effort failed to in-corporate Montreat workers for fear that this "would add greatly to the difficulty of preserving conditions" necessary to maintain segrega-tion.[33]

Montreat's policy of "non-segregation" was not without its inequi-ties in practice. Black participants in conferences or as delegates to the General Assembly were provided only segregated facilities. Critics ad-mitted that these were of a higher quality than in the past, but they were still inferior to those provided whites, particularly during the General Assembly. The Board of Women's Work requested in 1957 that the General Assembly examine several Montreat policies, includ-ing the use of the facilities by "all" Presbyterians. This board arranged for black delegates to attend the Women's Conference in 1958. In addi-tion, it scheduled the Reverend James H. Robinson, pastor of the Church of the Master in New York City, as speaker. The activities of this interracial congregation were highly offensive to conservative critics of further desegregation.[34]

The Montreat Board of Directors was again faced with the problem of desegregating its facilities. In 1959 it reaffirmed its 1950 decision to provide access to blacks at all conferences except those for young people. There were some differences in tone in the 1950 and 1959 statements, but both provided for the segregation of black participants in Fellowship Hall. The next year the board decided not to maintain any segregated conferences, which opened the way for black young people to use Montreat's facilities legitimately.[35] The struggle of many years over racial separation at Montreat ended.

During this period when youth were the last group to be absolutely segregated in Montreat, numerous activities involving them kept the issue before the church. PCUS college student efforts were organized as the Westminster Fellowship on campuses across the South. The leadership of these college groups and their adult advisers were concerned that the group at Stillman College be adequately represented. Lawrence Stell of the Board of Christian Education was responsible for making the arrangements for a 1955 Montreat conference for college-age students. The Westminster leadership had informed Stell it wanted the Stillman group represented. Montreat President J. Rupert Mc-Gregor responded that this would not be in accord with policy but noted that there might be some room for accommodation. Outside of Montreat some Westminster Fellowship groups made available their facilities to allow black delegates to participate in meetings. In other cases college groups sponsored programs on black-white relations.[36]

The PCUS World Missions Youth Conferences provided additional interracial contacts. The 1958 quadrennial event was held in Lexington, Kentucky, "in a completely non-segregated convention with no unpleasant incidents." At the next convention, which was held in Dallas, white delegates protested the housing patterns placing them in hotels and black delegates in dorms at Southern Methodist University. The convention director said this resulted from the policies of the hotels involved and that the eating and meeting facilities were desegregated.[37]

Local efforts to provide interracial contacts for students were also available, though not without controversy. During the spring of 1959, the campus minister at Alabama Polytechnic Institute in Auburn, Alabama, the Reverend George Telford, arranged for a supper and social program with a group from nearby Tuskegee Institute. The First Presbyterian Church of Selma and Tuscaloosa Presbytery were indignant at this act and petitioned the Synod of Alabama for corrective action, reporting (among other things) that "white girls were seated at the supper besides two colored boys." The Auburn church gave its full support to Telford's work. When the synod took up the matter, it merely suggested that the church's Campus Christian Life Committee keep the synod informed about changes in its policies.[38]

Youth programs were also at issue as other Presbyterian conference and camp facilities faced the question of desegregation. Brazos Presbytery experimented in the late-1950s with an interracial youth camp after previously operating segregated facilities. An inadequate number of white boys, however, created an imbalance of white girls and black boys which the leaders thought would harm the legitimacy of the program, and the camps were discontinued after 1960. Hanover Presbytery in Virginia established a camp facility of its own in the 1950s. The presbytery adopted a policy of integration from the beginning to accommodate the new black churches established in Richmond. This policy was resisted by a number of churches, including First Presbyterian, Richmond, which made the largest donations to the benevolence programs of the presbytery. Despite this church's considerable power and the discontent of other congregations, the policy was not changed.[39]

In other cases the desegregation of church courts did not result in the immediate desegregation of all church activities. Although Birmingham Presbytery accepted black churches in 1965, the same policy that approved this move also stipulated that the youth program of the presbytery would not be integrated until 1967, despite the presence of only two black churches. Central Mississippi Presbytery found itself embroiled in a controversy in 1969 over what to do with black churches and its youth camping program. At its spring meeting, the presbytery narrowly (38–35) adopted a policy prohibiting any integrated event at its Camp Calvin and requested advice on the disposition of the property. Several presbyters protested the action and initiated an appeal because such action did not conform to the denomination's stand and precluded the total involvement of two black churches in presbytery events. The Synod of Mississippi recommended that the presbytery be more inclusive in its program. Instead, the presbytery continued to consider disposing of its property to ensure that no integrated camp, youth or adult, could be held on presbytery property. The controversy adversely affected the camping program, contributing to low attendance and use, which were justifications for the sale of the camp. Despite protest from Trinity Presbyterian Church in Jackson, Mississippi, which had given sizable contributions to improve the facility, the presbytery authorized the sale of this property.[40]

Some attempts to desegregate facilities provoked threats of violence. One presbytery in Florida decided to sell its camping facility because of threats from local vigilantes and the lack of commitment by local law enforcement to ensure that private property would be adequately protected. Threats were not as pervasive elsewhere but were nonetheless abusive and annoying.[41]

Presbyterians have always been noted as a denomination concerned with education, but the desegregation of their educational institutions was a long process. The four PCUS seminaries all had adopted a policy of integration by 1951. The lack of adequate ministerial preparation for blacks and the phasing out of the Theology Department at Stillman brought about this situation. The ministerial training which blacks received for much of the period ignored the traditions and strengths of the larger black church.[42]

The 1954 General Assembly action condemning segregation had been directed in large part at the trustees and directors of Presbyterian colleges in the hopes they would adopt policies that eliminated race as a factor for admission. Some colleges, such as Hampden-Sydney College in Virginia and King College in Tennessee, did this. Two new Presbyterian colleges founded in the 1960s, St. Andrews in North Carolina and Florida Presbyterian (later Eckerd College), began with policies which made no mention of race as an admission criterion. Other colleges had much more difficult times coming to this decision. Davidson College in North Carolina, one of the oldest and most prestigious of the denominational colleges, had to overcome significant opposition both in the student body and among alumni, though many hailed the decision as long overdue when it finally came in 1962.[43]

The last educational institution to adopt desegregation policies did so to comply with federal regulations, not church positions. Belhaven College in Jackson, Mississippi, was the last Presbyterian college to eliminate race as a criterion for admissions. Had the college's board of trustees failed to do so, the school would have been denied student loan money available from the United States Department of Health,

Education, and Welfare. Die-hard segregationists challenged the college's new policy on the floor of the Synod of Mississippi in 1967, where their efforts failed.[44] If conscience could not motivate action in race relations, government policy and financial incentive could.

Some modest efforts at the desegregation of presbyteries were attempted prior to the 1960s. Snedecor Memorial Synod was abolished in 1952, when its constituent presbyteries were transferred to geographic presbyteries. Using the Negro Work Program, many denominational leaders sought to effect desegregation in presbyteries and local situations. Some of these efforts were more successful than others. To reach the goal of eliminating all racially segregated church courts, General Assembly action was necessary.[45]

A few ministers, both black and white, had worked in previously segregated presbyteries. Brazos Presbytery received the Reverend J. H. M. Boyce and the Reverend Hosea Rasberry from the segregated Central Louisiana Presbytery in 1951. The men worked to develop black churches in the Houston and Beaumont areas. Dr. Albert C. Winn, a white minister, was received by the segregated Central Alabama Presbytery at about the same time. Winn taught Bible at Stillman College and thought his act would be seen as one of solidarity with black Presbyterians. He noted in retrospect that it was a risky decision, not only with white Presbyterians, but with blacks, who could have seen it as unwarranted meddling. Fortunately for him, his actions were not seen in this way, but after the *Brown* decision his contacts with white Presbyterians were increasingly tense. Just when things seemed the worst, Winn was elected moderator of the Synod of Alabama, a development he attributed to the commissioners' freedom granted by Presbyterian polity.[46]

Church leadership in the 1960s began to press for membership of black churches in geographic presbyteries. The Division of Negro Work, together with the Boards of Church Extension and Christian Education, began to study the effects of segregated church courts. In November 1962 the Board of Church Extension asked that geographic presbyteries accept black churches into their bounds. Where this was not possible, the board urged that white presbyteries should accept more responsibility for black churches. (See map 1.)

Some synods and presbyteries were preparing for new developments. The Christian Relations Committee of the Synod of Alabama recommended that steps be instituted for the black churches to be trans-

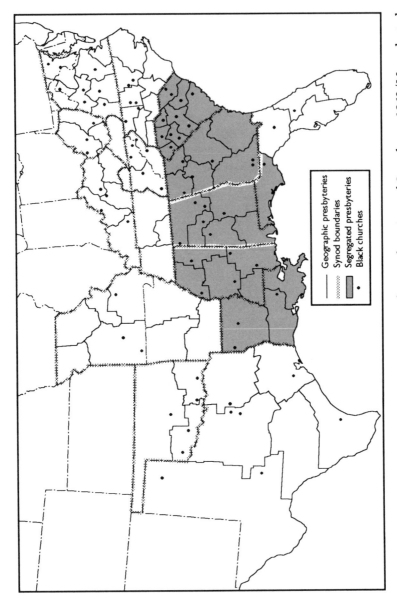

Map 1. Segregated Presbyteries Drawn over Geographic Presbyteries and Synods, ca. 1962 (Map adapted from Board of National Ministries materials, Presbyterian Church, Department of History, Montreat.)

ferred to white presbyteries in 1963. Red River Presbytery was looking "for the time when the colored churches in our area will become members of our presbytery." The Board of Christian Education conducted a study and determined that the system of segregated church courts was deterring a significant number of young men, both black and white, from entering the Presbyterian ministry.[47]

In 1964 several overtures were presented to the General Assembly requesting that black presbyteries be dismantled and that black churches be absorbed into the geographic presbyteries. Indeed, thirty-two of seventy-one black churches were then members of geographic presbyteries. The Synods of Alabama, Georgia, and Louisiana were instructed to receive the respective churches into the appropriate courts.[48] The presbyteries to be affected were not only those of the three synods mentioned but also those located in the synods of North Carolina, South Carolina, Florida, and Mississippi.

Presbyteries responded to these instructions in one of two ways. Either they indicated their willingness to comply, or they displayed reluctance bordering on hostility. The Presbyteries of Augusta-Macon and Florida indicated their general approval of the instructions by receiving the black churches within their bounds into membership at their summer and fall meetings in 1964. Some presbyteries, such as Louisiana, Fayetteville, and Birmingham, indicated a generally positive response to the action but did not receive black churches until 1965.[49]

Not all Presbyterians were pleased with the instructions to receive black churches. Several complained that the General Assembly could not tell them who should be members. The synod, argued Southwest Georgia Presbytery, was the only body which could instruct a presbytery regarding its composition. East Alabama Presbytery noted that the action was controversial and did nothing, pending the outcome of the 1965 General Assembly. The process of dismantling the segregated presbyteries which began in 1964 was not completed until 1968. (See table 2.) By March 1966 there were still twenty-two black churches left to be received by seven presbyteries: Tuscaloosa, East Alabama, South Mississippi, St. Andrews (in Mississippi), Central Mississippi, and Pee Dee and Harmony (in South Carolina).[50]

After initially taking the legalist position that the General Assembly action had no authoritative basis, these presbyteries argued that desegregation would not be in the "best interest" of all parties in-

Table 2. Transfer of Churches from Segregated to Geographic Presbyteries, 1962–1968

Date Transferred	Church name	Location	Year Organized	Presbytery left	Presbytery joined
May 23, 1962	Rice Memorial	Atlanta, Ga.	1923	Georgia-Carolina	Atlanta
May 23, 1962	Trinity	Decatur, Ga.	1944	Georgia-Carolina	Atlanta
May 23, 1962	Westhills	Atlanta, Ga.	1955	Georgia-Carolina	Atlanta
Apr. 16, 1963	Sardis	Jefferson, Ga.	1888	Georgia-Carolina	Athens
Apr. 16, 1963	Westside	Elberton, Ga.	1952(?)	Georgia-Carolina	Athens
Oct. 13, 1964	Bethel	Defuniak Springs, Fla.	1925	Central Alabama	Florida
Oct. 13, 1964	Pleasant Grove	Ponce de Leon, Fla.	1889	Central Alabama	Florida
Oct. 20, 1964	Peabody Heights	Eastman, Ga.	1962	Georgia-Carolina	Augusta-Macon
Oct. 20, 1964	Washington Street	Dublin, Ga.	1956	Georgia-Carolina	Augusta-Macon
Jan. 26, 1965	First	Scotlandville, La.	1924	Louisiana-Mississippi	Louisiana
Apr. 13, 1965	Nicholtown	Greenville, S.C.	1961	Georgia-Carolina	Enoree
May 1, 1965	Good Hope	Bessemer, Ala.	1913	Central Alabama	Birmingham
May 19, 1965	Carver Heights	Columbus, Ga.	1958	Georgia-Carolina	Southwest Georgia
May 19, 1965	Grant's Chapel	Darien, Ga.	1890	Georgia-Carolina	Savannah
July 13, 1965	Second	Thomasville, Ga.	1918	Georgia-Carolina	Southwest Georgia
Sept. 11, 1965	Good Hope	Frierson, La.	1877	Louisiana-Mississippi	Red River
Sept. 11, 1965	Holywood Heights	Shreveport, La.	1957[a]	Louisiana-Mississippi	Red River
Sept. 11, 1965	Red Lick	Mansfield, La.	1892	Louisiana-Mississippi	Red River
Sept. 12, 1965	Westminster	Birmingham, Ala.	1946	Central Alabama	Birmingham
1966	Ann Street	Mobile, Ala.	1911	Central Alabama	Mobile
June 18, 1966	Cleveland Avenue	Montgomery, Ala.	1890	Central Alabama	East Alabama

June 18, 1966	Westminster	Tuskegee, Ala.	1955	Central Alabama	East Alabama
Sept. 29, 1966	Amy's Chapel	Rowland, N.C.	1914	Georgia-Carolina	Fayetteville
Sept. 29, 1966	Mount Pelier	Maxton, N.C.	1881	Georgia-Carolina	Fayetteville
1967	Calvary	Greenville, Miss.	1952	Louisiana-Mississippi[b]	St. Andrews
1967	Community	Itta Bena, Miss.	1961	Louisiana-Mississippi	St. Andrews
1967	Enon Zion	Hattiesburg, Miss.	?	Louisiana-Mississippi	South Mississippi
1967	Fairview	Heidelberg, Miss.	1886	Louisiana-Mississippi	South Mississippi
1967	Garden of Eden	Okalona, Miss.	?	Louisiana-Mississippi	St. Andrews
1967	Gavins	Bay Springs, Miss.	1935	Louisiana-Mississippi	South Mississippi
1967	Greenfield	Waterford, Miss.	1898	Louisiana-Mississippi	St. Andrews
1967	Preston Chapel	Hattiesburg, Miss.	1915	Louisiana-Mississippi	South Mississippi
1968	Alexander	Kosciusko, Miss.	1910	Louisiana-Mississippi	Central Mississippi
1968	Faith	Jackson, Miss.	1948	Louisiana-Mississippi	Central Mississippi
1968	Mount Hebron	McColl, S.C.	?	Louisiana-Mississippi	Pee Dee
1968	Mount Pisgah	Hartsville, S.C.	1922	Louisiana-Mississippi	Pee Dee
1968	New Bethel	Dillon, S.C.	1964[c]	Louisiana-Mississippi	Pee Dee
1968	New Bethel	Florence, S.C.	1947	Louisiana-Mississippi	Pee Dee
1968	Old Bethel	Hamer, S.C.	1870	Louisiana-Mississippi	Pee Dee
1968	Pilgrim Grove	Newton, Miss.	1884	Louisiana-Mississippi	Central Mississippi
1969	Cousar Memorial	Bishopville, S.C.	1884	Synod of South Carolina	Harmony
1969	St. James	Kingstree, S.C.	?	Synod of South Carolina	Harmony

Source: Compiled from statistics in the PCUS General Assembly *Minutes*, 1963–69.

[a]Organized in 1957 from the Torrance Church, Shreveport, La.

[b]After the 1965 General Assembly, Louisiana-Mississippi was the only remaining segregated presbytery.

[c]New Bethel was organized in 1964 from the merger of the Bethel Church (organized in 1870), Hamer, S.C., and the New Liberty Church, Dillon, S.C.

volved. Central Mississippi Presbytery suggested creating a black presbytery within the synod to deal with the situation. The synod rejected
this approach as incompatible with General Assembly policy.[51]

Though the majority in these church courts succeeded in delaying
the implementation of desegregation, there were individuals working
toward opposite ends. In 1966, from a group including some of its most
conservative members, Central Mississippi Presbytery received a proposal that the black churches be received into membership; the effort,
however, was unsuccessful. At about the same time, the Pee Dee Presbytery was entertaining a similar motion, which opponents defeated
by a vote of 30–22.[52]

The reception of black churches into these remaining church courts
was a traumatic experience. The large majority of the presbyteries in
these areas had very conservative reputations. Indeed, Central Mississippi Presbytery voted against every major constitutional revision
which came before the PCUS. Given the situation in that presbytery,
the General Assembly was keenly interested in the reception there of
black churches. The 1966 assembly voted to establish a committee to
investigate the situation in the Synod of Mississippi. It was not specifically charged with acting on the matter of presbytery desegregation, but one observer believes that the intent of the committee was
to aid in the process by having differences aired and dealt with con-
structively. The committee, composed of five former moderators of
the General Assembly, made several trips to Mississippi and found an
anti-assembly attitude among a significant portion of the ministers
and elders. The strongest sentiment was in Central Mississippi Presbytery. Conservatives such as Morton Smith believed that the "Visi-
tation Committee," as it was called, was an undue usurpation of the
authority by the General Assembly. Smith argued, and many of his
peers in Mississippi agreed, that the General Assembly had wandered
from its historic doctrinal positions, thus provoking an anti-assembly
attitude.[53]

Central Mississippi Presbytery continued to resist efforts of the
General Assembly, although some in the state and within the presbytery opposed the recalcitrant leadership. The Reverend William Jones,
pastor of the Faith Presbyterian Church in Jackson, a congregation
founded with the help of the Negro Work Program, challenged readers
of the *Presbyterian Survey* in 1968 to hold the presbytery accountable.
This was a test of the integrity of the denomination. "It would seem

to me and the 200-plus Negro Presbyterians within Central Mississippi," wrote Jones, "that the General Assembly must make its position known. Either we are wanted or we are not." Jones hoped that this occasion would give the General Assembly the opportunity to exercise "its full authority in seeking to bring not only the Negro communicants of Central Mississippi into the mainstream of the church, but also white Presbyterians who [also] desire to serve the church."[54]

The issue of receiving black churches into geographic presbyteries became the basis of a power struggle. It was another case where individuals opposed to the action of the General Assembly were disheartened, while proponents were encouraged, as both sides claimed that biblical authority and justice were on their sides.

Earlier, there were some local efforts to integrate Presbyterian congregations. In 1949 Oak Cliff Church in Dallas received into membership a young black man who wanted to become a minister. The women's group in a Florida congregation also accepted a black woman as a member that year. In the wake of events in 1954, the Decatur Presbyterian Church, Decatur, Georgia, opened its doors to all who came to worship. The kneel-in movement, however, caused reconsideration of this policy, and black worshipers were segregated within the sanctuary for a period during the early 1960s.[55]

Other churches also received black members or claimed to have no barriers to attendance or membership based on race; the denomination as a whole, however, had no uniform policy. To alleviate the situation, the General Assembly acted in 1964 to amend its *Book of Church Order* to state explicitly that race could not be grounds for excluding individuals from worshiping in any Presbyterian church. Opponents claimed that the amendment was unnecessary, and proponents urged that clarification of previous policy was needed to remove any ambiguity from the church's rules. The amendment passed the General Assembly and was ratified by the presbyteries.[56]

The 1964 action was an attempt to correct inadequacies in the Presbyterian system. When black attendance at worship services became a reality, many churches reacted by adopting restrictive access policies. Congregations often took such action in opposition to the minister's position. One Mississippi church acknowledged that it was on dubious theological grounds by prefacing its exclusionary statement as follows: "Although we recognize that this is not what Jesus Christ would do, nevertheless . . . " and went on to establish a procedure by which blacks would be excluded, including the posting of church officers to act as sentries in the parking lot.[57]

The inclusion of a nondiscriminatory statement in the denomination's *Book of Church Order*, the rules which guided the conduct of ministers and churches, allowed for protest against discrimination. Emmett Barfield, pastor of First Presbyterian Church, Grenada, Mississippi, protested the exclusion of black worshipers from his congregation at a meeting of St. Andrews Presbytery in the summer of 1966. His motion to have the session of the church reconsider its position in light of General Assembly action was defeated. Two substitute motions asking for a study of conditions in the church and a general study of all racial matters before the presbytery passed. These motions, however, were followed by one to table consideration of all these matters. It passed.[58]

A similar situation had arisen the previous summer in Montgomery, Alabama. A racially mixed group of Presbyterians presented themselves at the Trinity Presbyterian Church to hear Leighton Ford preach. Ford was a Presbyterian minister affiliated with the Billy Graham Evangelistic Association and was in Montgomery to help with a Graham evangelistic crusade. When the integrated group presented itself at the door, it was refused admittance to the worship services. The group included Presbyterian ministers and elders as well as a black serviceman from Craig Air Force Base in Selma who stated a desire to hear Ford preach. A complaint against the church was filed with East Alabama Presbytery and the Synod of Alabama because the group was excluded from worship. The synod ruled that the denial of access was not in accord with practices approved by the denomination but held the integrated group responsible for precipitating a confrontation.[59]

During the troubled days of 1965, the session of the First Presbyterian Church in Selma, Alabama, asked for the guidance of Tuscaloosa Presbytery in the interpretation of the nonexclusionary rule. The presbytery took note of the extraordinary difficulty faced by the Selma congregation because of local circumstances and asked the session "to use every effort to bring conscience and vow together."[60]

Others also asked for direction in interpreting the provisions of denominational polity. Ben Lacy Rose, a professor at Union Seminary in Richmond and moderator of the 1971 General Assembly, wrote a popular question-and-answer column in the *Presbyterian Survey*. Even before the constitutional changes of 1964, he noted that the *Book of Church Order* did not confer the power to deny persons attendance at worship to officers or members of a congregation. Therefore, he argued, there was no such right for anyone. Moreover, there was ample scriptural justification to open the doors and welcome all "who labor and are heavy laden."[61]

The change in polity, however, did not guarantee a corresponding change in attitude. Just before Christmas 1969 two students from Morris College in Sumter, South Carolina, went to worship at First Presbyterian Church, Sumter. The session refused to allow them to attend the service because they were black. They returned on January 11, 1970, when a shoving incident resulted in their arrest, a fine of $100, and conviction for disorderly conduct. The elders feared the two would disrupt the service, perhaps by reading James Foreman's "Black Manifesto." Finally, on February 1, the pair returned to the church, which was as physically proximate to the campus as any other, and they attended without incident that day.[62]

Local interracial contact, which began slowly in the PCUS, continued in the 1950s and 1960s. Two churches in Memphis—Parkway Gardens (black) and St. Andrew's (white)—exchanged ministers in 1964. The Board of Church Extension granted a leave of absence to Lawrence Bottoms so that he could help begin an interracial congregation in Miami. Three churches (two black, one white) in the Dallas, Texas, area came together to share ministerial leadership and resources in 1968.[63] While these experiments in congregational interracial activity were the exception, the official barriers which had previously prevented such action were removed.

The desegregation of church courts generally paralleled changing racial attitudes in the denomination. When the General Assembly was held at Montreat, black commissioners were provided with lodging in the servants' quarters. These facilities were inferior by any standard, and the Mountain Retreat Association made some efforts to improve the situation. Eventually blacks were allowed to take meals in the main dining hall at Assembly Inn, the major hotel in Montreat, although their seating assignments were segregated. White liberals felt they were throwing down a gauntlet when they sat and ate with the black commissioners.[64]

The first "non-segregated" General Assembly occurred in 1950 at

Massanetta Springs, the conference ground of the Synod of Virginia near Harrisonburg. The Reverend James Marshall of Florida protested the arrangements and asked the assembly to segregate all church meetings. The request was denied, but the policy of segregation was not totally repudiated. Rather, the highest church body said that it did not make policy on segregation for synods and presbyteries. Thus Virginia Presbyterians could integrate their facilities if they desired.[65]

The *Brown v. Board of Education* decision restructured the environment for discussing race relations in the South. In its wake the PCUS General Assembly resolved that separation based on race was incompatible with Christian faith and ethics. The assembly recommended this statement to lower church courts for study and action.[66]

Some of these courts reacted favorably to the rejection of segregation, while others berated the assembly. Synods in Texas and Arkansas affirmed the decision and passed it on to the boards of their institutions to be considered as an institutional policy. Church courts in South Carolina and Mississippi vigorously denounced the assembly's position. The indignation of the Synod of Mississippi not only was based on scriptural and confessional grounds but included resistance to the authority of the General Assembly. The Synod of South Carolina refused to accept the General Assembly action as binding on its own practices. According to the synod, "It is in the best interest of harmonious relations between the white and Negro races in this section at this time that the present enrollment policies in the institutions under the control and support of Synod be continued."[67]

Rather than take a position immediately, the Synod of North Carolina asked Presbyterians in its jurisdiction to consider carefully the matter. After a year the synod decided that the 1954 General Assembly action should be accepted as a legitimate expression dealing with a complicated issue. The efforts of earnest individuals seeking worship opportunities should be recognized, but the existence of differing opinions could not be ignored.[68]

Some progress toward desegregating Presbyterian facilities and institutions was made in the 1960s, but it was limited at best. In the early 1960s the gap between profession and practice came to the attention of several church courts. The Synod of Virginia noted that ten years after it had endorsed the General Assembly statement of 1954 and the *Brown* decision, the church had said little about the practice of segregation. This silence occurred during the abolition of school systems and while economic pressures were forcing ministers and others who voiced their convictions out of communities around the state. Presbyterians in Texas noted that the synod had said the right things but had not made the issue vital for most communicants. Both church courts and the General Assembly called on their members to get involved by applying their convictions to daily events.[69]

Perhaps the most dramatic confrontation by the General Assembly over segregated facilities occurred in 1964 and 1965. The 1965 Assembly was scheduled to meet in the Second Presbyterian Church of Memphis, Tennessee, where the session had adopted an exclusionary membership and visitor policy in 1957. To ensure that Second Presbyterian Church complied with the General Assembly policy, Carl Pritchett, the minister of the Bethesda Presbyterian Church in Maryland, asked the 1964 General Assembly to apply the newly stated policy to its 1965 location, but definitive action was not taken. Reports began to circulate that Second Church would not conform to this policy and that it had in fact turned blacks away from worship services. Pritchett then contacted local leaders in Memphis and arranged to attend services on May 10, 1964. Most of the group that accompanied Pritchett were students, black and white. The arrangements were made by Dr. Vasco Smith, an elder at Parkway Gardens Presbyterian Church and vice-president of the Memphis NAACP, and the Reverend Lawrence Haygood, pastor at the Parkway Gardens Church. When the integrated group presented themselves for worship, they were prevented by an elder from entering the church building.[70]

The incident was well publicized, both in the denominational and in the secular press. Presbyterians immediately demanded that the 1965 General Assembly be relocated. The Synods of Virginia and North Carolina asked that the scheduled meeting be moved. Though not all Presbyterians or church courts opposed the position of the Second Church in Memphis, a sizable and weighty body of opinion condemned that church's position. John Leith, professor of theology at Union Theological Seminary in Virginia, published an article entitled "The Church and Race" for the *Presbyterian Outlook* in July 1964. Though he never mentioned the Memphis situation, his meaning was quite plain: "The conclusion is inescapable that when race is made a condition of worship, of receiving the sacrament from the Lord's Table, of participation in the life of the Lord's Church, the line is clearly drawn between apostasy and obedience, between heresy and orthodoxy, between pretentious fraud and the reality of the church."[71]

Memphis Presbytery became involved in the controversy and requested that the Second Church respond. The church session refused to reconsider any of its actions, despite considerable pressure from ministers, missionaries, and even some within the congregation itself. The moderator of the 1964 General Assembly, Felix Gear, a professor of theology at Columbia Theological Seminary, then used an extraordinary power to relocate the 1965 meeting to Montreat, North Carolina. There was irony in this turn of events, for Gear had pastored the Second Presbyterian Church from 1943 to 1947, but he saw that too much was at stake in 1965 for the denomination to be meeting in a segregated facility. He stated that this was not punishment of a particular congregation; rather, it was an action to prove denominational integrity. Shortly following this action, the elders of the Second Presbyterian Church reversed their exclusionary policy.[72]

The impact of the event on the General Assembly was obvious, but the action also had a tremendous effect on the particular church involved. The session, which at first had ruled that the Second Church would not allow blacks to worship, was composed of men who had been elected to serve lifetime terms. The PCUS allowed, but did not mandate, that churches rotate their session membership. Some church members who opposed the action of the session came together to form the Accord Committee in February 1965. It sought to implement the rotation of church officers in addition to changing church policy. The Accord Committee was successful in calling a congregational meeting on February 28, 1965, that approved the implementation of a rotating session membership. A large number of elders resigned following this action, and many left the church to form the Independent Presbyterian Church, which was openly segregationist and initially not affiliated with any ecclesiastical body. Throughout the turmoil of 1964–65 in the Memphis congregation, the program of the church was somehow maintained.[73]

The impact of these events on the Second Presbyterian Church is difficult to assess precisely. But when the history of the congregation was published in 1971, this part of the story was left untold. And though the congregation did remain in the PCUS and went into the reunited Presbyterian Church (U.S.A.) in 1983, they elected to withdraw from that body in 1989 and joined the Evangelical Presbyterian Church.[74] Though there is no documentable relationship with these later events and though they can never be held to be the exclusive cause of later action, it is reasonable here to hold that "the past is prologue."

Opening the doors of the Presbyterian Church in the United States took decades. The struggles happened in many different places and at different times in a denomination whose black membership constituted less than 1 percent of the total membership. Yet the PCUS could never escape the question of segregation in the church. When church courts did not want to deal with the issue, young people and women's groups did. Church polity permitted this diversity of reaction, although the survival of segregated organizations was permitted by that same church polity. When the courts decided to face the situation, policy was altered. In changing the policy, the denomination found that changes in polity and program were often necessary as well.

5

THE CIVIL RIGHTS MOVEMENT AND THE PRESBYTERIAN CHURCH, U.S., 1954–1973

T HE PREOCCUPATION of the PCUS with race relations and the condition of black Presbyterians is well illustrated by General Assembly action from the time of the establishment of Snedecor Memorial Synod in 1915 through the Negro Work Program. That program, as well as the debates over race and the desegregation of denominational facilities, had tremendous consequences for the denomination. These events occurred within the context of the civil rights movement. The denomination faced the issues in society at large partially by addressing matters of internal policy and polity, but it also had to address the implications of the larger movement.

Before 1954 the rights of black Americans were one concern among many for Southern Presbyterians. The Committee on Christian Relations had manifested this concern in reports to various church courts, dealing not only with race relations or the economic condition of blacks but also with alcohol, labor-management and church-state relations, marriage and divorce, and transitional problems confronting post–World War II society.[1]

Presbyterian ministers and laypeople became active in a multitude of racial situations. J. McDowell Richards, president of Columbia Theological Seminary in Decatur, Georgia, responded to the race-baiting tactics of Eugene Talmadge in a widely distributed sermon, "Brothers in Black." East Hanover Presbytery in Virginia and the Synod of North Carolina officially complained of the resurgence of the Ku Klux Klan and its violent practices in the postwar period. Other Southern Presbyterians became active in ecumenical and interracial work. A Dallas minister participated in a job-placement service with Northern blacks and Southern employers, a project which had limited success.

On a Sunday morning in February 1950, "Brady's Alley," a slum area in Davidson, North Carolina, burned. The next Sunday Carl Pritchett, minister of the local Presbyterian church, addressed the situation from the pulpit. This prompted a series of meetings on health and safety hazards in the area as well as exploration of sources of federal aid to help rebuild Brady's Alley.[2]

Examples of such activity must be placed in proper context. In the pre-1954 period many conservatives questioned the wisdom of interracial work which did anything beyond maintaining the status quo. This group feared that any such efforts would result in advances for the Communist movement. Critics of this view argued that only by such advances could blacks reasonably be expected to achieve the American dream. This dualism existed not only in the thoughts of church people but in society at large.[3]

Racial attitudes changed on a whole range of issues in the quarter century following the 1954 *Brown v. Board of Education* decision. In addition to education, these issues included access to public accommodations and to economic resources. Presbyterians had to confront these issues in their daily lives, as did all other Southerners. Some church members took this confrontation to heart and used their Christian faith as the basis for how they interacted with individuals and organizations advocating civil rights. Others brought issues before the various groups in the denomination. In both cases opposition to the involvement and study of civil rights issues was encountered. The first pivotal issue in redefining this struggle for civil rights was public education.

The National Association for the Advancement of Colored People led the attempt to remove segregation from the schools. The Southern Regional Council (SRC), based in Atlanta, supported the legal battle of the NAACP and promoted the desegregation of schools in its literature. The PCUS offered considerable support to educate Southern whites about the problems of segregation. The *Presbyterian Outlook* commended the SRC's reports to its readers, and the General Assembly's Division of Christian Relations and the Board of Women's Work sent a SRC pamphlet entitled *The Schools and the Courts* to ministers and women leaders during the autumn of 1953.[4]

Southern politicians encouraged disobedience to school desegregation court orders through "massive resistance." Their approach resulted in a number of states making desegregation illegal and condoning the abolition of public school systems to maintain a segregated society. This tactic mobilized a white power structure in direct opposition to the emerging black power structure in which economic reprisals and even violence often resulted.[5]

One of the most visible battles over the implementation of so-called massive resistance occurred in Virginia. The governor of Virginia appointed a commission to determine what to do with public education in the wake of the *Brown* decision. The Gray Commission, named after its chairman, presented the governor with several options, which included closing schools to avoid integration. Presbyterian clergy were among those who opposed such action, and segregationists blamed "white preachers" for the situation. Prince Edward County was flashpoint for the conflict over school closings to avoid integration. The county included Hampden-Sydney College, an old and respected Presbyterian-related institution, and a number of Presbyterian churches. Several members of the Farmville Presbyterian Church expressed distress at the endorsement of the *Brown* decision by the Synod of Virginia in 1954. The minister, the Reverend James R. Kennedy, was at odds with a number of parishioners, including the local superintendent of education, over the issue of keeping the schools open. Tension developed throughout the synod and was not always limited to the clergy-laity division, though many believed that was the best way to make sense of the conflict. The Christian Relations Committee of the synod tried to calm the conflict in 1957 with an appeal to patience and prayers based on an understanding of the larger issues involved.[6]

Atlanta was also the scene of a school desegregation conflict in the 1950s. When the school board tried to implement a court-ordered desegregation plan in 1957, eight ministers issued "A Call to Civil Obedience and Racial Goodwill." The Atlanta Manifesto, as it was called, supported the desegregation plan. It was heavily influenced by Herman L. Turner, pastor of the Covenant Presbyterian Church, a congregation of the Presbyterian Church in the U.S.A., and was written by J. McDowell Richards, president of Columbia Theological Seminary of the PCUS. Other PCUS ministers, including the moderator of the General Assembly, William M. Elliot, Jr., of the Highland Park Presbyterian Church in Dallas, endorsed the statement. The manifesto called for citizens to comply with court-ordered desegregation because of the necessity of public schools to the social and cultural life of the city. Moreover, the Christian faith should facilitate a "free exchange of ideas" among those of differing viewpoints rather than justifying bigotry and prejudice. The statement received a favorable reception in the Atlanta press, and eventually other ministers signed. A second such declaration in 1958 reinforced the concepts of the first.[7]

The desegregation of public schools in Little Rock, Arkansas, provoked local conflict and gained much national attention. The events there in the fall of 1957 resulted from a plan which did as little as possible to desegregate the city's schools. The Board of Education began planning for 1957 in the wake of the *Brown* decision. As the date approached for implementation of the modest plan, which would have allowed only a handful of black students at the white Central High School, community support was lacking. Orval Faubus, the governor of Arkansas, tried to prevent the implementation of desegregation by calling out the National Guard. The Eisenhower administration reacted by federalizing the National Guard and dispatching troops to ensure compliance with the desegregation plan.[8]

Faubus's actions prompted protests from a variety of sources, including various Arkansas ministers, among them prominent Presbyterians such as Marion Boggs and Dunbar Ogden, Jr. Boggs saw trouble on the horizon early in 1957 and set out to address it in a sermon entitled "A Time for Christian Citizenship." He condemned the practice of segregation as contradicting "the Christian doctrine of the dignity of man." Christians had a duty to provide moral and ethical leadership in troublesome times; therefore, obedience to the law was important. Boggs concluded by noting that there would be problems with the implementation of desegregation, although he probably did not envision the developments as they unfolded. Ogden also preached a notable sermon during this period, "The Teachings of Christ for Our Times," but he was more visible as president of the Little Rock Ministerial Association when he accompanied several black students to Central High School.[9]

Some Presbyterian laity supported the desegregation plan. One elder of the Second Presbyterian Church in Little Rock, representing the Arkansas Economic Council–State Chamber of Commerce, noted before a meeting of young people that future desegregation would be easier than it was in the 1950s. Obstruction of desegregation plans, said A. Walton Litz, came from adults, and he implied that if young people influenced policy, the transition would be easier.

Other Presbyterians reacted unfavorably to the idea of desegregation. A *Southern Presbyterian Journal* editorial placed the controversy in the context of struggles between the PCUS and the Presbyterian Church in the U.S.A. Both the stated clerk and the moderator of the PCUSA's General Assembly supported the move of the Eisenhower administration to enforce the law. The editor noted that some within the PCUS were wondering "whether this demand for the enforcement of integration at the point of a gun does not indicate less sympathy with Southern brethren than with the comrades in Moscow."[10]

Ernest Q. Campbell and Thomas Pettigrew conducted a now-famous sociological study of the ministry in Little Rock during the desegregation crisis, which they published in 1959. The sociologists found that the strongest pro-integration statement made during this time emanated from five Presbyterian ministers in Clarksville, Arkansas. Campbell and Pettigrew studied twenty-nine ministers, including several Presbyterians. These men were categorized as "Innovators," "Influentials," or "Inactives." The innovators protested against Faubus's actions, but they were generally considered failures, as the churches they pastored lost membership. The sociologists attributed this failure to liberal laity in the city who supported the words of innovators but whose membership was most often in a church pastored by an influential. The innovators pastored churches which were more defined by a neighborhood membership and smaller than those served by ministers of either of the other categories. The liberal laity could support the innovators only in public, not in the confines of the ministers' home church. There was a greater chance that the innovators' churches would have a congregational polity than churches with influential or inactive ministers. Perhaps the ministers' role was overestimated, for church women's groups led the religious community's reaction to the crisis and responded first to the statements of several national church governing bodies when they issued a general call to prayer before the ministers acted.[11]

Although Campbell and Pettigrew did not reveal the denominational affiliations of their participants, some Presbyterians were probably in one or another of their categories. Presbyterian ministers were active enough to be the subject of an attack by Governor Faubus, who charged that many Presbyterians were Communists. Washburn Presbytery categorically denied the charge and expressed its outrage at the governor's statement.[12]

The role played by the PCUS in the conflict over desegregation expanded during this period as some church people proposed to establish segregated private schools in churches. Various presbyteries and synods as well as the General Assembly overwhelmingly opposed this idea. Their statements recalled that church pronouncements since 1954 had favored desegregation in the church and in society, and they argued that creating church schools would violate the separation of church and state.[13]

Such official denominational stands did not endear the PCUS to segregationists. Frequently ministers and laity committed to the denomination's positions found themselves in adversarial relations with politicians and such groups as the White Citizens' Council.[14] The case of Arkansas's Washburn Presbytery shows just how emotional the conflicts could become.

The conflict intensified with the dawning of the 1960s. Even PCUS liberals had taken a dim view of direct action during the 1950s. An attitudinal change took place during the decade, however, and by 1960 it was quite evident in the reaction of the *Presbyterian Outlook* to the sit-in movement. An editorial noted that when blacks presented themselves at lunch counters, they could wait for service. "Yes, they could wait—but they have been waiting for 50, 75, 100 years. How long should they wait?" The alternative to waiting was to "present themselves calmly, in good humor and manner, and ask to be served."[15]

Richmond, the home of the *Presbyterian Outlook*, Union Theological Seminary, the Presbyterian School of Christian Education, and the denomination's Board of Christian Education, was the scene of several racial incidents in the early 1960s. Several employees of the Board of Christian Education and some seminary students participated in these incidents. Irvin Elligan, a black Presbyterian minister and board employee, recalled that when he and others went to a previously all-white restaurant, an elderly white woman told the group that they should be patronizing black restaurants, not integrating white ones. Elligan concluded that she bore him no personal malice but believed wholeheartedly in the system of segregation.[16]

The lunch counter sit-in movement began in Greensboro, North Carolina, on January 31, 1960. It quickly spread and reached Charlotte, North Carolina, within ten days. About 150 students from Johnson C. Smith University, a black college of the Presbyterian Church in the U.S.A. located in Charlotte, began that city's sit-in movement. A limited number of white students from nearby Davidson College, a PCUS institution, also participated. Davidson students were more affected, however, when a proposed YMCA program on the sit-in movement scheduled at the Davidson College Presbyterian Church was canceled by the session. The college administration then allowed the meeting to be held in a college building. John R. Cunningham, a former president at Davidson who was also affiliated with the Presbyterian Foundation, an institution to raise and manage funds for denominational purposes, was one of several other Presbyterians serving on a committee to study the problems leading to the sit-ins.[17]

The synods in both Virginia and North Carolina took notice of the effects of these events. In 1960 the Synod of Virginia noted that the witness of the Dutch Reformed Church in South Africa was seriously damaged because of apartheid, which should serve as a warning to the PCUS not to make the same mistake. North Carolina Presbyterians knew that the desegregation of lunch counters and schools would ultimately affect churches.[18]

The integration of the University of Mississippi by James Meredith in 1962 held national attention as the state's leadership displayed unbelievable intransigence to federal authority, a stance that resulted in a riot. Local pastors, led by the rector of the Episcopal Church, the Reverend Duncan M Gray, Jr., criticized the rioters. Murphy Wilds, pastor of Oxford's First Presbyterian Church, called for corporate as well as individual confession for the riot and reaction of state leaders, noting that "sins of omission over the years can be as serious as sins of commission over a few hours." The Presbytery of St. Andrews, in which Oxford was located, publicly deplored the riot and passed a statement urging all people to comply with appropriate legal authority and to examine individual attitudes which might promote racial strife. Another Presbyterian minister in Mississippi blamed, at least partially, ministers and church people. "The horror of Ole Miss," said Charles Stanford, "has been the result of Christian preachers who have not been preaching the whole counsel of God to the people of God."[19] Few Mississippians, however, accepted even the mildest of reproaches.

Events in Birmingham in 1963 presented yet another arena in which the cause of civil rights confronted segregation. A group of ministers, including Edward Ramage of the First Presbyterian Church, issued "An Appeal to Law and Order and Common Sense" in January. The moderate approach advocated in the "Appeal" was palatable to white Presbyterians. The ecumenical group followed its "Appeal" with a letter on April 12 to the black community which argued "that such actions as incite to hatred and violence, however technically peaceful those actions may be, have not contributed to the resolution of our local problems. We do not believe that these days of new hope are days when extreme measures are justified in Birmingham." Four days later Martin Luther King, Jr., responded to these clerical critics from the Birmingham jail.[20]

The trouble in Birmingham did not subside with King's march and jailing. That autumn, unknown persons bombed the Sixteenth Street Baptist Church, killing three young girls. Church courts and organizations as well as the rest of the nation were astonished by this violent act. The Synod of Georgia, Women of the Church, and Fayetteville Presbytery adopted resolutions of sorrow, and Potomac Presbytery collected an offering of $151.30 to send to the families of the victims.[21]

The civil rights movement effectively used mass marches to make its point, and numerous religious organizations and denominations participated. The March on Washington for Jobs and Freedom during the Labor Day weekend of 1963 organized a huge crowd. The National Council of Churches, of which the PCUS was a member, endorsed the march. Denominational representatives, however, were the only ones not to approve the council's participation. This did not prevent a number of Presbyterians from attending, including a group which proudly gathered under a banner identifying them as "Presbyterians, U.S." (See fig. 7). About 100 gathered at the Church of the Pilgrims, a PCUS congregation, for a prayer service before joining the hundreds of thousands of other marchers. Those who participated in the Washington march were convinced of the moral rightness of their act. Yet their participation did not come easily, because such an activist approach was not rooted in a strong denominational tradition.[22]

Others participated in the 1965 Selma march in Alabama. Most of the Presbyterians in the Selma march, however, did not live in the area. When asked why she participated, Rachel Henderlite replied that her first motive was to be able to answer satisfactorily the question, Where were you when concerned people were marching for justice and freedom? Moreover, Selma was not an isolated event. The events there, said Henderlite, could have occurred in any number of cities in the South, and the turnout from all over the nation was overwhelming, even if the local reception was disappointing. Prominent church leaders such as Ernest Trice Thompson and James L. Mays of Union Semi-

7. PCUS participants in the March on Washington for Jobs and Freedom, 1963 (Courtesy of Presbyterian Church [U.S.A.], Department of History, Montreat, North Carolina)

nary and Malcolm Calhoun of the Board of Christian Education participated in the march, as did other Presbyterians. Local Presbyterians were in a quandary over what to do about the marchers. After the march was over, they argued, many of the marchers left the citizens of Selma to face their problems alone. Others were infuriated and lashed out in retaliation. McBee Martin of Bristol, Virginia, complained about the inadequacy of the *Presbyterian Survey*'s coverage: "There is no reference to the sex orgies and other indecent behavior that went on during the March." "We seldom report," replied the editor with admirable restraint, "rumors of sex orgies in connection with religious events."[23]

When civil rights advocates marched in Washington, Congress was considering reform legislation. It still had not passed that legislation when the PCUS General Assembly met in 1964. Several overtures urged the highest court of the denomination to endorse this bill. The *Presbyterian Outlook* strongly supported it. Kenneth J. Foreman, Sr., noted that opponents of the civil rights legislation argued that its passage would threaten liberty. "The bare bones of the matter," he replied, "is that the Act (if and when it becomes one) is intended to destroy our liberty to *deny* liberty to others." The General Assembly stopped short of this endorsement. Instead, it issued a "Pastoral Letter to Local Sessions" which affirmed some of the precepts of the civil rights movement and the legitimacy of protests by black Americans, even if these caused social turmoil.[24]

This action did not satisfy a small but significant group of PCUS clergy and laity who thought that the denomination should take a more aggressive role. They organized three area meetings after the 1964 General Assembly to form a Fellowship of Concern. Its original purpose was to witness for the cause of civil rights within the denomination. The FOC presented a petition with 400 names supporting civil rights legislation to Senator Hubert Humphrey through J. Randolph Taylor, the pastor of the Church of the Pilgrims, a PCUS congregation in Washington. The goal of FOC remained racial reconciliation, although from time to time it discussed other related concerns. This group provided a PCUS presence in James Meredith's Mississippi march of 1966 and contributed $5,000 to the Division of Christian Action of the Board of Christian Education for the "specific endeavors in the area of racial reconciliation." These Southern Presbyterian liberals never fully identified with any one civil rights organization because they were more concerned with maintaining cooperation and contact with several different organizations.[25]

Gradually many conservative and moderate churchmen came to view the FOC as an interest group. It chose to disband in 1968 because at least some of its primary goals had been met and the position of the denomination on racial issues was more palatable. Disbanding also allowed members to seek other avenues for participating in social change.[26]

Martin Luther King, Jr., appeared upon the American scene in 1955 during the Montgomery bus boycott. Ten years and a Nobel Peace Prize later, he was the nation's most prominent civil rights leader. King addressed the PCUS when he spoke at a Christian Action Conference at Montreat in 1965.

Planning for this August 1965 conference began early in the year. Other speakers included James McBride Dabbs, Gayraud Wilmore, a black Presbyterian minister in the Presbyterian Church in the U.S.A., and a representative from the United States Department of Justice. Preconference publicity brought many negative comments. The problem was compounded when King hesitated to attend because of rioting in the Watts section of Los Angeles, California, just before the scheduled beginning of the Montreat conference. He did come, though he needed police protection to traverse safely portions of Buncombe County.[27]

Several church courts reacted negatively to the announcement of the 1965 Christian Action Conference. The Sessions of the First Presbyterian Church of Bainbridge, Georgia, and the First (Scots) Presbyterian Church of Charleston, South Carolina, took occasion to lambast General Assembly policies on this issue as well as matters which were only partially related. Both complained about the General Assembly's 1965 position paper on civil disobedience and the denomination's continued participation in the National Council of Churches. In addition, the Charleston session denounced the recently developed "equalization" funding proposal for church agencies, which would, they feared, greatly enhance the contributions of the PCUS to agencies such as the NCC. Presbyteries in Alabama and South Carolina also objected to King's invitation. After the conference, Tuscaloosa Presbytery received information that Gayraud Wilmore discussed racial intermarriage, which further fueled their opposition to the entire proceeding.[28]

The 1965 General Assembly met four months before the conference but had to deal with the issue. Numerous requests were received to withdraw the King invitation. It ruled that board and agency personnel should make specific plans for Montreat conferences. A writer in the *Presbyterian Outlook* argued that this decision made especially good sense, for one of the leaders of the civil rights movement was eminently qualified to present his cause to Presbyterians.[29]

The Board of Christian Education, which was sponsoring the conference, thus received a clarification of its authority, but it also received many complaints. Both ministers and laity wrote objecting to King's participation, not fathoming how "good" Christians could participate in a program with King. Several pointed to an interview in the December 30, 1963, *National Observer* which portrayed the civil rights leader as unconcerned with traditional theological issues such as the virgin birth, the divinity of Christ, and his bodily resurrection. Others charged that King was nothing but a Communist and a troublemaker. The task of interpreting, if not defending, the conference and King's participation in it fell to Marshall Dendy, executive secretary of the Board of Christian Education, who pointed out that King was a "recognized leader" of an important social movement. The board knew that resolution of the conflict would not occur at this or other similar meetings. Rather, the task was to help Presbyterians understand the church's role in such controversial issues in "the light of our understanding of the Word of God and the full meaning of God's love for all people."[30]

When King finally arrived at the 1965 Christian Action conference in Montreat, he did not present a blueprint for the PCUS to follow in dealing with the civil rights movement. His presentation, entitled "The Church on the Frontier of Racial Tension," sketched the socioeconomic plight of black America and noted the demise of segregation. King urged churches to move beyond social reform to help create changes in the hearts and minds of people so they could accept individuals without prejudice.[31] (See fig. 8.)

Several of the objections to King's appearance at Montreat also protested activities of the National Council of Churches. King was independent of the NCC, but this ecumenical agency was vitally concerned with the civil rights movement. Even before the 1960s there had been a great deal of controversy in the denomination over how deeply the PCUS should be involved in it. The *Southern Presbyterian Journal* frequently criticized the NCC and its predecessor, the Federal

8. Martin Luther King, Jr. (right) and Malcolm Calhoun at the Christian Action Conference, Montreat, North Carolina, August 1965 (Courtesy of Margaret Calhoun)

Council of Churches, for stands on social issues, giving heavy emphasis to their positions against segregation.[32]

The connection between ecumenism and civil rights advocacy seemed ironclad to opponents of denominational policy. As the church's official publication, the *Presbyterian Survey* presented articles congruent with the various pronouncements of the General Assembly. These drew much segregationist fire. "Your magazine," wrote H. L. Duke of Havana, Florida, "has become a publication of integration, not inspiration." Mrs. James H. Townsend of Miami Shores, Florida, spoke directly to the ecumenical–civil rights axis: "*Survey* is slanted in favor of integration, the National Council of Churches and the swallowing up of Presbyterianism by ecumenism."

Conservatives during the 1950s and 1960s sent a constant flow of overtures to presbyteries and the General Assembly requesting that the denomination cease its affiliation with the NCC. These requests were consistently refused. Other church courts, as well as individuals, approved of NCC action, though at times they disagreed over specifics. They defended the ecumenical agency as helping present a united front for American Protestantism, if not American Christianity.[33]

The NCC developed several programs to assist the civil rights movement. These came under the authority of the Commission on Religion and Race. One of the most controversial was the Delta Ministry, which was initially a project to identify indigenous black leadership in Mississippi and assist in the development of economic solutions for blacks and other poor people in the state. Programs of the Delta Ministry involved a number of citizenship and literacy training events as well as planning fair employment campaigns and school desegregation. Often Delta Ministry personnel shared facilities with the staffs of other civil rights organizations.[34]

The program was inaugurated in 1964, just in time to assist hundreds of civil rights workers as they made their way to participate in the Mississippi Summer Project. The initial program helped train these workers, providing volunteer clergy to help establish communication with local clergy and legal assistance to the volunteers. But confusion existed over the proper relationship of the NCC program to civil rights organizations, the role of volunteers, and the ability to obtain assistance from both blacks and whites in Mississippi. Obviously, any activity which promoted community development in Mississippi in the 1960s would be closely related to civil rights.[35]

Many within the PCUS attacked the Delta Ministry. Some used it as the pretext to issue additional calls for the denomination to withdraw from the NCC. Paul Tudor Jones, pastor of Memphis's Idlewild Church, responded by asking that some reasonable evaluation be made of the Delta Ministry and the 1964 Mississippi Summer Project. The goals of the project, as Jones understood them, were relief work for the local black population, literacy training, and voter registration. In Memphis the Rotary Club had promoted a literacy training program which used public transit facilities and had many black students. Memphis churches had been willing participants in a number of relief efforts sponsored by ecumenical agencies as well as the Red Cross. Jones had been recently approached by an official of the Republican party in Memphis to help publicize a voter registration drive through the church. No one had objected to any one of these involvements, but when the same kind of activities were carried out as part of a civil rights program, there was an outcry. Jones concluded that the advice

Gamaliel gave the Sanhedrin in the fifth chapter of Acts when the apostles Peter and John appeared before them was still valid: "Refrain from these men, and let them alone: for if this counsel or this work be of men, it will come to nought, but if it be of God, ye cannot overthrow it; lest haply ye be found even to fight against God."[36]

The PCUS did not hasten to support the work of the Delta Ministry, but gradually its caution gave way to curiosity about the program. The 1966 General Assembly authorized two separate investigations to determine what the denomination should do in regard to the Delta Ministry. As a result of this reevaluation the Board of Church Extension contributed $25,000 to its support for 1968. A $7,000 advance on this grant had to be made in late 1967 because of financial difficulties which had plagued the operation from its inception.[37]

As a participating member in the NCC, the PCUS was entitled to representation on the governing board of the Delta Ministry. James McBride Dabbs was chosen for this task in 1967. He accepted and became an advocate of the Delta Ministry within the denomination. Its work held out hope for Mississippi, he thought. "This is Christianity at the grass roots. The church should be supporting this kind of activity across the South."[38]

Not all Presbyterians were convinced that the Delta Ministry should receive the denomination's support. During the winter of 1966, a group of Delta Ministry staff and members "invaded" an abandoned Air Force installation in Greenville, Mississippi. They claimed that they were entitled to this property as United States citizens. This advocacy of collective ownership proved to the *Presbyterian Journal* that the Delta Ministry was really a communist organization, communist "with a small 'c' perhaps, but of the same breed as its big brother."

Numerous correspondents to the *Presbyterian Survey* also voiced their opposition to the Delta Ministry and called for the PCUS to get out of the NCC. "The mission of the church is saving men's souls," claimed Hugh J. Harper of Birmingham. Change comes only through the individual and by God's grace, "not by the NAACP, CORE, NCC or UN programs." Ultimately such efforts as the Delta Ministry would lead to Communism.[39]

Mississippi's white religious leaders were also upset at the establishment of the Delta Ministry. The Methodist bishop, Edward Pendergrass, charged that its staff was paternalistic, denying leadership to all white Mississippians. Others noted that this exclusion cost the possibility of any white support for the project, however slight that was.[40]

Mississippi Presbyterians were exasperated with the Delta Ministry. Briarwood Presbyterian Church in Jackson adopted a resolution protesting the NCC activity in the Delta area of the state. "We must insist," noted the elders, "that such actions will certainly result in violence and bloodshed, and possibly death. The preaching of the Word of God would be seriously hindered, and relations between the races disrupted." Central Mississippi Presbytery adopted this resolution and declared that it would not recognize any statements the NCC made as binding; it requested that statements regarding the Delta Ministry cease. First Presbyterian Church in Corinth asked St. Andrews Presbytery to demand that the General Assembly withdraw from the NCC in 1966 because of the Delta Ministry. The presbytery concurred, noting that the NCC project engaged in work which most Presbyterians considered far afield of the church's "spiritual ministry."[41]

The Synod of Mississippi tried to organize a constructive response to the Delta Ministry. The General Assembly recognized the sensitivity of Mississippians when the synod recommended that the church abstain from contributing to the program. A minister in Greenwood even suggested that the $25,000 grant the Board of Church Extension made to the Delta Ministry for 1968 be made contingent on incorporating a local Presbyterian minister in the administrative process to enhance communication.[42]

By 1967 the synod had decided to embark on its own program. It appointed a Committee on Special Ministries to the People of Mississippi to explore the needs of nontraditional ministries in the state. The Board of National Ministries approved the project and agreed to pay a staff member's salary up to $12,500 per year in addition to matching any other expense up to $25,000 per year. The new ministry was to investigate food and clothing distribution, child care services, personal evangelism, vocational counseling and job services, family counseling, and health and legal services. The synod then created a new vehicle to implement these programs, the Presbyterian Council on Special Ministries.[43]

Several programs were funded under this new arrangement. Vacation Bible schools were established in black communities in Jackson and the Delta region in 1968 and 1969. The council participated in relief efforts in the wake of Hurricane Camille in 1969. Presbyterians sponsored programs for young adult blacks in Hattiesburg and another Vacation Bible school in Sumner, Mississippi.[44]

In 1970 the Board of National Ministries found it necessary to eliminate the Presbyterian Council on Special Ministries from its budget because of a decline in giving for benevolences. The synod tried to maintain the program, however, with special offerings. By the 1971 annual meeting, this proved to be an ineffective way to fund the operation. The director of the council then joined the staff of South Mississippi Presbytery, although the council was officially continued as a clearinghouse for information. Special ministry projects continued to be reported in various churches and presbyteries in Mississippi until 1973. Their remaining funds were then distributed among the three presbyteries for special programs.[45]

By the mid-1960s the legitimacy of the civil rights movement was firmly established, as new cases of injustice were constantly being brought to light. The rioting in Watts showed that not everyone interested in guaranteeing civil rights was willing to wait for the fruits of nonviolence. The *Presbyterian Outlook*, whose position on civil rights issues was well known, wondered what benefit could be derived from its continued "preaching to the converted" on the matter, since the mass media also reported events, though it continued to report on matters affecting Presbyterians.

The congruence of the passage of the Civil Rights Acts of 1964 and 1965 with the discovery of racial prejudice and turmoil in other parts of the nation led to a rethinking of the situation. Ben Hartley, editor of the *Presbyterian Survey*, called for everyone to "get off Alabama's back." Let those who had always said Southerners knew how to handle race relations have their chance with the new laws in place. The advice was roundly criticized and, as events developed, the adversarial editorial position was maintained.[46]

The church now had to determine what was appropriate as protest in the mid-1960s. The 1966 General Assembly refined previous statements on civil disobedience to include approval of such activity only after "other peaceful means" had been exhausted. The *Presbyterian Journal* even reconsidered its position. A 1967 article approved the theory of civil disobedience but excluded civil rights activities from the scope of appropriate action. The Synods of North Carolina and Mississippi condemned violent organizations such as the Ku Klux Klan and also the bombings of churches and homes. North Carolina Presbyterians attempted to understand the reasons for violence in the black community. Such understanding did not remove individual responsibility but acknowledged that problems existed. The real solution cited in pronoucements and from the pulpit lay in allowing all people into the church's fellowship without regard to race, country of origin, or economic circumstances.[47]

Secular events and their perception by Presbyterians fueled the belief that the church and nation were confronting a crisis. Two programs illustrate this understanding: "A Declaration about the Crisis in American Society," adopted by the Board of Christian Education on October 20, 1967, and the NCC program "Crisis in the Nation," issued in 1967 and incorporated into the PCUS in February 1968.

"A Declaration about the Crisis in American Society" set forth two related problems which the church and nation had to confront: the war in Vietnam and rioting. The declaration was adopted during the escalation of United States involvement in Vietnam and in the wake of rioting in Detroit. The Board of Christian Education sought to have Presbyterians help:

- to arouse the conscience of the church and nation about our national crisis;
- to express in effective action in society the concern that is aroused; and
- to intensify our ministry for reconciliation of men with God and one another.[48]

Several churches indicated that they deeply appreciated the declaration. The session of the Iroquois Presbyterian Church in Louisville, Kentucky, instructed its Service Committee to evaluate the statement and work for its implementation at the local level. Other churches were antagonized. Sessions and individuals were concerned that this document had taken the board away from its legitimate work into areas where it had no real expertise. The session of the First Presbyterian Church, Lake City, Florida, claimed that the statement did nothing to help clarify the problems it cited.[49]

The NCC's General Board adopted a "Resolution on the Crisis in the Nation" at its September 1967 meeting. It charged that racism was a pervasive problem for all Americans and that the churches must do something to help educate their membership about it. They should begin to work with "aggrieved" peoples and encourage racial reconciliation by establishing programs to alleviate the problems of racism.

The NCC called on constituent denominations to assist in this effort with their own programs.[50]

The Board of National Ministries responded for the PCUS. It approved a "Master Plan for 1968 Participation in the 'Crisis in the Nation'" at the February 28, 1968, meeting. This called for the creation of a youth and adult study module to be distributed to all interested churches. To introduce the materials, the executive secretaries of the Boards of Women's Work, World Mission, National Ministries, and Christian Education sent a special-delivery letter to all the pastors and directors of Christian Education on March 20, 1968. The packet included a variety of printed and audio material by people both within and without the church which sought to explain the problems faced by black America and encourage groups to become observers/participants in their local communities.[51]

The project encountered immediate opposition, followed by some praise. Critics began by objecting to the funds that were necessary to send the letters special delivery. Others complained that church school material should be biblically rooted, not based on contemporary issues. Whatever was done in such curriculum "should be directed towards pressing the claims of the Gospel to change human nature through personal faith." Other opponents protested that the General Assembly did not approve the material. The board, however, did receive favorable responses. A North Carolina pastor found that the curriculum had facilitated a number of discussions and even drawn local leaders into discussions with the church about community problems.[52]

Results were mixed, at best. The "Crisis in the Nation" materials were available from the Board of Christian Education at a reasonable cost and were not distributed freely to all churches. The board evaluation of the program indicated that churches in the Synods of Texas and Virginia were most likely to order the materials and that churches within the Synods of Alabama, Appalachia, Georgia, Mississippi, and South Carolina were least likely to do so. Within these areas urban churches were more disposed to accept the packets. The evaluation identified 1,400 study groups involving a minimum of 18,000 communicants. This represented only 2 percent of the denomination's total membership. Of this group only 0.3 percent incorporated study tours of their communities into their curriculum. The report evaluators rejoiced that there were Presbyterians who wanted to study community problems but were disheartened that even fewer "are willing to act upon their learnings and involve themselves in the mission to today's world. Even then they seem to do so as individuals and not as groups within the Body of Christ."[53]

A major ecumenical civil rights activity was Project Equality. This program was initiated by the National Catholic Conference for Racial Justice in May 1965. Its purpose was to encourage the employment of minorities in business and other sectors of society on the basis of their qualifications. The project conducted its first programs in St. Louis and Detroit. Soon thereafter, it became interdenominational. When a local group started in Nashville in 1967, Nashville Presbytery at first declined to join but reversed that decision in 1968. The PCUS Board of World Missions, located in Nashville, had opted to participate in May 1967.[54]

One of the major civil rights organizations in the 1950s and 1960s was the Southern Christian Leadership Conference (SCLC) of Martin Luther King, Jr. The Fellowship of Concern donated $1,000 to the Board of Christian Education in 1967 for it to forward on to SCLC in support of that organization's work. This was simply a transfer of funds and involved no denominational money.[55]

Several leaders in the denominational bureaucracy recognized that at some point the denomination might want to support the work of the SCLC. George Chauncy, on the staff of the Office of Church and Society of the board, was delegated to find out more about King's organization and interpret it to the church. During the budgeting process for 1968, the board explored the possibility of presenting a small grant to the SCLC, a civil rights group which was not being consumed by the emerging Black Power movement. While the board knew it could not approve all of the activity of the SCLC, it considered much of its work constructive. A grant of $750 was sent on April 5, 1968, the day after King was assassinated in Memphis.[56]

When knowledge of this grant became public, the board was beseiged with criticism. James O. Speed wrote to William B. Kennedy that he had defended several controversial board decisions in the past, but the SCLC grant seemed to cut out any ground for such defense. Such a mild reprimand was not the end. The board received several notices that benevolence giving would suffer as a result of its action. Harmony Presbytery charged that SCLC activity led to violence and petitioned the General Assembly to withdraw the board's support. The session of the North Avenue Presbyterian Church in Atlanta alleged both a lack of proper authorization and the political nature of the grant as reasons to withdraw it.[57]

Board officials again had to respond. They reiterated that the SCLC was a beneficial civil rights group. William Kadel noted that the grant was perceived as part of the church's response to the "Crisis in the Nation" program, and some officials argued that it was simply a legitimate gift.[58]

Another denominational response to the civil rights movement came with the encouragement of "special ministries," the impetus for which had several sources. It derived partially from the "Crisis in the Nation" program and was partially influenced by ecumenical contacts. The Board of National Ministries had a long history of making grants to develop new churches or support missionary endeavors, but this new direction placed emphasis on community development by church groups, not all of which could claim strong denominational affiliations. In 1966 the board approved a tricultural (Hispanic, white, and black) church in Miami, an interracial church under way in St. Petersburg, Florida, and a black church in New Orleans which was developing an inner-city ministry that included youth programs and literacy training. Moreover, the board encouraged churches to participate in a variety of community development programs with both public and private funding.[59]

Church courts at other levels took up this challenge. Potomac Presbytery developed an ongoing commitment to Washington, D.C. inner-city work in the late 1960s. In Lynchburg, Virginia, Westminster Presbyterian Church developed a ministry for youth in the downtown area which provided some religious training. It was designed to demonstrate that "a Christian community is concerned about the youngsters, regardless of their academic or economic status, regardless of the color of their skin or the profession of faith or lack of faith of their parents." Both of these efforts also reveal the direction in which the Synod of Virginia was moving.[60]

Another local special ministries project occurred in Auburn, Alabama. The First Presbyterian Church of that town began to investigate ways to make federal money available for housing projects in the community. This resulted in the establishment of the Presbyterian Community Ministry. The session combined $5,000 from the 1969 budget with $10,000 from the Board of National Ministries. This initial grant was to be augmented by additional gifts from interested persons, not all of whom were Presbyterians. Plans called for eight to ten houses to be built in 1969 for needy families who were willing to make a series of monthly payments in order to relocate to adequate housing.[61]

None of the PCUS's special ministries drew as much attention as that in Memphis during a sanitation workers' strike in the spring of 1968. Many of the strikers were unable to arrange for adequate resources to support themselves and their families during this period. The Parkway Gardens Presbyterian Church set up an emergency food service for the strikers. When it requested an emergency $5,000 grant from the Board of National Ministries, the board dispatched Lawrence Bottoms to evaluate the situation. He reported to John Anderson, the board's executive secretary, that the money should be sent immediately in order to maintain the denomination's credibility. The board bypassed the normal review process, appropriating the money from a $40,000 contingency fund.[62]

The distinction between meeting human need and providing assistance to the strikers was lost on many. Critics immediately charged that this action actively supported the strikers. It was, they said, a highly questionable gesture in such a tension-packed situation. Ben Lacy Rose, chairman of the Board of National Ministries, tried to explain the grant. He defended the action because it was the last resort to continue a temporary hunger project in Memphis, and the money did come from a contingency fund. Moreover, the board was not trying to take sides in the strike. "Remembering Matthew 25," wrote Rose, " 'Inasmuch as ye have done it unto one of the least of these my brethren . . . ,' we were simply trying to meet human need."[63]

The situation was all the more volatile because it was during this strike that Martin Luther King, Jr., was assassinated. All official pronouncements from Southern Presbyterians expressed shock. John Anderson noted that King had lived only six years longer than Jesus Christ. "In that time he was led by his Christ to demonstrate more love than most people show in 89 years." Even the *Presbyterian Journal*, which opposed King, his methods, and his movement, expressed sadness at this turn of events. Even though the *Journal* believed the worst that the Federal Bureau of Investigation printed about King, he was nevertheless "the most effective champion of the principles he stood for" and "the one Negro leader whose public image was one of moderation, if not strictly of non-violence."

The breadth of reaction to Martin Luther King, Jr., and how Presbyterians understood him and the entire movement may best be gauged by the June 1968 issue of the *Presbyterian Survey*. Thousands of subscribers were met with a full-page picture of King's mule-drawn casket on the front-page cover with the theme imprinted: LOVE SHALL OVERCOME. The editorial question of the issue was clearly stated: "How can the white Christian deal with his own racism, individually and institutionally, and with the racism of fellow whites, all at the same time? If, psychologically speaking, change of heart follows change of behavior, how and when does he begin to change his behavior? If, theologically speaking, change of heart begins with repentance, how can he repent of his terrible sin and be freed of his terrible, terrible guilt?" The issue probed these questions and included a story on the sanitation workers' strike and how Presbyterians were involved there.

The reaction to the issue was highly charged. Letters to the editor were carried for the remainder of the year. Few carried the emotional sting and zing of those in the August issue. The letters that month began with a thoroughly supportive epistle from some faculty at Union Seminary in Richmond. But the tone of all letters ran two to one against the issue. And nothing could hide the deep-seated racism of many. "I am a segregationist 100%," proudly proclaimed Mrs. Isla Margaret Milner of Quincy, Florida, a community that was 75 percent black, she explained. Racial problems did not arise from what the white population did. Rather, she continued, "it is a matter of their [blacks'] sorryness, laziness and lack of self pride and not enough gumption to get out and work for what they want." Others protested through their actions: "DO NOT SEND THIS EXECRABLE PERIODICAL TO ME *EVER* AGAIN."

In the following months many people wrote to express their horror at the racist rhetoric of these and other letters. Such a reaction was typified by Elizabeth Drake of Gastonia, North Carolina, who started by saying she was not in complete agreement with everything in the June issue, but "I certainly do not condone the narrowmindedness displayed by a good many white Christians."

But the criticism kept coming. There was so much that Ben Hartley, the editor, ran his own personal question-and-answer editorial:

Q: Do you believe Martin Luther King was a Christian?
A: Yes.
Q: Do you believe Martin Luther King was a Communist?

A: No. And the only evidence I've seen attempts to support such charges using guilt by association and other smear techniques.[64]

At the same time there were efforts to strengthen the resolve of the denomination and individuals of like mind to obtain the support of the PCUS for the SCLC's Poor People's March. The General Assembly declined to issue an endorsement, but numerous individuals within the assembly meeting registered their support. The executive secretaries of several boards agreed that they would find some means to travel to Washington as a symbol of such support. John Anderson's board reminded him that he could not go as an official representative of the PCUS, adding that if the executive secretary was on vacation, the board could not tell him what to do with his time.[65]

After the executive secretaries made their pilgrimage to Washington, conservative Presbyterians unleashed another round of criticism against them. The Presbyterian Church in Weaverville, North Carolina, thought the action a violation of the General Assembly's instructions and believed it condoned disobedience of the law. T. Watson Street, of the Board of World Missions, replied that the marchers had complied with the letter of the law by obtaining permits and other necessary documents. He and the others were trying to call attention to the general plight of the poor by their brief trip to Washington.[66]

Though the General Assembly did not endorse the march, other church courts did. The Synod of Virginia endorsed the march to provide appropriate identification with the poor. Representatives were authorized to attend the Day of Solidarity observance and report back to synod. Mecklenburg Presbytery's Christian Action Committee donated $1,000 from an anonymous source to the Poor People's March. The *Presbyterian Outlook* reported that this was not an endorsement of the march, but it was presented as a ministry to the hungry.[67]

Many of these actions can be related to a sense of guilt on the part of white Southern Presbyterians, which is seen in the 1969 report of the Synod of Virginia's Committee on Justice and Mercy. The paper dealt with race as it affected the public school situation in the state. Noting a lack of consistent direction in its previous statements, the synod "unambiguously declared" its support of all individuals who were suffering harassment for the cause of racial equality and educational opportunity and asked the "forgiveness of those parents who

have agonized in loneliness as they have watched children being excluded from the benefits of the best and strongest educational opportunities." The synod deplored the situation of Virginia public education in the 1950s and 1960s. Presbyterians could only ask forgiveness
for their part in it and redirect their attention to improving the situation. It directed specific attention to Prince Edward County, where
schools were closed from 1959 to 1964 to avoid desegregation.[68]

Education faced new challenges at the same time. Busing as a means
to achieve integration of schools was becoming a court-mandated
policy in many areas. Two major cases involved Richmond, Virginia,
and Charlotte, North Carolina. Both synods in these states argued that
the problems caused by busing were preferable to those faced with the
segregated system it sought to replace. Their presbyteries received requests for establishing private schools, but the church courts counseled churches not to yield to this option. More important than busing
was the public good represented in public education. It deserved support even in the face of drastic actions.[69]

The small number of black Southern Presbyterians were concerned
with public education as well as with the civil rights movement. They
felt isolated in a denomination so predominantly white. The special
ministries programs highlighted some of their problems. Several white
leaders, such as John Anderson, felt that there must be some vehicle
for black Presbyterians to present their case. The Board of National
Ministries appropriated $15,000 to help organize the Black Presbyte-
rian Leadership Conference (BPLC) in September 1969 on the campus
of the Interdenominational Theological Center in Atlanta. This small
group of ministers and elders advocated causes of concern to blacks
within the denomination, including the recruitment of black ministers and staff for General Assembly agencies, more support for Stillman College, appropriate "social and political action programs" to address racism in church and society, and the establishment of a Black
Affairs office within the church.

The pattern of previous PCUS involvement with black churches and
ministers was to incorporate them into various structures. These efforts did not allow for independent action but tied the work of the
programs to denominational priorities. The Negro Work Program of
the 1940s and 1950s was remarkable in that it provided a dual rationale
for continuing such work. Segregationists saw it as the development of
churches *for* blacks, while more moderate to liberal proponents could

take encouragement from the inclusion of black churches in geographic presbyteries, thus "desegregating" the denomination. But the program was not independent.

The BPLC saw this feature of previous efforts as a major weakness. The flaw of these programs was that they were "a regular agent of the structure, as well as a reflection of the system, which dehumanized and fragmented the community." The BPLC intended to stay independent of the structure and thus be able to speak without fear of compromise.[70]

The BPLC presented a paper entitled "Black Expectations" to the 1970 General Assembly, noting its reasons for organizing. The assembly responded by authorizing $25,000 for its operation, sanctioning a special offering for the organization on October 18, 1970, and receiving the paper to be printed in the minutes. At that time the concerns of black Presbyterians paralleled those of other minority groups within the church. Hispanics and black Presbyterians began to see themselves in competition for church attention and resources, a result of PCUS missionary efforts among minorities.[71]

The BPLC bluntly challenged their white brothers and sisters. Its 1972 report to the General Assembly noted the need for unity in the denomination. "TOWARD AT-ONE-MENT" charged that despite statements to the contrary, most Presbyterians did not want to share their pew with blacks, "and in order to salvage their consciences, white Presbyterians engage in social service projects demeaning to blacks who are only perceived as 'objects of mission.'"[72]

The expenses of the BPLC rapidly increased in the early 1970s as it became more involved with economic development programs, including some bad loans. The General Assembly approved $30,000 for the group in 1972, and the organization then requested $113,600 for 1973.[73]

Many thought that the BPLC was less than successful in achieving its goals. The independent structure of the organization created unease among denominational leaders. Regardless of racial concerns, organizations tend to fear what they cannot control. The PCUS was no different in this than any other denomination. Although it became involved in a number of programs which did not fare well, the organization did help give black Presbyterians a sense of identity and furthered the cause of minority and ethnic concern within the denomination.[74]

The BPLC was being formed while James Foreman was prominent

in the public eye with his "Black Manifesto," a declaration that the churches of America owed black Americans something in return for supporting slavery and segregation. It was a religious version of the Black Power movement and was labeled Marxist by numerous critics. Several denominations, including the United Presbyterian Church, USA, and the Episcopal Church, along with the NCC, received the "Black Manifesto" favorably and responded with grant programs. The PCUS was not ignorant of this development. The *Presbyterian Survey* devoted a major article by Jeff Rogers, a black PCUS minister, to Black Power. Its significance may be measured in the three pages of readers' response devoted to the article and subject in a subsequent issue. The PCUS General Assembly staff wanted to respond in such a way that the denomination could make a witness without appearing to submit to pressure. Therefore the staff rejected the Marxist theory of the "Black Manifesto" but acknowledged white racism. The General Assembly also tried to ensure that the manifesto received a fair hearing in church circles, although some critics saw no way to reconcile it with the teachings of the denomination. At the same time, the BPLC offered a mechanism by which the denomination could deal with the issues of the "Black Manifesto." It approved a number of remedial programs, some of which were never funded, while others continued the community development work already being done. In addition, a major base of support for Stillman College was mobilized at an opportune time.[75]

Though the BPLC did not endorse Foreman's contention that white churches should pay reparations to blacks for the centuries of slavery, segregation, and injustice that they inflicted or at least supported, it did claim a biblical tradition whereby the oppressor came to the aid of the oppressed. Initially it was not possible for the BPLC to join Foreman's organization, the Interreligious Foundation for Community Organization (IFCO). After a period of time and changes in IFCO leadership, however, the BPLC became a supporting member in 1973.[76]

The official PCUS response to civil rights issues after 1954 was favorable to the cause but faced significant internal challenges from conservative members. In the 1960s the denomination reacted like many other mainline Protestant denominations with a variety of programs to promote community development. Although these responses did not place it at the heart of the civil rights movement, they did make the issues of the movement palpable within the denomination.

The impact of this knowledge varied according to the level at which it was received and was usually greater in the higher courts than in the lower ones. Concern for and identification with civil rights issues were not absent from local churches or individuals, but these cases were the exception rather than the rule. Black Presbyterians also helped focus denominational attention on problems facing black America by highlighting the problems of a minority within an overwhelmingly white denomination.

6

RACE, SCHISM, AND REUNION

THE BOUNDARIES that had so well delineated the origins and history of the PCUS had been breached by the early 1970s. The territorial limits of the denomination's ecclesiology were penetrated in 1969 with the authorization for "union" presbyteries between the church courts of the PCUS and related regional presbyteries of the United Presbyterian Church, USA. In 1969 the General Assembly also authorized the first set of talks with the UPCUSA on union since 1955.[1] The process set in motion culminated in 1983 with the reunion of the two denominations in the Presbyterian Church (U.S.A.).

Conservative members in the 1970s refused to compromise with the direction of action. The Continuing Church Movement was organized in the 1940s to oppose union at that time. The *Southern Presbyterian Journal* was organized as part of this opposition, which continued into the 1970s. Each year a "Journal Day" was held in Weaverville, North Carolina, as a rally for this opposition. In 1970 W. Jack Williamson of Greenville, Alabama, articulated the feelings of many when he said: "Radicals, determined ecumenists, have a timetable for the liquidation of the historic witness of the PCUS." The Reverend Frank Barker of Birmingham summarized the intensity of the moment cryptically: "Brethren, we are at war."[2]

Efforts were made to try to reconcile those identified as conservatives and liberals. Some thought that having a layman as moderator of the General Assembly could help resolve the friction. Dr. L. Nelson Bell, a former medical missionary to China and a founder of the *Southern Presbyterian Journal*, was elected moderator in 1972, despite his well-known opposition to union with the UPCUSA.[3]

But this effort to heal the divisions was inadequate. On December 4, 1972, the National Presbyterian Church in America was formed. This occurred 112 years to the day after the formation of the Presbyterian Church in the Confederate States of America. Unlike Bell, the ministers and elders who met at the Briarwood Presbyterian Church in Birmingham, Alabama, were unwilling to continue working in the PCUS. "We have reluctantly accepted the necessity of separation," they declared, "deeming loyalty to Christ to take precedence over relationships to any earthly institution, even a visible branch of the Church of Christ." According to the new denomination, which soon became known as the Presbyterian Church in America (PCA), the PCUS had abandoned the Bible and the historic Reformed creeds and based its authority on human reason and not divine will.[4]

The commissioners in Birmingham claimed to be in the theological lineage of their forefathers who gathered in Augusta, Georgia, in 1861. The Confederates made their case in a document written by James Henley Thornwell known as "Address . . . to all the Churches of Jesus Christ throughout the Earth." Like their ancestors, the 1973 commissioners sent "A Message to All Churches of Jesus Christ throughout the World."

On two occasions the 1973 "Message" quoted the 1861 "Address." Both matters were seen as critical in providing a rationale for the new denomination and merit analysis. The first citation was relative to the authority of the Scriptures, and the second concerned church government.

The 1861 meeting occurred subsequent to the Old School General Assembly action known as the Gardiner Spring's Resolution. This statement, proposed by the pastor of the Brick Presbyterian Church in New York City, declared the support of the Old School General Assembly for the action of the federal government in dealing with the states threatening to secede from the national union. Many commissioners from the South did not attend the meeting in Philadelphia because of the difficulty in travel and the uncertain political situation. Those who did attend did not share the view of the resolution. They opted to walk out of the assembly. Subsequently another group of commissioners gathered in Augusta to make their own statement of events in the "Address." Much of this document was given over to restating the course of events, and then to positing the question: "Is slavery, then, a sin?"[5]

By contrast, there is no one single issue addressed in the 1973 "Message." Nor was the political state of affairs so chaotic that separate governments had been founded. The commissioners in Birmingham took a 112-year-old statement and used it to support a particular point of view of scriptural authority, rather than using the Bible to answer specific questions as in 1861: "Do the scriptures directly or indirectly condemn slavery as a sin?" Instead, the 1973 commissioners attacked "change in the Presbyterian Church in the United States" which "came as a gradual thing and its ascendancy in the denomination, over a long period of time. We confess that it should not have been permitted."

The situations of 1861 and 1973, however, were quite different. In the first, Scripture was asserted as an authority and then examined in light of the question. That question was answered in the negative as other grounds of eliminating slavery (e.g., human rights) were also rejected. But in 1973 Scripture was asserted only as an authority without a predicate to examine, except for the nebulous "change" and the failure of the church courts to "exercise discipline."

A second difference is that the intellectual world of 1861 was beginning to wrestle with the challenges of new scholarship, which included Darwin's theory of evolution and higher critical study of the Scriptures.[6] By 1973 those challenges had been confronted many times over. In such a situation, the commissioners in Birmingham tried to answer the questions of their day with answers from a previous time.

The second appeal of the Birmingham commissioners to those in Augusta was in the area of church government. The "Message" quoted the "Address" in its preface: "As a church, we consciously seek to return to the historic Presbyterian view of Church government." In 1861 the commissioners gathered in Augusta felt they had no recourse, given the political developments of their time. It was unwise and unsafe to maintain meeting as one body when travel was dangerous and foreboding because of hostilities. This practicality was bolstered by the argument that "the unity of the church does not require a formal bond of union among all the congregations of believers throughout the earth." Because of the circumstances of 1861, the Southerners did not see themselves as having forced a "breach of charity," yet they were forced out of the denomination as "sinners." Consequently they understood there was no recourse but to form another denomination, retaining in it the marks of Old School Presbyterianism.[7]

One hundred and twelve years later the context of sectional discord and conflict over the role of interdenominational voluntary societies had changed to the modern ecumenical movement. As with their forebears, the 1973 commissioners chose to reject the current situation of church cooperation in favor of a tradition of denominational autonomy.

The "Message" of 1973 was more a document of willful departure than the "Address" had been. The political reality of armed conflict gave a different tenor to the meeting in 1861. The conclusion that slavery was not sinful is a case study in the hermeneutics of racism. By ignoring the context of their ancestors, the PCA missed an opportunity to assess the relationship of scriptural authority and racial ideology. In 1861 church government was simply a means to an end, but by 1973 the preservation of the system had become more important.

In analyzing the PCA split, we can explain the ecclesiastical division in terms of the theological development of fundamentalism. Recent treatment of this movement in the Presbyterian Church in the U.S.A. by J. Bradley Longfield describes the struggle between fundamentalists, modernists, and those who sought to hold the middle together against the pressures of either end. One of the chief warriors against modernism was J. Gresham Machen. Those who led the way out of the PCUS in 1973 were decidedly influenced by Machen.[8]

Interestingly enough, Machen was a product of the "Southern" Presbyterian Church. He grew up in a PCUS congregation in Baltimore, the Franklin Street Presbyterian Church. His religious mentors in youth were well grounded in the Calvinism of Thornwell's tradition. Moreover, Machen's family background was rooted in the quasi-religion of the Lost Cause.

Machen was educated at Johns Hopkins University and Princeton Theological Seminary. He studied in Germany at Marsburg and Göttingen and returned to teach at Princeton in 1906. While studying abroad, Machen was tempted to turn from Old School Presbyterianism and adopt the modernism of the university. After some period of turmoil and upon his return to Princeton, he rejected this option and became an exponent of the so-called Princeton theology, a theological heritage similar to the Thornwellian position below the Mason-Dixon line.

Gradually Machen's rejection of modernism was sharpened and became the basis for *Christianity and Liberalism*, published in 1923. This book set the parameters for conflict in the General Assemblies of the 1920s. Longfield contends that Machen's regional heritage provided its own unique solution to ecclesiastical conflict: secession. Eventually he came to exercise that option.[9]

Machen and his later adherents in the PCUS were committed to the philosophical approach of commonsense realism. The scientific method of this approach was found in the inductive methods of Francis Bacon. The method began with particular "facts" that could be established and moved to general statements by induction. Theologically speaking, this meant that "facts" about God, humanity, and nature were to be found in the Bible. They were facts because of where they were found. Once the facts of the Bible were established, then it was possible to make general statements about God, humanity, and nature which would become indisputable. Over time the traditional use of the term "infallible" to describe the Scripture was changed to "inerrant" as the need arose to establish that the original facts were without fault.[10]

The advocates of separation in 1973 were the heirs of this tradition. They thought that the theological changes of the twentieth century had torn the true faith from its only source. Increasingly, however, theology questioned the original "facts" as critical methods of biblical study developed. Such methods frustrated the conservatives and fundamentalists, who saw the modern critical method as leading to the dilution of the truth of the Christian faith.[11]

Conservatives in general, and fundamentalists in particular, have been ridiculed in popular culture ever since the Scopes "Monkey Trial" in 1925, but this ridicule has not extinguished this subculture. As cultural change quickened after World War II, the establishment of segregation came under attack, as did many other practices. The fundamentalists' worldview often was not challenged by segregation.

Responding to the 1954 General Assembly report "The Church and Segregation," Morton Smith claimed that there was no biblical condemnation of segregation, a case that sounded strangely like Thornwell's answer to the question on the sinfulness of slavery. "The fact is that God segregated Israel from the Canaanite," wrote Smith in 1973. "It is debatable as to whether the Church should get into the matter of trying to change that particular pattern, and branding one form of culture as sinful as opposed to another."

This reasoning was in fact derived from the 1861 case. The Bible did not condemn slavery, Thornwell had argued, and neither did it condemn segregation, said Smith. Therefore as the Bible was the source of particular "facts" about reality and relationships, both personal and social, Christians had no biblical grounds to oppose these practices.[12]

Initially almost 41,000 communicants in 260 churches joined in the PCA exodus. The new denomination represented those most discontented with the PCUS, but not all conservatives left. Ministers and churches in Mississippi, Alabama, and South Carolina represented the largest number of churches in the new denomination (171 of 260 churches and 108 of 191 ministers).[13] (See map 2.)

One of the first effects of the schism was seen in the election of the moderator of the PCUS General Assembly in 1974. Lawrence Bottoms was nominated, as were Kenneth Phifer and Albert Kissling. All were considered liberal ministers. Bottoms had spent his adult professional life in the ministry of the PCUS working with boards and agencies for the establishment and support of black churches. There was no significant disagreement between Bottoms and the others on such issues as Vietnam war resisters, abortion, church union, or the development of a new confession of faith for the denomination.[14]

The effect of race in the PCA split is debated. There was no major racial issue before the denomination in 1973 as there had been in the 1960s. Since the 1940s, however, race had been an important element in defining liberalism and conservatism in the PCUS. Leaders of the schism had criticized one or another of the denomination's positions on race relations or human rights. Racial concerns had also been a factor in the structuring of church programs and thus an element in denominational politics. Race was a factor as it defined the attitudes, ideas, and responses of both liberals and conservatives for several generations. The epitome of this relationship between race and polity was Central Mississippi Presbytery, which combined a stringent conservative theology with segregationist ideology. It voted against every major constitutional change of the PCUS prior to the vote for reunion with the UPCUSA in 1983.[15]

While the intensity of racial issues diminished as an element in denominational struggles, black Presbyterians did not disappear. In the 1970s the PCUS struggled with the question of the identity of blacks within the church. The concept of ethnic variety emerged as one of the results of the civil rights movement for many denominations. As the PCUS began to plan for a new General Assembly organizational structure in the 1970s, the racial minorities were grouped together to consolidate resources and help increase awareness of minority concern. This organizational strategy included the development of "a rationale for a racially inclusive society" as well as working toward this goal with various programs.[16]

The Black Presbyterian Leadership Caucus continued to sponsor

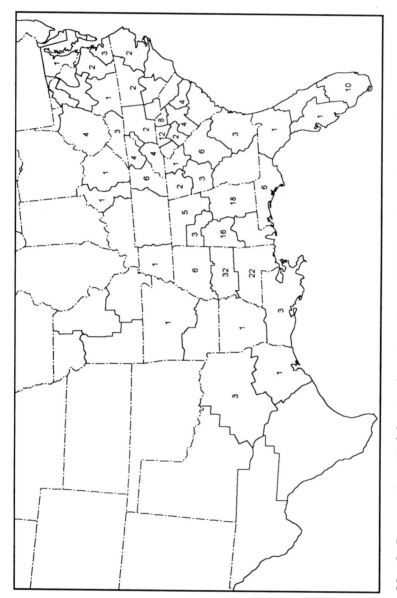

Map 2. Congregations Withdrawing from the PCUS and Joining the Presbyterian Church in America, 1973–1974 (Arabic numerals indicate the number of churches that withdrew from each presbytery. Boundaries of the presbyteries do not necessarily reflect county lines.)

programs for youth, women, and campus ministries until the Division of Corporate and Social Ministries assumed these functions in 1975. The division also incorporated Hispanic and Native American programs into its ethnic affairs work. The establishment of ethnic congregations remained part of the Division of National Mission, but the division pursued this goal without the zeal of the days of the Negro Work Program.[17]

The denomination's unease with ethnic issues was well illustrated in the arrangements for the churchwide Consultation on Mission held at Montreat in February 1978. This event was designed and promoted to plan denominational mission objectives and activities for the remainder of the twentieth century. Of the 270 official representatives invited, only five were minority representatives. Such a forum should have been the occasion to highlight ethnic involvement, noted black Presbyterian Randolph R. Ratliff. But considerable time and effort were still needed to make white Presbyterians aware that just because the 1960s were over, concerns by black Presbyterians had not disappeared. The consultation document that resulted emphasized the need for "Ethnic Ministry Imperatives," which were described as the necessity "to develop ways for the PCUS to live in solidarity and in full partnership in mission with ethnic minorities."[18]

Leadership opportunities continued to elude many talented black leaders. Rumors persisted of racial prejudice limiting opportunites. And in cases where blacks assumed leadership positions, they found their opportunities limited. When John Anderson was executive secretary of the Board of National Ministries, he brought on his staff a black Presbyterian minister from New Jersey, Joe Roberts. But opportunities within both the PCUS and the UPCUSA were limited. When Roberts left the employment of the board, he stayed in Atlanta as pastor of the Ebenezer Baptist Church, the church of Martin Luther King, Jr.[19]

Unlike the talks of union in the 1950s, the discussion of "reunion" from 1969 to 1983 had different results. Race as a polity and policy issue was seen in a different light. Many American churches turned their social consciences toward South Africa in the 1970s, and the PCUS was no exception. Specifically, the PCUS and other denominations called for American companies to divest their South African holdings. The process often took the form of shareholder resolutions, as did the action of the General Assembly Mission Board in December

1976 that called for Citibank to stop making loans to South Africa. This action, which would have been highly contentious a decade before, passed with only one dissenting vote.[20]

Focusing attention on South Africa meant that racial concerns were more widely distributed. Black Presbyterians and their allies, however, continued to hold the denomination accountable for racism. The General Assembly established a Committee on Church and Race in 1976. While this was a positive step, noted Elias S. Hardge, Jr., in the *Presbyterian Survey*, "It is most unfortunate that at this time such a committee is necessary."[21]

Increasingly, racial issues, including the racial dimension of the union plan, were discussed within the denomination as a matter of representation. Some complained that this was a quota system. Yet Hardge replied, "What is more Presbyterian than quotas?"[22] Indeed, Presbyterian polity has historically relied on the parity of "teaching elders" (ministers) and "ruling elders" (lay leaders). Both are given the same office, but each fulfills a specific function. There is a sense in which some would say this is a quota, giving the clergy more of a determination on an issue than the total number of church members.

As the plan for union was refined, a mechanism to report racial and gender representation was established. Each presbytery and synod as well as the General Assembly would establish a committee of representation that would monitor nominees to various committees, agencies, and assignments, giving specific attention to race, ethnic background, gender, age, and disabilities. This committee would be the guarantee that no one was prevented from service in the new denomination.[23]

Simultaneously, developments within the union talks had a positive result among conservative critics of the PCUS, not all of whom left with the PCA. The Concerned Presbyterians organization remained viable until 1976, when it decided it could no longer effectively challenge PCUS policy or actions. (See fig. 9.) But a new organization emerged known as the Covenant Fellowship of Presbyterians. This group was unofficially designated as the primary evangelical PCUS organization. It was consulted in the union discussion and presented thirteen guidelines for the direction of these conversations. When the Committee on Union presented its plan in 1981, the Board of Directors of the Covenant Fellowship overwhelmingly endorsed it.[24]

Several conclusions about the Presbyterian Church in the United States and race relations since World War II are possible.

EXPEDITING "MISSION"

9. Cartoon in the *Concerned Presbyterian* (Sanford, N.C.), ca. summer 1974. "G.E.B." stands for General Executive Board, formed in 1972 in the last major denominational restructuring. (Courtesy of Presbyterian Church [U.S.A.], Department of History, Montreat, North Carolina)

First, the denomination's orientation to black Presbyterians was strongly influenced by its nineteenth-century evangelization efforts, which were paternalistic—some would even say, racist. Most of the efforts before the Negro Work Program could be considered in this genre, though some participants had different views. Increasingly, those who did not hold to the church's paternalism made their views known, which fostered a debate over racial ideology. The intensity of this debate climaxed in the 1960s as the civil rights movement made the case for equal rights. Although the denomination was officially on the periphery of the movement, numerous individuals in the General Assembly as well as some of its agencies were deeply concerned. Several participated in direct action campaigns or other events.

Second, racial ideology, and to a lesser extent segregation in the church, affected ecumenical activity of the PCUS. This was particularly true of discussions about church union in the 1950s and about membership in the National Council of Churches. The interrelationship of ecumenical activity and race is illustrated in the careers of three ministers.

J. Randolph Taylor served as pastor of the Church of the Pilgrims in Washington, D.C., in the 1960s. He was active in civil rights activities, including the 1963 March for Freedom and Jobs. He later cochaired the Joint Committee on Presbyterian Union and in 1983 was elected the first moderator of the newly formed Presbyterian Church (U.S.A.).

Donald W. Shriver served as president of the Assembly's Youth Council in 1950–51 when it negotiated with Montreat authorities over allowing the attendance of Snedecor Synod delegates at Youth Council meetings. When Montreat refused to allow this, the council met at nearby Warren Wilson College. Shriver later edited *The Unsilent South*, a collection of sermons on race and civil rights, and has spent much of his career in various academic posts, including having served as president of Union Theological Seminary in New York City.

In contrast to Taylor and Shriver is Morton Smith. Smith taught first at Belhaven College in Jackson, Mississippi, and later at Reformed Theological Seminary in the same city. He was a constant critic of denominational policy and programs as well as a defender of the racial status quo. His critique of the PCUS was published with a subtitle: *The Decline of the Presbyterian Church, U.S., As Reflected in Its*

Assembly Actions. Smith was elected as the stated clerk of the PCA General Assembly in 1973.

Third, groups of women and youth raised concerns over racial issues and provided the most sympathetic and serious hearing for these concerns before the 1950s. The last group to deal with race as a matter of church policy was the church court system itself. Before 1965 this was a system composed solely of men. As young people assumed leadership positions and women expanded their role in the denomination in ordained office, they were able to help make the changes in policy and polity which led to the desegregation of the church.

Fourth, the Negro Work Program, which began in 1946, provided the opportunity to strengthen the black constituency in the denomination to the point where desegregation did not bring about the disappearance of the constituency. Before that time, black Presbyterians had insufficient numbers and leadership to deal successfully with incorporation into larger church life. The Negro Work Program helped develop leadership through the establishment of congregations and the revitalization of Stillman College. The success of the program may be the reason for its abolition, as by the early 1960s numerous black congregations were established. While the majority of these were found in predominantly white presbyteries, some were organized as part of exclusively black presbyteries. The time had arrived to end race as a category of program and polity, and both the Negro Work Program and black presbyteries were abandoned.

This change was not accomplished without some pain to all parties. Segregationists complained of violations of church law, while others feared the eventual disappearance of a black constituency. Church law accommodated itself the changes, and General Assembly rulings prevailed over presbytery and session recalcitrance in much the same way that congressional action overrode state and local ordinances. Fears that the black minority would disappear from the denomination were not realized, but tension was present as the limits of goodwill were to be tested.

Finally, the statements of the PCUS after World War II on race and, to a degree, some of its actions as well as other trends and developments represent its change from a regional denomination into one that had taken its place within the mainstream of American Protestantism. Ernest Trice Thompson arranges the third volume of his *Presbyterians in the South* in two divisions: "Out of the Backwater" and "Into the Mainstream." This classification has molded much of the discussion and thought both within and without the PCUS relative to the denomination's effectiveness in various endeavors.[25]

Moving into the mainstream of twentieth-century Protestantism, however, has not been easy, nor should it be assumed that the mainstream has always been correct. The series The Presbyterian Presence (1990–92) evaluates the course of the mainstream Presbyterian Church in various denominational forms throughout this century.[26] The Presbyterian experience in America has often revealed a concern with authority. Central to this concern is the authority of the Scriptures. But also at issue are the nature and extent of personal and group authority. The debate and conflict that raged in the PCUS after 1945 about and around racial issues were part of this conflict of authority and the struggle for control.

George Marsden recently noted parallels between J. Gresham Machen and Karl Barth. Both studied under Wilhelm Hermann at Marsburg. In fact, by only two years they missed overlapping in their studies. Both made critiques of the modernism their teacher advocated and found it lacking. This is significant for the PCUS, as those who departed in 1973 were heavily indebted to Machen's critique, while Barthian influence became commonplace in PCUS (and UPCUSA) seminaries in the 1950s and 1960s. The events described here were part of the drama being played out in the larger religious and social culture.[27]

Explicitly racial issues receded from the forefront of church life in the 1970s as the institution of segregation was more or less dismantled. Concern for racial issues, however, remained close to the heart of many people, both black and white. The denomination was committed to build inclusive structures, yet commitment did not guarantee results. Isaac Crosby, the first black to receive a doctoral degree from Union Theological Seminary in Virginia, urged the continued identification of racial issues at the beginning of the 1980s.[28] It seemed ironic that just as the church sought to be inclusive, racial designations were dropped, and it became more difficult to identify race as a factor for consideration in denominational life.

The PCUS experience with race as a matter of racial ideology and church polity after World War II was a prism for the rest of Southern society. As the only major denomination still bounded by its Civil War borders, and noted as well for its social power, the Presbyterian Church in the United States was an important part of Southern history and society. This peculiar conjunction makes this denominational experience in racial affairs a unique one in America's continuing struggle for racial justice. Although only part of the story, it represents a significant part as it chronicles how black and white people of a common religious commitment variously interpreted and practiced that religion in their own time and place.

NOTES

1. "An Agony" for the Presbyterian Church, U.S.

1. *Presbyterians in the South* 117 (June 10, 1942): 3, 15; Presbyterian Church in the United States (hereafter PCUS), *Minutes of the Eighty-Second General Assembly* (hereafter *Mins.———GA*), 1942, p. 95, and *Mins. 83d GA*, 1943, p. 33. Note that throughout this book I often follow Presbyterian practice in using no definite article with the name of a specific synod or presbytery (e.g., "Bouchelion, of [the] Central Louisiana Presbytery").

2. Paul Carter, *The Decline and Revival of the Social Gospel: Social and Political Liberalism in American Protestant Churches, 1920–1940* (Ithaca, N.Y.: Cornell University Press, 1954), p. 4.

3. Presbyterian Church in the United States, *Book of Church Order*, rev. ed. (N.p.: Board of Christian Education for the General Assembly of the Presbyterian Church in the United States, 1961), chaps. 13 and 14.

4. Walter L. Lingle and John W. Kuykendall, *Presbyterians: Their History and Beliefs*, 4th ed. (Atlanta: John Knox Press, 1978), pp. 80–82; Ernest T. Thompson, *Presbyterians in the South*, 3 vols. (Richmond: John Knox Press, 1963–73), 1:51–71 passim, and 2:13–35 passim; Morton H. Smith, *"How Is the Gold Become Dim" (Lamentations 4:1): The Decline of the Presbyterian Church, U.S., As Reflected in Its Assembly Actions*, 2d ed. (Jackson, Miss.: Premier Printing, 1973), pp. 1–22; C. Bruce Staiger, "Abolitionism and the Presbyterian Schism of 1837–1838," *Mississippi Valley Historical Review* 36 (1949–50): 395; George M. Marsden, *The Evangelical Mind and the New School Experience* (New Haven: Yale University Press, 1970), pp. 250–51; Victor B. Howard, "The Anti-Slavery Movement in the Presbyterian Church, 1835–1861" (Ph.D. diss., Ohio State University, 1961), pp. 8–12. The denomination formed in 1861 was originally known as the Presbyterian Church in the Confederate States of America. In 1865 the name was changed to the Presbyterian Church in the United States.

5. Brooks Holifield, *The Gentlemen Theologians: American Theology in Southern Culture, 1795–1860* (Durham, N.C.: Duke University Press, 1978), pp. 111–12.

6. Sir Walter Hamilton, *Lectures in Metaphysics*, 2 vols. (Boston, 1859), 1:34, 2:530, as quoted in Holifield, *Gentlemen Theologians*, p. 118.

7. James Oscar Farmer, Jr., *The Metaphysical Confederacy: James Henley Thornwell and the Synthesis of Southern Values* (Macon, Ga.: Mercer University Press, 1986), pp. 91–97.

8. Ibid.; Holifield, *Gentlemen Theologians*, pp. 121–22.

9. Bradley J. Longfield, *The Presbyterian Controversy: Fundamentalists, Modernists, and Moderates* (New York: Oxford University Press, 1991), pp. 32–37.

10. Ernest Trice Thompson, *The Spirituality of the Church* (Richmond: John Knox Press, 1961).

11. Thompson, *Presbyterians in the South*, 2:373–77, 380–81.

12. Ibid., 274–301 passim; Donald W. Shriver, Jr., ed., *The Unsilent South: Prophetic Preaching in Racial Crisis* (Richmond: John Knox Press, 1965), p. 14; Dwyn Mecklin Mounger, "Racial Attitudes in the Presbyterian Church, U.S. 1944–1954" (B.D. thesis, Princeton Theological Seminary, 1965), p. iv. The last effort at union prior to the success of 1983 was in 1954–55. At that time the merger of three denominations—Presbyterian Church in the United States of America, Presbyterian Church in the United States, and the United Presbyterian Church in North America—was before the respective church courts. The PCUS defeated the proposition, but the other two bodies merged into the United Presbyterian Church in the United States of America (UPCUSA) in 1958. The 1983 union occurred between the PCUS (Southern) and the UPCUSA (Northern).

13. Samuel S. Hill, Jr., *Southern Churches in Crisis* (New York: Holt, Rinehart and Winston, 1967), pp. 24, 76–77, 106–7, 119–20; PCUS, *Mins. 110th GA*, 1970, pp. 283–85.

14. Gayraud S. Wilmore, Jr., "Identity and Integration: Black Presbyterians and Their Allies in the Twentieth Century," in *The Presbyterian Predicament: Six Perspectives*, ed. Milton J Coalter, John M. Mulder, and Louis B. Weeks, The Presbyterian Presence (Louisville: Westminster/John Knox Press, 1990), pp. 109–10.

15. Kenneth K. Bailey, "The Post–Civil War Racial Separations in Southern Protestantism: Another Look," *Church History* 46 (December 1977): 455–73; H. Richard Niebuhr, *The Social Sources of American Denominationalism* (New York: New American Library, 1975), pp. 261–62; Gunnar Myrdal, *An American Dilemma: The Negro Problem and Modern Democracy*, 2 vols. (New York: Pantheon Books, 1972), 2:860, 870–71.

16. George Tindall, *The Emergence of the New South, 1913–1945*, A History of the South, vol. 10 (Baton Rouge: Louisiana State University Press, Louisiana Paperbacks, 1970), 145–75; Jacquelyn Dowd Hall, *Revolt against Chivalry: Jessie Daniel Ames and the Women's Campaign against Lynching* (New York: Columbia University Press, 1979), pp. 55–56, 59.

17. Tindall, *Emergence of the New South*, pp. 175–76, 550–51; Ann Wells Ellis, "The Commission on Interracial Cooperation, 1919–1944: Its Activities and Results" (Ph.D. diss., Georgia State University, 1975), pp. 358–69.

18. David M. Reimers, *White Protestantism and the Negro* (New York: Oxford University Press, 1965), pp. 86–88, 161–63; Robert Moats Miller, "The Attitude of American Protestantism toward the Negro, 1919–1939," in *The Negro in Depression and War: Prelude to Revolution*, ed. Bernard

Sternsher (Chicago: Quadrangle Books, 1969), p. 123; Carter, *Social Gospel*, pp. 148–49; Ellis, "Commission on Interracial Cooperation," pp. 379–82.

19. Reimers, *White Protestantism*, p. 95; W. Edward Orser, "Racial Attitudes in Wartime: The Protestant Churches during the Second World War," *Church History* 41 (September 1972): 344–45; Carter, *Social Gospel*, pp. 130–32.

20. Benjamin Muse, *The American Negro Revolution: From Nonviolence to Black Power, 1963–1967* (Bloomington: Indiana University Press, 1969), p. 81; Orser, "Racial Attitudes in Wartime," pp. 337, 345; C. Vann Woodward, *The Strange Career of Jim Crow*, 3d rev. ed. (New York: Oxford University Press, 1974), pp. 130–34.

21. Ralph McGill, *The South and the Southerner* (Boston: Little, Brown, 1963), pp. 130–34; Aldon D. Morris, in his *Origins of the Civil Rights Movement: Black Communities Organizing for Change* (New York: Free Press, 1984), pp. 17–25, points out that the roots of the movement antedate 1954 and specifically discusses the Baton Rouge boycott of 1953; Richard Kluger, in his *Simple Justice: The History of Brown v. Board of Education and Black America's Struggle for Equality* (New York: Alfred A. Knopf, 1976), details the development of the *Brown* case; see also Woodward, *Strange Career*, pp. 8–10, 134–35, 152–55.

22. Woodward, *Strange Career*, pp. 104, 170; James McBride Dabbs, *Who Speaks for the South?* (New York: Funk and Wagnalls, 1964), p. 363; Florence Mars, *Witness at Philadelphia* (Baton Rouge: Louisiana State University Press, 1977).

23. Woodward, *Strange Career*, pp. 193–94.

24. Muse, *American Negro Revolution*, pp. 78–79, 172.

25. Aldon D. Morris, "The Rise of the Civil Rights Movement and the Movement's Black Power Structure, 1953–1963" (Ph.D. diss., State University of New York, Stony Brook, 1979), pp. 171, 542–43; Gayraud Wilmore, Jr., " 'The New Negro' and the Protestant Churches," in *Freedom Now: The Civil Rights Struggle in America*, ed. Alan F. Westin (New York: Basic Books, 1964), pp. 302–4.

26. Robert Wuthnow, *The Restructuring of American Religion: Society and Faith since World War II* (Princeton: Princeton University Press, 1988), see chap. 7, "The Great Divide," pp. 133–72. See also Wuthnow, "The Restructuring of American Presbyterianism: Turmoil in One Denomination," in *The Presbyterian Predicament: Six Perspectives*, ed. Milton J Coalter, John M. Mulder, and Louis B. Weeks, The Presbyterian Presence (Louisville: Westminster/John Knox Press, 1990), pp. 27–48.

27. Joel L. Alvis, Jr., "Racial Turmoil and Religious Reaction: The Rt. Rev. John M. Allin," *Historical Magazine of the Protestant Episcopal Church* 50 (March 1981): 84–89.

28. Henry J. Pratt, "The Growth of Political Activism in the National Council of Churches," *Review of Politics* 34 (July 1972): 330; Muse, *American Negro Revolution*, p. 52.

29. Pratt, "Growth of Political Activism," pp. 333–40; Pratt, *The Liberalization of American Protestantism: A Case Study in Complex Organizations* (Detroit: Wayne State University Press, 1972), pp. 195–96, 240.

30. Woodward, *Strange Career*, pp. 125–26; Woodward himself argues that the Social Gospel movement had little effect on the South in an earlier period (C. Vann Woodward, *Origins of the New South*, A History of the South, vol. 9 [Baton Rouge: Louisiana State University Press, Louisiana Paperbacks, 1971], 450). Other scholars, such as Samuel S. Hill, Jr., argue that Southern churches' basic social concern was in the socialization process (Hill, *Southern Churches in Crisis*, pp. 76–77, 106–7). This argument has been countered by examples of such activity; see Wayne Flynt, "Dissent in Zion: Alabama Baptists and Social Issues, 1900–1914," *Journal of Southern History* 35 (November 1967): 523–42, and Flynt, "One in the Spirit, Many in the Flesh: Southern Evangelicals," in *Varieties of Southern Evangelicalism*, ed. Edwin Harrell (Macon, Ga.: Mercer University Press, 1981), pp. 23–44. The significance of this Southern Social Gospel is questioned by John Boles, "Religion in the South: Recent Historiography" (paper given at the Southern Historical Association, Memphis, Tennessee, November 6, 1982). The most extensive case for such a movement is John P. McDowell, *The Social Gospel in the South: The Woman's Home Mission Movement in the Methodist Episcopal Church, South, 1886–1939* (Baton Rouge: Louisiana State University Press, 1982), and the best treatment of the Social Gospel in the PCUS is Flynt, "Feeding the Hungry and Ministering to the Broken-Hearted: The Presbyterian Church in the United States and the Social Gospel, 1900–1920," in *Religion in the South*, ed. Charles Reagan Wilson (Jackson, Miss.: University Press of Mississippi, 1985), pp. 83–138.

31. Reimers, *White Protestantism*, p. 185; Muse, *American Negro Revolution*, pp. 48–52.

32. Muse, *American Negro Revolution*, p. 88.

33. Jeffery K. Hadden, "Clergy Involvement in Civil Rights," *Annals of the American Academy of Political and Social Science* 387 (January 1970): 119–21; Kenneth K. Bailey, *Southern White Protestantism in the Twentieth Century* (New York: Harper and Row, 1964), pp. 145–46, which cites the 1954 General Assembly of the PCUS statement on segregation and the refusal of the 1954 Synod of Mississippi to comply as part of the clergy-lay conflict. All PCUS church courts had clerical and lay representatives. One of the strongest Mississippi proponents for rejecting the General Assembly's stand was Dr. G. T. Gillespie, a minister and president of the denominationally affiliated Belhaven College in Jackson.

34. Miller, "Attitude of American Protestantism," p. 107; Dabbs, *Who Speaks for the South?* p. 331; G. T. Gillespie, *A Christian View on Segregation*, reprint of an address before the Synod of Mississippi of the PCUS, November 4, 1954 (Greenwood, Miss.: Citizen's Council, n.d.).

35. Jeffery K. Hadden, *The Gathering Storm in the Churches* (Garden

City, N.Y.: Doubleday, 1969), p. 5; Robert Lee, "Social Sources of the Radical Right," *Christian Century* 79 (May 9, 1962): 595–97.

36. "The Agony of the Church," *Christian Century* 79 (October 10, 1962): 1215–16.

2. Jim Crow, Jacob's Ladder, and the Negro Work Program

1. Ernest Trice Thompson, *Presbyterian Missions in the Southern United States* (Richmond: Presbyterian Committee on Publication, 1934), pp. 183–88; see also Erskine Clarke, *Wrestlin' Jacob* (Atlanta: John Knox Press, 1978), and Donald Mathews, "Charles Colcock Jones and the Southern Evangelical Crusade to Form a Biracial Community," *Journal of Southern History* 41 (August 1975): 299–320.

2. Willis D. Weatherford, *American Churches and the Negro* (Boston: Christopher Publishing House, 1957), p. 195; Thompson, *Presbyterian Missions*, pp. 190–94; Bailey, "Post–Civil War Racial Separations," pp. 453–73.

3. Thompson, *Presbyterians in the South*, 2:313–20; Thompson, "Black Presbyterians: Education and Evangelism after the Civil War," *Journal of Presbyterian History* 51 (Summer 1973): 179–83.

4. Thompson, *Presbyterians in the South*, 2:310–11; Paul W. Terry and L. Tennant Lee, *A Study of Stillman Institute: A Junior College for Negroes* (University: University of Alabama Press, 1946), pp. 52–53.

5. Thompson, *Presbyterians in the South*, 2:320–25.

6. Ibid.

7. Oscar B. Wilson, Diary, January 20, 1899, Presbyterian Church (U.S.A.), Department of History, Montreat, North Carolina (hereafter DH, Montreat).

8. Thompson, *Presbyterians in the South*, 3:89.

9. R. Douglas Brackenridge and Francisco O. Garcia-Treto, *Iglesia Presbiteriana: A History of Mexican-Americans in the Southwest* (San Antonio, Tex.: Trinity University Press, 1974), pp. 87–89.

10. Willard C. Mellin, "Theological and Non-theological Factors in the Development of Policy and Action of the United Presbyterian Church Regarding the Negro, 1900–1965" (Ph.D. diss., Union Theological Seminary, New York, 1975), pp. 75–77.

11. Executive Committee on Home Missions, *Annual Report*, 1921, pp. 28–29; 1923, p. 17.

12. Executive Committee on Home Missions, *Annual Report*, 1930, pp. 13–15; 1936, pp. 19–20; 1924, pp. 18–19; Benjamin A. Lynt, "I Visited Seventeenth Street," *Presbyterian Outlook* 127 (February 26, 1945): 12.

13. Executive Committee on Home Missions, *Annual Report*, 1944, pp. 34–35; Synod of Alabama, *Minutes*, 1944, pp. 451–54; interview with Ruth Douglas See, Montreat, North Carolina, January 27, 1983; *Presbyte-*

rian Outlook 127 (February 26, 1946): 15; interview with Ernest Trice Thompson, Richmond, Virginia, July 18, 1983.

14. PCUS, *Mins. 85th GA*, 1945, p. 87, and *Mins. 86th GA*, 1946, p. 91; Executive Committee on Home Missions, *Annual Report*, 1947, pp. 52–54, 60–61; *Presbyterian Outlook* 128 (June 29, 1946): 11; Thompson interview.

15. Synod of Mississippi, *Minutes*, 1948, pp. 699–700.

16. Alexander R. Batchelor, *Jacob's Ladder: Negro Work in the Presbyterian Church in the United States* (Atlanta: Board of Christian Education, 1953), pp. 47, 65–76; Batchelor to H. V. Lofquist (copy), September 9, 1949, Mountain Retreat Association File, 1949–59, C. Grier Davis Papers, DH, Montreat; Note Book Material File, Division of Negro Work, General Correspondence Series, Board of National Ministries, PCUS, DH, Montreat (hereafter DNW-GCS).

17. *Presbyterian Outlook* 128 (June 10, 1946): 8–9; PCUS, *Mins. 86th GA*, 1946, p. 91.

18. *Presbyterian Outlook* 128 (June 10, 1946): 10–11 and (July 15, 1946): 5–6.

19. Snedecor Memorial Synod, *Minutes*, September 22–24, 1946, p. 6; Letters to the Editor, *Presbyterian Outlook* 128 (July 29, 1946): 2; (August 5, 1946): 2; (August 12, 1946): 2; (September 9, 1946): 2; *Southern Presbyterian Journal* 9 (June 15, 1950): 2–3.

20. Assembly's Committee on Negro Work, *Minutes*, January 8, 1947, p. 19, DH, Montreat; *Presbyterian Outlook* 129 (June 16, 1947): 12.

21. Wilmore, "Identity and Integration," pp. 109–10.

22. *Presbyterian Outlook* 128 (June 10, 1946): 10; Thompson interview; Ruth D. See interview; Executive Committee on Home Missions, *Annual Report*, 1947, pp. 60–61.

23. Sara Barry, "The Role of the Presbyterian Church in the United States in a Segregated Society" (M.R.E. thesis, Biblical Seminary in New York, 1955), pp. 67–68; "The Reorganization: Board of Church Extension, Negro Work," *Presbyterian Outlook* 132 (March 20, 1950): 8–9; interview with Lawrence W. Bottoms, Louisville, Kentucky, March 22, 1983; Reamers, *White Protestantism*, p. 123; E. C. Scott, *Ministerial Directory of the Presbyterian Church, U.S., 1861–1941; Revised and Supplemented, 1942–1950* (Atlanta: Hubbard Printing, 1950), p. 39.

24. PCUS, *Mins. 88th GA*, 1949, pp. 143–44; Thompson, *Presbyterians in the South*, 3:367–68; Weatherford, *American Churches and the Negro*, pp. 258–62.

25. Assembly's Committee on Negro Work, Manual adopted January 7–8, 1949, DH, Montreat.

26. *Presbyterian Outlook* 128 (April 26, 1946): 8; 135 (June 29, 1953): 10–11.

27. *Presbyterian Outlook* 137 (February 7, 1955): 5.

28. Bottoms interview; Board of Church Extension, *Annual Report*,

1962, pp. 28–29; Lawrence Bottoms to Donald Miller, June 3, 1954, Misc. "M" File, DNW-GCS.

29. PCUS, *Mins. 86th GA*, 1946, pp. 35, 76.

30. *Christian Observer* 138 (March 29, 1950): 2–3; Flynt, "Feeding the Hungry," pp. 83–138.

31. PCUS, *Mins. 90th GA*, 1950, p. 70; *Presbyterian Outlook* 132 (April 10, 1950): 8; "The Dissolution of Snedecor Memorial Synod," Snedecor Region—General File, DNW-GCS; Mecklenberg Presbytery, *Minutes*, October 19, 1948, p. 43.

32. PCUS, *Mins. 91st GA*, 1951, p. 80; Board of Church Extension, *Minutes*, April 1951, pp. 99–101; *Presbyterian Outlook* 132 (May 11, 1950): 4; Thompson interview.

33. *Presbyterian Outlook* 133 (February 5, 1951): 1; (June 4, 1951): 10; (June 25, 1951): 11–12, 15; (July 25, 1951): 4; Synod of Louisiana, *Minutes*, 1951, p. 247; Synod of Georgia, *Minutes*, 1952, p. 11; Board of Church Extension, *Annual Report*, 1953, pp. 48–49.

34. Batchelor, *Jacob's Ladder*, p. 85; Board of Church Extension, *Minutes*, April 1951, pp. 102–3, and April 1952, pp. 150–53; Lawrence W. Bottoms to William I. Reeves, September 23, 1954, Institute File, DNW-GCS; Bottoms interview.

35. Irvin Elligan to All Ministers (circular letter), December 17, 1954, Race Relations File, DNW-GCS; "Facts about Our Negro Churches from Our Negro Churches for Our Negro Churches," ca. February 1956, ibid.

36. Institute File, DNW-CGS; Board of Women's Work, *Minutes*, November 1950, p. 7; Barry, "Presbyterian Church in the United States in Segregated Society," pp. 76–77.

37. *Presbyterian Outlook* 133 (October 29, 1951): 8; Albert C. Winn to James J. Alexander, August 27, 1956, Central Alabama Presbytery, Church Extension File, DNW-GCS; Lawrence Bottoms to Norman Cook, March 23, 1956, Snedecor Region—Christian Education File, Division of Negro Work, Subject Correspondence Series, DH, Montreat (hereafter DNW-SCC); Board of Church Extension, *Minutes*, November 1957, p. 166.

38. *Minutes* of the Committee to Study the Snedecor Regional Plan, May 7, 1957, Snedecor Region File, DNW-GCS.

39. Assembly's Committee on Negro Work, *Minutes*, December 1, 1949. The consolidation took place on December 2, 1949.

40. Board of Church Extension, *Minutes*, July 1952, p. 179; Bottoms interview.

41. Board of Church Extension, *Minutes*, February 1956, pp. 81–82, and July 1956, p. 9; Brazos Presbytery, *Minutes*, September 12, 1957, p. 34.

42. *Presbyterian Outlook* 138 (September 17, 1956): 8; 145 (March 4, 1963): 3; Board of Church Extension, *Minutes*, February 1963, p. 47, and July 1963, p. 61.

43. Andrew Murray, *Presbyterians and the Negro—A History* (Philadelphia: Presbyterian Historical Society, 1966), pp. 176–94 passim; Board

of Church Extension, *Minutes*, October 1961, p. 179; Marshall L. Smith to Alexander Batchelor, November 10, 1953, and Batchelor to Smith, November 14, 1952, Requests for Surveys in the Communities File, DNW-GCS; Alexander Batchelor to Robert L. Peters, Sr., January 7, 1954, Misc. "P" File, ibid.; Jas. C. Ruffin to Alexander Batchelor, April 15, 1954, and Batchelor to Ruffin, April 26, 1954, Misc. "R" File, ibid.

44. PCUS, *Mins. 89th GA*, 1949, pp. 72–73; Southwest Georgia Presbytery, *Minutes*, October 16, 1951, p. 26; *Southern Presbyterian Journal* 10 (March 26, 1952): 15; Bottoms interview.

45. *Southern Presbyterian Journal* 8 (February 15, 1950): 16; Board of Church Extension, *Minutes*, November 1953, p. 258; PCUS, *Mins. 93d GA*, 1953, p. 94.

46. W. C. Jamison to Alexander Batchelor, September 16, 1954, Misc. "J" File, DNW-GCS; Fayetteville Presbytery, *Minutes*, October 23, 1953, p. 375, and January 20, 1953, p. 43; Memphis Presbytery, *Minutes*, January 2, 1952, p. 11; Louisiana Presbytery, *Minutes*, April 20, 1954, pp. 9–10; Savannah Presbytery, *Minutes*, September 14, 1954, p. 6; Mecklenburg Presbytery, *Minutes*, January 27, 1959, p. 40; Red River Presbytery, *Minutes*, September 12, 1961, p. 528; East Hanover Presbytery, *Minutes*, April 20, 1948, pp. 46–47; All Souls Presbyterian Church, Manuscript History, 1952–1956, Local Church History Program, DH, Montreat (hereafter cited as LCHP).

47. Alexander R. Batchelor to Richard O. Flinn, April 24, 1953, Survey File, and Schedule for Survey Workshop, May 25–27, 1953 File, and Survey Procedures, List of Surveys Conducted in Past Two Years as of February 8, 1954 File, DNW-GCS.

48. PCUS, *Mins. 88th GA*, 1948, pp. 141–42; Synod of Alabama, *Minutes*, 1946, p. 31; *Presbyterian Outlook* 29 (January 20, 1947): 15; Synod of Arkansas, *Minutes*, 1947, p. 13, and 1949, p. 29; Synod of Virginia, *Minutes*, 1948, pp. 343–45; Synod of Alabama, *Minutes*, 1948, p. 19, and 1949, p. 16; Synod of Georgia, *Minutes*, 1948, pp. 39–40; Synod of Florida, *Minutes*, 1949, p. 40; Red River Presbytery, *Minutes*, April 20–21, 1948, pp. 32–33; Brazos Presbytery, *Minutes*, April 19, 1949, p. 48; Synod of Mississippi, *Minutes*, 1950, pp. 118–20; Synod of North Carolina, *Minutes*, 1952, pp. 81–84.

49. Synod of Mississippi, *Minutes*, 1952, pp. 242–43; Harmony Presbytery, *Minutes*, April 10, 1951, p. 25; Enoree Presbytery, *Minutes*, January 8, 1963, pp. 16–17.

50. Synod of Georgia, *Minutes*, 1953, p. 22; 1956, p. 27; and 1958, p. 17; Synod of Mississippi, *Minutes*, 1958, p. 26; Louisiana Presbytery, *Minutes*, January 19, 1955, p. 58; Florida Presbytery, *Minutes*, April 1, 1958, pp. 26–28; Red River Presbytery, *Minutes*, September 9, 1958, p. 309; Synod of Alabama, *Minutes*, 1957, p. 16; Synod of Texas, *Minutes*, 1957, p. 201, and 1958, p. 394; Synod of Arkansas, *Minutes*, 1961, pp. 46–55; Hanover Presbytery, *Minutes*, January 26, 1960, p. 17; Red River Presbytery, *Minutes*, September 10, 1963, p. 23.

51. Bottoms interview; Synod of North Carolina, *Minutes*, 1950, p. 379; Board of Church Extension, *Annual Report*, 1957, pp. 11–12; Synod of Texas, *Minutes*, 1952, pp. 148–49; Synod of Florida, *Minutes*, 1956, p. 31; Synod of Arkansas, *Minutes*, 1959, p. 31; Synod of North Carolina, *Minutes*, 1960, pp. 113, 115; Brazos Presbytery, *Minutes*, February 10, 1960, p. 15.

52. Louisiana Presbytery, *Minutes*, January 21, 1958, p. 57; Alexander R. Batchelor to Mrs. Thomas D. Hopkins, March 12, 1954, Misc. "H" File, DNW-GCS; Synod of Texas, *Minutes*, 1960, p. 698; Florida Presbytery, *Minutes*, April 20, 1954, p. 9, and April 1, 1958, pp. 18–19; interview with Albert C. Winn, Decatur, Georgia, June 2, 1982; Albert C. Winn to Lawrence W. Bottoms and James J. Alexander, January 23, 1956, Central Alabama Presbytery File, DNW-GCS; and H. L. Gladney to Lawrence W. Bottoms, January 7, 1958, Georgia-Carolina File, ibid.

53. Interview with Irvin Elligan, Jr., Atlanta, Georgia, June 6, 1983; Thompson interview; East Hanover Presbytery, *Minutes*, April 19, 1949, p. 36; October 18, 1949, pp. 32–33; April 15, 1952, p. 14; and October 21, 1952, p. 19; Synod of Virginia, *Minutes*, 1953, p. 283.

54. Synod of Virginia, *Minutes*, 1955, p. 57; East Hanover Presbytery, *Minutes*, January 24, 1956, pp. 18–19, and January 22, 1957, p. 23; All Souls Presbyterian Church, Richmond, Virginia, Resume 1952–1956, LCHP; Thompson interview.

55. Elligan interview; Thompson interview.

56. East Hanover Presbytery, *Minutes*, January 26, 1954, pp. 21–22, and April 20, 1954, pp. 36–37; Hanover Presbytery, *Minutes*, February 10, 1959, p. 32, and September 30, 1958, p. 28.

57. Synod of Texas, *Minutes*, 1951, p. 68, and 1953, pp. 279–80; Brazos Presbytery, *Minutes*, April 22, 1953, p. 20; March 9, 1954, pp. 2–13; January 24, 1958, p. 79; and September 27, 1960, p. 45; Pioneer Presbyterian Church, Beaumont, Texas, Resume 1948–1953, LCHP.

58. Memphis Presbytery, *Minutes*, October 28, 1952, p. 22; April 28, 1953, pp. 27–28, 36; and October 26, 1954, p. 37; Parkway Gardens Presbyterian Church, Memphis, Tennessee, 1953 and 1963, LCHP.

59. *Presbyterian Survey* 43 (June 1953): 24–26; *Southern Presbyterian Journal* 7 (February 15, 1949): 18–19; Robert McNeill, *God Wills Us Free: The Ordeal of a Southern Minister* (New York: Hill and Wang, 1965), pp. 124–29.

60. Augusta-Macon Presbytery, *Minutes*, September 11, 1956, p. 23; October 23, 1956, p. 37; and January 22, 1957, p. 10.

61. Interview with Albert H. Freundt, Jr., Montreat, North Carolina, August 31, 1983; interview with Spencer C. Murray, Montreat, North Carolina, October 13, 1983; *Presbyterian Outlook* 133 (February 5, 1951): 10–11; Faith Presbyterian Church, Jackson, Mississippi, 1944–1949 and 1952–1953 histories, LCHP.

62. Florida Presbytery, *Minutes*, October 27, 1953, p. 19; Synod of Alabama, *Minutes*, 1958, p. 49; Birmingham Presbytery, *Minutes*, April 14–

15, 1952, p. 25; April 13–14, 1953, p. 26; February 23, 1955, p. 20; March 14, 1957, p. 35; January 21–22, 1957, p. 20; and January 20–21, 1958, pp. 29–30.

63. Board of Church Extension, *Annual Report*, 1955, p. 49; Bottoms interview; Synod of Texas, *Minutes*, 1952, p. 149; Donald Smith, "Black Ministers, Presbyterian Church, U.S., with an update on Black Churches" (Tuscaloosa, Ala.: Stillman College Office of Institutional Planning, November 5, 1975).

64. Bottoms interview; Elligan interview; East Hanover Presbytery, *Minutes*, July 15, 1952, p. 11; Memphis Presbytery, *Minutes*, October 15, 1952, p. 14; Lawrence W. Bottoms to Mrs. John K. Orr, February 3, 1954, Misc. "O" File, DNW-GCS; Bottoms to Jawells Carr, November 15, 1956, Louisiana-Mississippi Presbytery File, DNW-SCC.

65. Report of Church Extension Committee, February 2–3, 1957, Central Alabama Church Extension File, DNW-SCC; Synod of Florida, *Minutes*, 1957, pp. 21–22; Harvard Sitkoff, *The Struggle for Black Equality, 1954–1980* (New York: Hill and Wang, 1981), p. 64.

66. Red River Presbytery, *Minutes*, September 11, 1956, p. 184; Winn interview; interview with John F. Anderson, Montreat, North Carolina, December 8, 1983.

67. Board of Women's Work, *Minutes*, July 5, 1945, p. 18; July 10, 1945, p. 20; July 16, 1946, p. 11; June 23, 1947, p. 4; March 1947 meeting, Exhibit F; November 1947 meeting, Exhibit N; and October 22, 1959, p. 3.

68. Fayetteville Presbytery, *Minutes*, April 18, 1950, p. 224; Board of Women's Work, *Minutes*, November 1952 meeting, Exhibit J, p. 34, and July 14, 1958, p. 4; Report of Presbyterial Training Schools in All Negro Presbyteries for 1959 and 1960, Re: Negro Work File, Interracial Work Subject Files, Board of Women's Work, PCUS, DH, Montreat (hereafter cited as BWW).

69. *Southern Presbyterian Journal* 5 (August 1, 1946), pp. 13–14; Synod of Florida, Women of the Church, *Minutes*, 1948, p. 38, and 1949, pp. 35–36; Synod of Alabama, Women of the Church, *Minutes*, 1948, p. 23.

70. Augusta-Macon Presbytery, *Minutes*, April 21, 1952, p. 14; Synod of Florida, Women of the Church, *Minutes*, 1947, pp. 32–33; 1954, p. 22; and 1956, p. 21; Synod of Virginia, Women of the Church, 1954, p. 34; Synod of Texas, *Minutes*, 1952, p. 163, and 1955, p. 110; Fayetteville Presbytery, *Minutes*, July 17, 1951, pp. 354–55; Brazos Presbytery, *Minutes*, September 22, 1955, p. 29; Synod of South Carolina, Women of the Church, *Minutes*, 1950, p. 16; Synod of Texas, Women of the Church, *Minutes*, 1942, pp. 34–35, and 1955, p. 33; Synod of Florida, Women of the Church, *Minutes*, 1956, p. 21; Washington Shore Presbyterian Church, Orlando, Florida, 1958 history, LCHP.

71. Manual for Intergroup Work and Manual for Directors of Interdenominational Conferences, Intergroup Work File, Interracial Subject Work Files, BWW; Board of Women's Work, *Minutes*, November 5–7, 1946, Exhibit Z; *Southern Presbyterian Journal* 11 (June 25, 1952): 16; Fayetteville

Presbytery, *Minutes*, April 18, 1950, p. 227; Synod of Mississippi, *Minutes*, 1947, pp. 24–25, and 1948, p. 28; Synod of North Carolina, Women of the Church, *Minutes*, 1947, p. 19, and 1949, p. 33; Annie Tait Jenkins to Mrs. J. C. Garrison, March 4, 1955, Board of Women's Work, Miscellaneous File, DNW-GCS.

72. Synod of Arkansas, Women of the Church, *Minutes*, 1951, p. 25; 1952, p. 27; 1956, p. 27; and 1963, p. 18; Synod of Virginia, Women of the Church, *Minutes*, 1948, p. 37; 1949, p. 36; 1950, p. 39; 1951, p. 40; 1952, p. 45; and 1953, pp. 28, 44; Louisiana-Mississippi Presbyterial, 1953 history, LCHP; Synod of Mississippi, Women of the Church, *Minutes*, 1954, pp. 28–29; Synod of South Carolina, Women of the Church, *Minutes*, 1957, p. 17, and 1967, p. 28; Synod of South Carolina, *Minutes*, 1953, pp. 44–45, and 1959, p. 51; Synod of Alabama, Women of the Church, *Minutes*, 1950, pp. 21–22; Synod of Georgia, Women of the Church, *Minutes*, 1950, p. 27, and 1955, p. 30; Synod of North Carolina, Women of the Church, *Minutes*, 1954, p. 53, and 1968, p. 22.

73. The Conference for Negro Women sponsored by the Synodical of North Carolina as reported in the Synod of North Carolina, Women of the Church, *Minutes*, illustrates the trend:

Year	Attendance	Year	Attendance
1952	229	1961	166
1953	257	1962	163
1954	249	1963	156
1955	252	1964	159
1956	215	1965	126
1957	N/A	1966	100
1958	220	1967	96
1959	N/A	1968	98
1960	167	1969	93

See also Synod of Georgia, Women of the Church, *Minutes*, 1959, p. 13; Synod of South Carolina, *Minutes*, 1962, p. 57; Synod of Arkansas, Women of the Church, *Minutes*, 1964, p. 10; Synod of Arkansas, *Minutes*, 1964, p. 56; Synod of North Carolina, Women of the Church, *Minutes*, 1969, p. 16.

74. Board of Women's Work, *Minutes*, November 9, 1945; November 1950, Exhibits, p. 27; March 5, 1953, p. 9; April 1954, Exhibits, p. 21; June 28, 1954, pp. 7–8; and February 1966, Exhibit G, p. 16; Synod of Arkansas, *Minutes*, 1955, p. 39; Synod of Georgia, Women of the Church, *Minutes*, 1955, p. 31.

75. Assembly's Committee on Negro Work, *Minutes*, October 8, 1947, p. 40, and October 29, 1948, pp. 75–76; Lawrence Bottoms to Ernest A. Andrews, Jr., April 14, 1956, Misc. "A" File, DNW-GCS; Synod of Florida,

Minutes, 1948, p. 24, and 1952, p. 21; Synod of South Carolina, *Minutes*, 1954, pp. 37–38; Red River Presbytery, *Minutes*, April 22–23, 1952, p. 285, and September 30, 1960, pp. 461–62; Tuscaloosa Presbytery, *Minutes*, April 21, 1952, p. 406; Barry, "Presbyterian Church in the United States in a Segregated Society," p. 85; George W. Gore, Jr., to Alexander Batchelor, March 6, 1953, and Carl M. Hill to Batchelor, July 18, 1953, Student Work–Tallahassee, Florida, File, DNW-GCS; Isabel Rogers to Lawrence Bottoms, January 19, 1955; Bottoms to Rogers, January 27, 1955; and Bottoms to Elizabeth McWhorter, June 15, 1955, Student Work File, DNW-GCS.

76. Batchelor, *Jacob's Ladder*, pp. 127–35; *Presbyterian Outlook* 130 (February 9, 1948): 3, and 131 (February 7, 1949): 5–6.

77. PCUS, *Mins. 88th GA*, 1948, pp. 144–45, and *Mins. 90th GA*, 1950, p. 69; Assembly's Negro Work Committee, *Minutes*, October 29, 1948, p. 76; Board of Church Extension, *Minutes*, April 1950, p. 35; Samuel Burney Hay to Lawrence Bottoms, April 6, 1954, Stillman College File, DNW-GCS; *Southern Presbyterian Journal* 10 (February 27, 1952): 1; Bottoms interview; Barry, "PCUS in a Segregated Society," p. 86.

78. Board of Women's Work, *Minutes*, November 10, 1948, p. 46; Patricia Houck Sprinkle, *The Birthday Book: First Fifty Years* (Atlanta: Board of Women's Work, PCUS, 1972), pp. 1–2, 259–66; *Southern Presbyterian Journal* 10 (April 23, 1952): 13, and 11 (May 21, 1952): 14–15; interview with Samuel Burney Hay, conducted by Florence F. Corley, Covington, Georgia, October 14 and 21, 1979 (deposited at DH, Montreat).

79. PCUS, *Mins. 92d GA*, 1952, pp. 168–70, and *Mins. 93d GA*, 1953, p. 86; Board of Church Extension, *Minutes*, July 1953, p. 234.

80. *Presbyterian Outlook* 135 (May 11, 1953): 8; *Southern Presbyterian Journal* 11 (April 1, 1953): 4–5, and 12 (June 24, 1953): 14; H. F. Reinhardt to Lawrence Bottoms, February 14, 1952, Stillman Campaign File, DNW-GCS; Synod of Louisiana, *Minutes*, 1952, p. 310; Synod of North Carolina, *Minutes*, 1953, pp. 98–99; Synod of South Carolina, *Minutes*, 1953, pp. 55–56; Synod of Texas, *Minutes*, 1953, p. 279, and 1958, p. 363; Birmingham Presbytery, *Minutes*, April 13–14, 1953, pp. 31–32, and October 13–14, 1953, p. 29; Brazos Presbytery, *Minutes*, April 22, 1953, pp. 29–31; January 28, 1954, p. 52; September 22, 1955, p. 29; January 25, 1957, p. 95; and October 14, 1958, p. 46; East Alabama Presbytery, *Minutes*, April 15, 1952, p. 28; Harmony Presbytery, *Minutes*, January 20, 1953, p. 8; Red River Presbytery, *Minutes*, October 21, 1952, p. 326, and September 20, 1955, p. 138; Southwest Georgia Presbytery, *Minutes*, October 21, 1952, p. 32, and June 30, 1953, p. 14; First Presbyterian Church, Auburn, Alabama, Minutes of Session, February 20, 1953, and March 9, 1955 (microfilm copy available in the Auburn University Archives, Auburn, Alabama); All Souls Presbyterian Church, Richmond, Virginia, History Resume, 1952–1956, LCHP.

81. PCUS, *Mins. 94th GA*, 1954, p. 199, and *Mins. 96th GA*, 1956, p. 70; Board of Church Extension, *Annual Report*, 1956, pp. 39–40; Board of

Church Extension, *Minutes*, February 1956, p. 79; *Presbyterian Outlook* 138 (January 30, 1956): 2, and 139 (February 11, 1957): 8.

82. PCUS, *Mins. 95th GA*, 1955, pp. 73–74; Charles E. Raynal, Jr., to Alexander Batchelor, June 4, 1954, and T. R. Robinson to Batchelor, October 17, 1954, Misc. "R" File; Corthan G. Smith to Batchelor, November 2, 1954, and William I. Reeves to Leonard A. Stidley, May 24, 1954, Misc. "S" File, DNW-GCS.

83. Winn interview.

84. Bottoms interview; Isaac Crosby, "From Conformity to Transformation," *Presbyterian Survey* 72 (May 1982): 35–36.

3. Ecclesiastical Equivalents for Liberals and Conservatives

1. Thomas Cary Johnson, *A History of the Presbyterian Church South*, American Church History Series, vol. 11 (New York: Christian Literature, 1894), pp. 422–34; Thompson, *Spirituality of the Church*, pp. 24–26. The standard interpretation of the origins of the distinctive doctrine has been challenged by Jack P. Maddex, "From Theocracy to Spirituality: The Southern Presbyterian Reversal on Church and State," *Journal of Presbyterian History* 54 (Winter 1976): 438–58, where he argues that the idea of a "non-secular" church was not a part of Thornwell's theology at all but an adaptation of Presbyterians in border states, fully developed during the Civil War and urged on the Southern church through several unions in the 1860s and 1870s. Maddex's interpretation has been challenged by James Farmer in *The Metaphysical Confederacy*, who notes that without the doctrine of the spirituality of the church, the maintenance of the Old School General Assembly prior to the Civil War would not have been possible (pp. 280–84).

2. Thompson, *Presbyterians in the South*, 2:262–63; Thomas Hugh Spence, Jr., "The Southern Presbyterian Church and the Spirituality of the Church" (S.T.D. thesis, Biblical Seminary, New York, 1929), pp. 221–53.

3. Thompson, *Presbyterians in the South*, 3:265–72; Thompson interview.

4. George Marsden, *Understanding Fundamentalism and Evangelicalism* (Grand Rapids, Mich.: William B. Eerdmans Publishing, 1991), pp. 57–61; Marsden, *Fundamentalism and American Culture: The Shaping of Twentieth-Century Evangelicalism, 1870–1925* (New York: Oxford University Press, 1980), pp. 11–21. This theological doctrine held that the Bible reveals certain ages, or "dispensations," which God had established with a variety of covenants. The PCUS rejected this theological notion by General Assembly action in 1944. Cf. PCUS, *A Digest of the Acts and Proceedings of the General Assembly of the Presbyterian Church in the United States, 1861–1965* (Atlanta: Office of the General Assembly, 1966), pp. 45–59.

5. Interview with Robert H. Walkup, Montreat, North Carolina, June

28, 1983. The most vehement conservative attack on liberal policies was Morton H. Smith's *"How Is the Gold Become Dim."* Smith wrote this critique in the early 1970s, and it was influential in the split that led to the formation of the Presbyterian Church in America.

6. Carter, *Decline and Revival of the Social Gospel*, p. 175; PCUS, *Mins. 74th GA*, 1934, p. 39; James H. Smylie, "The Bible, Race, and the Changing South," *Journal of Presbyterian History* 59 (Summer 1981): 201–3; Dwyn M. Mounger, "Racial Attitudes in the Presbyterian Church in the United States, 1944–1954," *Journal of Presbyterian History* 48 (Winter 1970): 51.

7. PCUS, *Mins. 75th GA*, 1935, pp. 93–95, and *Mins. 76th GA*, 1936, pp. 99–100; Thompson interview; Robert Moats Miller, *American Protestantism and Social Issues* (Chapel Hill: University of North Carolina Press, 1958), p. 310; Thompson, *Presbyterians in the South*, 3:530.

8. PCUS, *Mins. 76th GA*, 1936, p. 24; *Mins. 78th GA*, 1938, p. 46; *Mins. 79th GA*, 1939, p. 72; Smith, *"How Is the Gold Become Dim,"* pp. 137, 181; Thompson, *Spirituality of the Church*, pp. 41–42.

9. PCUS, *Mins. 83d GA*, 1943, p. 144, and *Mins. 84th GA*, 1944, pp. 150–51.

10. Numan V. Bartley, *The Rise of Massive Resistance: Race and Politics in the South during the 1950's* (Baton Rouge: Louisiana State University Press, 1969), pp. 295–305; Reamers, *White Protestantism*, pp. 115–16.

11. Ansley C. Moore, Racial Issues File, Ansley C. Moore Papers, DH, Montreat; "Macon Presbytery on Race Relations," *Presbyterian Outlook* 130 (February 2, 1948): 8; (March 8, 1948): 10; Barry, "PCUS in a Segregated Society," pp. 25–34.

12. "Dr. Scherer Offers a Motion," *Presbyterian Outlook* 139 (June 29, 1953): 10; Mrs. Howard Holmes to Editor, ibid., 132 (November 27, 1950): 2; Muriel M. Weisiger to Editor, ibid. 140 (January 13, 1958): 2.

13. Elligan interview; John Haddon Leith, "Ernest Trice Thompson . . . Churchman," in *Ernest Trice Thompson: An Appreciation* (Richmond: Union Theological Seminary in Virginia, 1964), pp. 30–48.

14. Mounger, "Racial Attitudes" (B.D. thesis), pp. 54–61. Morton Sosna, *In Search of the Silent South: Southern Liberals and the Race Issue* (New York: Columbia University Press, 1977), pp. vii–xi, discusses the various ways in which "liberal" has been used in Southern history. See also Mounger, "Racial Attitudes," pp. 39–40. "Southern" was dropped from the *Journal*'s title in 1959 (*Presbyterian Journal* 18 [October 8, 1959]: 3), indicating that the influence and appeal of the periodical were no longer exclusively regional. The name change was accompanied by the retirement of Henry B. Dendy as editor and the appointment of a new editor, G. Aiken Taylor.

15. "A Look to the Rock Whence We Were Hewn," *Presbyterian Outlook* 143 (February 20, 1961): 8; Mounger, "Racial Attitudes" (*Journal*), p. 51.

16. *Presbyterian Outlook* 132 (July 10, 1950): 6; 136 (January 25, 1954):

6–7; (February 1, 1954): 5; (February 8, 1954): 5; 139 (February 4, 1957): 4–5; (February 25, 1957): 5–8; 149 (March 6, 1967): 9.

17. Carl F. Hutcheson to Editor, *Presbyterian Outlook* 132 (November 20, 1950): 2; W. A. Henry to Editor, ibid. 139 (March 11, 1957): 2; Paul Hudgins to Editor, ibid. 140 (March 3, 1958): 2.

18. L. Nelson Bell, "Why," *Southern Presbyterian Journal* 1 (May 1942): 2–3; Thompson interview.

19. Julia Kirk Blackwelder, "Southern White Fundamentalists and the Civil Rights Movement," *Phylon* 40 (December 1979): 335; Blackwelder, "Fundamentalist Reactions to the Civil Rights Movement to 1969" (Ph.D. diss., Emory University, 1972), pp. 132–34; Mounger, "Racial Attitudes" (*Journal*), pp. 40–51; L. Nelson Bell, "A Layman Looks at Liberalism," *Southern Presbyterian Journal* 4 (September 15, 1945): 3–4; Bell, "What Is the Gospel?" ibid. 5 (August 1, 1946): 3. Bell was the father-in-law of evangelist Billy Graham.

20. Bell, "Race Relations—Whither?" *Southern Presbyterian Journal* 2 (March 1944): 4–5; Bell, "Racial Tensions: Let Us Decrease—Not Increase Them," ibid. 5 (February 15, 1947): 2–3; Bell, "Racial Tensions: Some Little Things That Will Help," ibid. 6 (June 2, 1947): 3–4; Bell, "No Moratorium on Courtesy," ibid. 14 (April 11, 1956): 3; J. E. Flow, "Is Segregation Unchristian?" ibid. 10 (August 29, 1951): 4–5; Bell, "Some Needed Distinctions," ibid. 16 (June 5, 1957): 2–3.

21. "Weaverville Statement," *Presbyterian Outlook* 139 (September 2, 1957): 8; Thompson, *Presbyterians in the South*, 3:540. Previous statements in the *Presbyterian Outlook* had also endorsed "voluntary segregation" in the pre-1954 period; see J. McDowell Richards to Editor, *Presbyterian Outlook* 132 (January 30, 1950): 2, and "Handwriting on the Wall," ibid., p. 8; *Presbyterian Journal* 25 (November 23, 1966): 9–10.

22. *Presbyterian Survey* 53 (August 1963): 4–5.

23. Billy Don Sherman, "The Ideology of American Segregationism" (Th.D. diss., Southwestern Baptist Theological Seminary, 1966), pp. 142–59; J. David Simpson, "Non-Segregation Means Eventual Intermarriage," *Southern Presbyterian Journal* 6 (March 15, 1948): 7; Morton H. Smith, "The Racial Problem Facing America," *Presbyterian Guardian* 33 (October 1964): 125–27.

24. Gillespie, *Christian View on Segregation*; Sherman, "Ideology of Segregationism," pp. 141–42; Blackwelder, "Fundamentalist Reactions," p. 130.

25. Cecil K. Brown, *The Southern Position with Respect to the Bi-racial System* (Waco, Tex. [ca. 1956]); Ella Morrison Lucas to Editor, *Presbyterian Outlook* 137 (April 4, 1955): 2.

26. Donald G. Miller, "Shall We Then Hear the Word of God and Do It?" *Presbyterian Outlook* 137 (March 14, 1955): 10–14.

27. East Alabama Presbytery, *Minutes*, June 19, 1956, pp. 5–8. Peter's vision of clean and unclean foods (Acts 10) is generally understood to be the turning point in the life of first-century Christianity. Jewish laws pro-

scribed a large number of foods, including pork and shellfish, as unclean for human consumption. In Peter's vision, God commanded him to eat these foods. Immediately after the vision, Peter was called to the home of a Roman soldier, Cornelius. The conjunction of the vision and the visit represents an opening of the message of Christ to non-Jews.

28. Ernest Trice Thompson, "The Struggle for Social Justice," *Presbyterian Outlook* 129 (May 12, 1947): 13–14; "Bible Study: Christian Relations among the Races," ibid. 133 (August 20, 1951): 13–14; "The Bible for Today," ibid. 134 (February 11, 1952): 8; "Paul Said 'Made of One,' " ibid. 137 (March 14, 1954): 9; "The Gospel for All Men" (Sunday School Lesson for May 13, 1956), ibid. 138 (April 30, 1956): 13–14; "Social Justice Then and Now" (Sunday School Lesson for July 10, 1960), ibid. 142 (June 27, 1960): 11–12; Ben Lacy Rose, *Racial Segregation in the Church* (Richmond: Outlook Publishers, 1957); Albert C. Winn, "Segregation and Bible Teachings," *Presbyterian Outlook* 137 (June 27, 1955): 5; Kenneth J. Foreman, "Why Did God Create the Races?" ibid. 141 (January 26, 1959): 9; J. Sherrard Rice, "Challenge of the Negro to the Church," ibid. 143 (February 6, 1961): 5–6; Robert Lawrence, "God Plays No Favorites," ibid. 147 (March 1, 1965): 5–6; Robert F. Davenport, "We Cannot Afford 'A Nigger,' " ibid. 148 (November 28, 1966): 5.

29. PCUS, *Mins. 86th GA*, 1946, pp. 39, 81.

30. PCUS, *Mins. 89th GA*, 1949, pp. 177–93; Thompson, *Presbyterians in the South*, 3:532–33; Smylie, "Bible, Race, and the Changing South," pp. 205–6.

31. *Southern Presbyterian Journal* 8 (June 1, 1949): 3 and (June 15, 1949): 15.

32. Synod of South Carolina, *Minutes*, 1948, pp. 47–49; Synod of Alabama, *Minutes*, 1948, p. 32; Red River Presbytery, *Minutes*, October 18–19, 1949, pp. 128–29; Synod of Alabama, *Minutes*, 1950, pp. 35–39; "The Alabama Report," *Presbyterian Outlook* 132 (October 16, 1950): 8; Robert McNeill, *God Wills Us Free* (New York: Hill and Wang, 1965), pp. 86–90.

33. "Ewart Amendment," *Presbyterian Outlook* 135 (June 29, 1953): 10; Barry, "PCUS in a Segregated Society," pp. 69–71; Mounger, "Racial Attitudes" (*Journal*), pp. 63–65; PCUS, *Mins. 93d GA*, 1954, pp. 188–97; Smylie, "Bible, Race, and the Changing Church," pp. 206–8.

34. Thompson, *Presbyterians in the South*, 3:539–40; Smith, "*How Is the Gold Become Dim*," pp. 151–53.

35. *Southern Presbyterian Journal* 13 (June 9, 1954): 7; *Presbyterian Outlook* 136 (July 12, 1954): 3, 4; Thompson, *Presbyterians in the South*, 3:540–41; Tuscaloosa Presbytery, *Minutes*, July 20, 1954, pp. 464–65; South Highland Presbyterian Church, Birmingham, Alabama, LCHP; Synod of Georgia, *Minutes*, 1954, p. 20; Fayetteville Presbytery, *Minutes*, July 20, 1954, pp. 192–93; Bottoms interview; Synod of Texas, *Minutes*, 1954, pp. 346, 401; Bailey, *Southern White Protestantism*, pp. 142–43.

36. Thompson, *Presbyterians in the South*, 3:539–40; PCUS, *Mins. 95th GA*, 1955, pp. 36–38, and *Mins. 96th GA*, 1956, pp. 33, 75.

37. "Kingstree, S.C., Effort Proposes to Screen Men's Group Speakers,"

Presbyterian Outlook 137 (November 28, 1955): 3; "S.C. Men's Group Seeks Conformity," ibid. (December 12, 1955): 2–3; "S. Car. Men Urge Conformity," ibid. 138 (January 9, 1956): 10–11; Howard H. Kemp to Editor, ibid. (February 6, 1956): 2; First Presbyterian Church, Auburn, Alabama, *Minutes of Session*, July 14 and October 13, 1957; Kathleen L. Moore, "John Haddon Leith: The Auburn Years" (paper for Dr. W. David Lewis, Auburn University, May 30, 1980, copy in possession of author), pp. 15–16.

38. Thomas Lindeman Johnson, "James McBride Dabbs—A Life Story" (Ph.D. diss., University of South Carolina, 1980), p. 349.

39. Frances Furlow, "Gentleman from South Carolina," *Presbyterian Survey* 56 (October 1966): 22–23; Fred Hobson, "James McBride Dabbs: Isaac McCaslin in South Carolina," *Virginia Quarterly Review* 53 (Autumn 1977): 642–45. Hobson calls *The Lasting South* "self-consciously Southern."

40. Furlow, "Gentleman from South Carolina," pp. 20–23; James McBride Dabbs, "The Faith That Is in Us," *Presbyterian Outlook* 140 (September 8, 1958): 5; "An Open Future for the South," ibid. 142 (September 5, 1960): 8; "Speak Now," ibid. 145 (December 9, 1963): 4.

41. Johnson, "Dabbs—Life Story," pp. 398ff.; Kluger, *Simple Justice*, pp. 3–26; R. Wilbur Cousar, "A Mild Reply to James McBride Dabbs in the *Presbyterian Outlook* on 'The Last Stronghold of Segregation,' " *Southern Presbyterian Journal* 10 (August 8, 1951): 4–5; R. W. Cousar to James McBride Dabbs, October 9, 1951, James McBride Dabbs Papers, in the Southern Historical Collection, University of North Carolina Library, Chapel Hill, North Carolina.

42. Bailey, *Southern White Protestantism*, pp. 126–27; David M. Reimers, "The Race Problem and Presbyterian Union," *Church History* 31 (June 1962): 207–9.

43. Reimers, "Race and Union," pp. 207–9; Anderson interview; Sanford M. Dornbusch and Roger D. Irle, "The Failure of Presbyterian Union," *American Journal of Sociology* 64 (January 1959): 352–55.

44. *Presbyterian Outlook* 141 (February 23, 1959): 5–7; "Sociologists and Union," ibid., p. 8; Harold J. Dudley to Editor, ibid. (March 23, 1959): 2.

45. *Southern Presbyterian Journal* 4 (December 15, 1945): 5–6; "A Loyal Southern Presbyterian" to Editor, *Presbyterian Outlook* 139 (December 9, 1957): 2.

46. Frances Pickens Miller, *Man from the Valley of Virginia* (Chapel Hill: University of North Carolina Press, 1971), pp. 210–15.

47. Randolph B. Lee, "An Open Letter to the Officers and Members of the Presbyterian Church in the United States," *Southern Presbyterian Journal* 5 (March 15, 1947): 4; W. H. Frazer, "Why I Favor Preserving the Southern Church," ibid. 11 (July 23, 1952): 7; "Disturbing," ibid. 12 (March 10, 1954): 1; Joseph S. Jones, *The Ku Klux Klan, the NAACP, and the Presbyterian Church* (Burlington, N.C. [ca. 1957]).

48. Lawrence W. Bottoms to Frances P. Miller, October 8, 1954, Bot-

toms Personal File, DNW-GCS; Mellin, "Theological and Non-Theological Factors," pp. 229–33; Murray, *Presbyterian and the Negro*, pp. 212–13; Elligan interview.

49. Freundt interview; Murray interview; Synod of Mississippi, *Minutes*, 1971, p. 28.

50. Shriver, *Unsilent South*, pp. 15–17; Kenneth J. Foreman, "Do You Believe in the Integration of the Races?" *Presbyterian Outlook* 139 (July 22, 1957): 9–10; Marion A. Boggs, "Lessons for Pastors Arising out of the Little Rock Crisis" (chapel talk, Columbia Theological Seminary, Decatur, Georgia, ca. fall 1961).

51. Anderson interview; McNeill, *God Wills Us Free*, p. 198; Shriver, *Unsilent South*, pp. 84–85.

52. Reimers, *White Protestantism*, pp. 170–71; R. J. McMullen to E. C. Scott, February 10, 1953, and Complaint of Chapel Hill Presbyterian Church to the Synod of North Carolina, April 25, 1953, in Chapel Hill Presbyterian Church, Chapel Hill, North Carolina, Records, DH, Montreat.

53. L. Nelson Bell, "Some Facts in the Jones Case," *Southern Presbyterian Journal* 11 (April 15, 1953): 9–10; R. J. McMullen to Frank Graham, January 16, 1953, Chapel Hill Presbyterian Church Records.

54. McNeill, *God Wills Us Free*, pp. 117–50; First Presbyterian Church, Columbus, Georgia, 1952 history, LCHP.

55. McNeill, *God Wills Us Free*, pp. 151–83.

56. Ibid.; First Presbyterian Church, Columbus, Georgia, 1958 history, LCHP.

57. McGill, *The South and the Southerner*, pp. 273–75; "The Columbus Case," *Presbyterian Outlook* 141 (June 29, 1959): 8.

58. Central Mississippi Presbytery, *Minutes*, April 19, 1962, pp. 64–65. Whenever a minister relocated from one church to another, he was presented to the presbytery of which the church was a member. The new presbytery would examine and then accept him as a member. Though presbyteries did have the right of refusing a minister, such action was out of the ordinary. This particular case is all the more ironic because Hart had been ordained in Mississippi Presbytery in 1953.

59. Ibid., June 18, 1962, p. 27; Synod of Mississippi, *Minutes*, 1963, pp. 109–10.

60. Central Mississippi Presbytery, "The Re-examination of the Reverend A. M. Hart" (transcript, July 9, 1964); PCUS, *Mins. 104th GA*, 1964, pp. 50–57; Synod of Mississippi, *Minutes*, 1965, pp. 133–57, and 1966, pp. 101–2; Central Mississippi Presbytery, *Minutes*, July 21, 1966, pp. 38–40.

61. Central Mississippi Presbytery, *Minutes*, April 19, 1962, pp. 79–83; October 18, 1962, pp. 12–13; February 28, 1963, p. 112; February 28, 1963, pp. 65, 104–6, 112; September 10, 1963, pp. 12–13; January 16, 1964, p. 30; Freundt interview; Murray interview.

62. Freundt interview; Murray interview. The major figures in presbytery affairs were Dr. John Reed Miller, pastor of First Presbyterian Church,

Jackson, Mississippi, and the Rev. W. A. Gamble, stated clerk of the Central Mississippi Presbytery.

63. Synod of South Carolina, *Minutes*, 1947, pp. 44–49; J. M. Walker to Editor, *Presbyterian Outlook* 129 (February 24, 1947): 2; R. E. McAlpine to Editor, ibid. (March 24, 1947): 2; H. Kerr Taylor to Editor, ibid. (April 7, 1947): 2.

64. W. H. Frazer, "Some Questions about Segregation," *Southern Presbyterian Journal* 10 (November 7, 1951): 3–4; Gillespie, "Christian View," pp. 2–3; Morton H. Smith, "The Racial Problem Facing America," *Presbyterian Guardian* 33 (October 1964): 127–28.

65. John H. Marion, "Segregation Sells America Short," *Presbyterian Outlook* 137 (March 14, 1955): 15; Martha Leslie to Editor, ibid. 139 (December 23, 1957): 2; Barry, "PCUS in a Segregated Society," pp. 34–39.

66. "Crucial Test," *Presbyterian Outlook* 139 (September 16, 1957): 8; ibid. (January 21, 1957): 8.

67. Shriver, *Unsilent South*, pp. 15–17; interview with Donald W. Shriver, Jr., Atlanta, Georgia, June 6, 1983.

68. Robert Walkup, "Not Race But Grace," in *The Unsilent South* (Richmond: John Knox Press, 1965), pp. 59–63. The following sermons in this volume also address the issue in one form or another: George Chauncy, "The Worship God Wants"; Joe S. McLure, "Facing the Truth"; Lawrence F. Haygood, "The Triumphant Life of the Poor in Spirit"; Jeffery P. Rogers, "Capitulation to Ceasar"; and J. Will Ormond, "Foundations."

69. "UTS Professors and Civil Rights," *Presbyterian Outlook* 146 (June 8, 1964): 7; Carl Pritchett, "Law and Order and Race Relations," in Bethesda Presbyterian Church, Bethesda, Maryland, 1964, LCHP.

70. "Violence Is Not Good—or New," *Presbyterian Outlook* 145 (September 30, 1963): 8; Matthew Lynn, "The Christian and Civil Disobedience," ibid., 147 (June 28, 1965): 7; John S. Brown, "On Civil Disobedience," ibid., pp. 5–6.

71. PCUS, *Mins. 105th GA*, 1965, pp. 156–61, and *Mins. 108th GA*, 1968, p. 99; "Civil Disobedience," *Presbyterian Outlook* 148 (April 14, 1966): 8.

72. Smith, *"How Is the Gold Become Dim,"* pp. 135–81 (quotation on p. 181).

73. Bruce T. Dickson, "What about Civil Disobedience?" *Presbyterian Journal* 26 (June 14, 1967): 10–12; Blackwelder, "Fundamentalist Reactions," p. 71; *Presbyterian Survey* 53 (November 1963): 8; 55 (July 1965): 4–5; and 58 (April 1968): 25.

74. W. G. Foster, "Young People's Department: Vesper Topics for January, Meet an African," *Southern Presbyterian Journal* 6 (December 15, 1947): 15; Stanley Shaloff, *Reform in Leopold's Congo* (Richmond: John Knox Press, 1970).

75. Katherine Myers Bassett to Editor, *Presbyterian Outlook* 130 (August 30, 1948): 2; James Peck, "And in Samaria," in *The Unsilent South* (Richmond: John Knox Press, 1965), p. 33; Marion Boggs, *What Does God*

Require—in Race Relations! The Covenant Life Curriculum (Richmond: CLC Press, 1964), p. 43; "202 Missionaries Appeal to Their Home Church," *Presbyterian Outlook* 146 (April 27, 1964): 5; Freundt interview.

76. John Allen MacLean, "What Southern Presbyterian Liberals Believe," *Presbyterian Outlook* 126 (August 20, 1945): 4–6; MacLean, "What Southern Presbyterian Liberals Are Driving At," ibid. (August 27, 1945): 5–7; Thompson interview.

77. Reimers, "Race and Union," pp. 211–12; William Childs Robinson, "What Is the Difference between 'the Liberal' and 'the Conservative'?" *Presbyterian Journal* 18 (July 29, 1959): 4–5; "Both 'Extremes' Equally Bad?" ibid. 21 (December 19, 1962): 11; "The Assembly Acted . . . ," ibid. 25 (May 11, 1966): 9–10; Ernest E. Mason, "The Fallacy of the Social Concept of Salvation," ibid. (January 25, 1967): 9–10.

78. "A Fellowship of Concern," *Presbyterian Outlook* 146 (January 6, 1964): 1; "More than 120 Laymen and Ministers Form a Fellowship of Concern," ibid., p. 3; "Fellowship of Concern," ibid., p. 8; "FOC Regional Meeting Urges More Specific Objectives," ibid. (January 27, 1964): 3–4; "Fellowship of Concern," ibid. (March 23, 1964): 4.

79. "Concerned Presbyterians," *Presbyterian Journal* 23 (July 1, 1964): 12.

80. "An Open Letter to the Church," *Presbyterian Outlook* 149 (March 20, 1967): 5; "A Response . . . to the Open Letter on Page 5," ibid., pp. 6–7; J. Randolph Taylor, Wellford Hobbie, Vance Barron, William Smith to Editor, ibid. (April 10, 1967): 7; Letters to the Editor, ibid.; "Presbyteries React to 'Open Letter,' " ibid. (May 8, 1967): 3.

81. William H. Kadel, "In a Time of Tension," *Presbyterian Outlook* 147 (October 11, 1965): 8; Marshall C. Dendy, "To a Fellowship of Concern," ibid. 149 (October 2, 1967): 6–7.

82. "Two and Two Makes Four, If the Twos Are Really Two," *Presbyterian Outlook* 149 (October 9, 1967): 8; "Counsel to the 'Concerned,' " ibid. (December 11, 1967): 9; "A Moderator's Meeting," ibid. 150 (February 5, 1968): 4–6; *FOCUS: Newsletter of FOC* [ca. 1967] and the *Concerned Presbyterian* (newsletter, May 1968), in Fellowship of Concern Newsletter File, Office of Church and Society Records, Board of Christian Education, DH, Montreat. Church union was articulated as the primary issue by the leaders of Concerned Presbyterians.

83. "Fellowship of Concern," *Presbyterian Outlook* 150 (February 5, 1968): 6; "FOC Dissolution Voted by Leaders," ibid. (June 3, 1968): 11; Board of National Ministries, *Minutes*, November 1968, pp. 4–6.

84. Freundt interview; Frank Joseph Smith, *The History of the Presbyterian Church in America: The Continuing Church Movement* (Manassas, Va.: Reformation Education Foundation, 1985), pp. 14–15.

4. Opening Closed Doors

1. Mecklenburg Presbytery, *Minutes*, October 19, 1948, pp. 43–45.

2. Hallie Paxson Winnsborough, *The Woman's Auxiliary—Presby-*

terian Church, U.S. (Richmond: Committee of Publication, 1927), pp. 31–46.

3. Batchelor, *Jacob's Ladder*, pp. 103–15; Hay interview; Hallie Paxson Winnsborough, *Yesteryears* (Atlanta: Assembly's Committee on Woman's Work, 1937), pp. 143–48, 150; Woman's Auxiliary, *Annual Report*, 1920, n.p., and 1925, p. 7; *Southern Presbyterian Journal* 3 (September 1944): 18–19.

4. Charlotte A. Taylor, "A Study of the Contribution of the Presbyterian Church in the United States to the Life of the Negro Woman of the South" (M.R.E. thesis, Biblical Seminary in New York, 1938), p. 74; Committee on Women's Work, *Annual Report*, 1938, p. 15; Synod of Alabama, *Minutes*, 1944, p. 451; *Southern Presbyterian Journal* 3 (September 1944): 18–19.

5. Woman's Auxiliary, *Annual Report*, 1920, n.p., and 1922, pp. 9–10; Board of Woman's Work, *Minutes*, March 23, 1938, pp. 6–7.

6. Winnsborough, *Yesteryears*, p. 141; Taylor, "Study of the Contribution," p. 76; *Presbyterian Outlook* 130 (November 8, 1948): 10.

7. Taylor, "Study of the Contribution," p. 69; Winnsborough, *Yesteryears*, pp. 154–56; Woman's Auxiliary, Presbyterian Church in the United States, *Annual Report*, 1920, n.p.; William Marion Sikes, "The Historical Development of Stillman Institute" (M.A. thesis, University of Alabama, 1930), pp. 59–60.

8. *Hallie Paxson Winnsborough* (Atlanta: Committee on Woman's Work, 1941), n.p.; Negro Work File, Interracial Work Subject Files, BWW; Woman's Auxiliary, *Annual Report*, 1923, p. 11.

9. Hall, *Revolt against Chivalry*, p. 126; Winnsborough, *Yesteryears*, pp. 137–38; Alabama Experiment File, Interracial Subject Work Files, BWW.

10. Hall, *Revolt against Chivalry*, pp. 176–77; Frances Louise Mays, "Our Heritage: A Challenge," in *Presbyterian Women of South Carolina*, ed. Margaret A. Gist (n.p.: Woman's Auxiliary of South Carolina, 1929), p. xix.

11. Negro Work File, Interracial Work Subject Files, BWW.

12. Reimers, *White Protestantism and the Negro*, pp. 86–88; Board of Women's Work, *Minutes*, March 23, 1938, pp. 6–7; *Presbyterian Outlook* 129 (January 13, 1947): 10.

13. Synod of Alabama, *Minutes*, 1959, p. 9; Annie Tait Jenkins, "Negro Work, Past, Present, and Future," Snedecor Region—General File, General Correspondence Series, Board of National Ministries records, DH, Montreat; Board of Church Extension, *Annual Report*, 1958, pp. 20–24; Board of Women's Work, *Minutes*, October 15, 1958, p. 2.

14. Synod of Alabama, Women of the Church, *Minutes*, 1961, p. 10; Synod of Georgia, Women of the Church, *Minutes*, 1963, p. 26; Synod of North Carolina, Women of the Church, *Minutes*, 1963, p. 32.

15. Synod of Georgia, Women of the Church, *Minutes*, 1964, p. 22, and 1967, p. 19.

16. Board of Women's Work, *Minutes*, October 19, 1960, pp. 5, 17; No-

vember 10, 1965, pp. 3, 8; November 9–10, 1966, p. 14; and February 22–23, 1967, pp. 9–10; Alyce Martin to Evelyn Green, June 20, 1963; Louise R. McKinney to Elizabeth R. Lollard, July 28, 1964; and Evelyn Green to Mrs. E. N. Callaway, March 4, 1964, in WOC: Workshop—Alabama Women, Interracial, June 1964, file, Evelyn L. Green Papers, DH, Montreat; Minutes of Planning Committee for Interracial Workshop, Women of Alabama, June 28–July 2, 1964 [sic], WOC: Workshop—Alabama Women, June 1965, File, Green Papers.

17. Ruth D. See interview; Assembly's Youth Council, *Minutes*, July 13–20, 1934, p. 3, and July 10, 1936, pp. 1–2, in Board of Christian Education, Presbyterian Church (U.S.A.), DH, Montreat (hereafter Assembly's Youth Council).

18. Assembly's Youth Council, *Minutes*, July 22, 1932, p. 3, and July 19, 1934, p. 8; Wallace McPherson Alston, "A History of Young People's Work in the Presbyterian Church in the United States" (Th.D. diss., Union Theological Seminary in Virginia, 1943), pp. 367–68; Executive Committee on Home Missions, *Annual Report*, 1939, p. 15; Taylor, "Study of the Contribution," pp. 109–10; Ruth D. See interview.

19. Assembly's Youth Council, *Minutes*, July 14, 1936, pp. 14–15; July 21, 1936, pp. 19–21; and Appendix 6, "Findings"; Alston, "History of Young People's Work," pp. 460–61.

20. Assembly's Youth Council, *Minutes*, July 23, 1937, pp. 5–6, and July 16, 1939, p. 26.

21. Assembly's Youth Council, *Minutes*, July 11, 1940, pp. 18–19; July 10, 1938, p. 3; and August 8, 1941, p. 3.

22. Assembly's Youth Council, *Minutes*, August 10, 1942, p. 29; August 8, 1943, p. 23; and January 15, 1944, p. 4.

23. Assembly's Youth Council, *Minutes*, November 12, 1944, p. 15, and July 20, 1946, p. 23; Ruth D. See interview.

24. Assembly's Youth Council, *Minutes*, July 16, 1939, p. 26; July 31, 1943, p. 8; July 9, 1945, p. 20; and July 15, 1946, p. 9.

25. Shriver interview; John S. McMullen to J. Rupert McGregor, February 20, 1950, Negro Question file, C. Grier Davis Papers, DH, Montreat; Assembly's Youth Council, *Minutes*, July 29, 1948, pp. 27–28, and July 22, 1950, pp. 5, 40–41, 42–43.

26. Assembly's Youth Council, *Minutes*, July 20, 1951, p. 4, and July 28, 1942, pp. 41–43; Shriver interview.

27. Shriver interview; Anderson interview; Ruth D. See interview; Winn interview.

28. Carl Pritchett to Editor, *Presbyterian Outlook* 128 (December 23, 1946): 2; Elizabeth Witherspoon to Editor, ibid. 129 (January 13, 1947): 2; Clyde Foushee to Editor, ibid.; R. E. McAlpine to Editor, ibid. (January 27, 1947): 2; Watson Street to Editor, ibid.; Kenneth G. Phifer to Editor, ibid. (February 10, 1947): 2.

29. Stuart Oglesby, "Montreat and the New Policy," *Presbyterian Outlook* 132 (July 10, 1950): 6; Edward H. Grant to Lawrence W. Bottoms, June 26, 1950, Snedecor Region—General File, DNW-GCS.

30. Leslie H. Patterson to J. Rupert McGregor, July 17, 1950; E. D. Witherspoon to McGregor, July 19, 1950; W. R. Willauer to McGregor, July 20, 1950; and L. A. Taylor to McGregor, August 2, 1950, all in Davis Papers; Henry B. Dendy to John S. McMullen, August 4, 1950, Assembly's Youth Council Correspondence Series, Board of Christian Education, DH, Montreat (hereafter Assembly's Youth Council Correspondence Series).

31. David B. Walthall to C. Grier Davis, June 15, 1950; Charles H. Gibboney to Davis, June 15, 1950; Alexander Batchelor to Davis, July 15, 1950; Vernon Broyles to Davis, June 20, 1950; P. J. Cumming to Davis, June 19, 1950; Walter Lingle to Davis, June 15, 1950; and Vernon Broyles to J. Rupert McGregor, July 24, 1950, all in Negro Question File, Davis Papers; John S. McMullen to Edward Grant, June 7, 1950; C. Grier Davis to Edward Grant, March 22, 1951; and John S. McMullen to Lawrence Bottoms, May 10, 1951, all in Assembly's Youth Council Correspondence Series.

32. J. Rupert McGregor to J. G. Anderson, Jr., January 14, 1952, Negro Question File, Davis Papers.

33. "Disappointment at Montreat," *Presbyterian Outlook* 136 (August 30, 1954): 8; *Southern Presbyterian Journal* 13 (September 15, 1954): 3. The second article was written by L. Nelson Bell, a resident of Montreat, one of the trustees in question, and an editor for the *Journal*. See Marshall Dendy to C. Grier Davis and J. Rupert McGregor, October 20, 1954, and McGregor to Dendy, November 10, 1954, Negro Question File, Davis Papers.

34. "Assembly Evaluation," *Presbyterian Outlook* 138 (June 25, 1956): 8, and "Montreat and the Church's Women," ibid. 139 (April 22, 1957): 3; Paul Hastings, "Strange Guests," *Southern Presbyterian Journal* 16 (January 15, 1958): 9–10.

35. Mountain Retreat Association Executive Committee, *Minutes*, January 3, 1959, pp. 2–3, DH, Montreat; Frank W. Price, "Montreat's Race Relations Policy," *Presbyterian Outlook* 141 (August 24, 1959): 8; "Montreat Directors Plan for Important Advances," ibid. 142 (September 5, 1960): 4.

36. Lawrence Stell to C. Grier Davis, August 3, 1954, and J. Rupert McGregor to Stell, August 7, 1954, Davis Papers; First Presbyterian Church, Auburn, Alabama, *Minutes of Session*, January 20, 1950, and February 27, 1962; Bethesda Presbyterian Church, Bethesda, Maryland, 1964, LCHP.

37. "Lexington Meeting Surpasses Quota," *Presbyterian Outlook* 140 (January 13, 1958): 3; "Students Protest Segregated Living Arrangement in Dallas," ibid. 143 (January 16, 1961): 3.

38. First Presbyterian Church, Auburn, Alabama, *Minutes of Session*, April 21 and 26, 1959; Tuscaloosa Presbytery, *Minutes*, April 21, 1959, pp. 702–3; Synod of Alabama, *Minutes*, 1959, pp. 29–31.

39. Brazos Presbytery, *Minutes*, October 13, 1959, p. 44, and September 27, 1960, p. 45; Hanover Presbytery, *Minutes*, January 28, 1958, pp. 31–32; May 26, 1959, p. 43; and October 20, 1959, p. 39; "Presbytery Upholds

Policy of Integration at Camps," *Presbyterian Outlook* 140 (June 9, 1958): 7; Thompson interview.

40. Birmingham Presbytery, *Minutes*, January 18, 1965, p. 18; Central Mississippi Presbytery, *Minutes*, April 17, 1969, pp. 13–14, 15–16; June 4, 1969, pp. 30–31; October 16, 1969, p. 13; July 16, 1970, pp. 38–39; and July 15, 1971, pp. 23–24; Synod of Mississippi, *Minutes*, 1969, pp. 30–32.

41. Brazos Presbytery, *Minutes*, October 1, 1954, pp. 29–30; Anderson interview.

42. Reimers, *White Protestantism*, pp. 127–28; Winn interview.

43. *Presbyterian Outlook* 136 (July 19, 1954): 11; ibid. (September 20, 1954): 3; "Florida Presbyterian Has No Racial Ban," ibid. 144 (November 5, 1962): 3; William B. Abbot to Editor, ibid. 141 (November 9, 1959): 2, and 143 (March 13, 1961): 2; "37 Students Have Their Say on Integration Policy," ibid. 142 (March 7, 1960): 4; "Davidson Advance," ibid. 144 (June 11, 1962): 9.

44. Synod of Mississippi, *Minutes*, 1967, pp. 65–66; Thompson, *Presbyterians in the South*, 3:546.

45. Thompson, *Spirituality of the Church*, p. 36; Thompson interview.

46. Winn interview; Brazos Presbytery, *Minutes*, April 17, 1951, pp. 19–20.

47. Board of Church Extension, *Minutes*, November 1962, p. 26; ibid., *Annual Report*, 1960, p. 31; Synod of Alabama, *Minutes*, 1963, p. 25; Red River Presbytery, *Minutes*, September 11, 1962, p. 584; "Racial Presbyteries' Recruiting Deterrent," *Presbyterian Outlook* 145 (March 18, 1963): 4.

48. PCUS, *Mins. 104th GA*, 1964, pp. 27–28; "Overtures," *Presbyterian Outlook* 146 (April 20, 1964): 10.

49. Florida Presbytery, *Minutes*, July 14, 1964, p. 35; Augusta-Macon Presbytery, *Minutes*, June 30, 1964, pp. 5–7; Louisiana Presbytery, *Minutes*, September 29, 1964, p. 27; Fayetteville Presbytery, *Minutes*, June 30, 1964, pp. 32–33; Birmingham Presbytery, *Minutes*, May 12, 1964, pp. 10–11, and August 5, 1965, pp. 2–3.

50. Southwest Georgia Presbytery, *Minutes*, July 14, 1964, pp. 14–15, 20–21; East Alabama Presbytery, *Minutes*, May 24, 1964, pp. 39–40, and January 26, 1965, pp. 24–32; PCUS: Reception of Negro Churches File, Office of Church and Society, Board of Christian Education records, DH, Montreat.

51. Harmony Presbytery, *Minutes*, May 19, 1964, pp. 3–4, and September 21, 1965, p. 34; Pee Dee Presbytery, *Minutes*, July 9, 1968, p. 40; Central Mississippi Presbytery, *Minutes*, January 21, 1965, pp. 33–34; July 21, 1966, p. 30; and June 3, 1968, pp. 2, 22; Tuscaloosa Presbytery, *Minutes*, May 12, 1964, pp. 976–77; Synod of Louisiana, *Minutes*, 1969, p. 45; Synod of South Carolina, *Minutes*, 1969, p. 27; Synod of Mississippi, *Minutes*, 1966, p. 83.

52. Central Mississippi Presbytery, *Minutes*, March 7, 1966, pp. 13–14; Pee Dee Presbytery, *Minutes*, January 25, 1966, p. 24.

53. Albert H. Freundt, Jr., "An Approach to Open and Honest Political Decision Making in the Presbytery of Central Mississippi in Connection with the Vote on Presbyterian Reunion" (D.Min. major project, McCormick Theological Seminary, 1984), pp. 2–3; Bottoms interview; Freundt interview; PCUS, *Mins. 107th GA*, 1967, pp. 149–50; Smith, "*How Is the Gold Become Dim?*" pp. 89, 91–92.

54. Wayne Rutherford to Editor, *Presbyterian Survey* 58 (March 1968): 4; William Jones to Editor, ibid. (June 1968): 37; "Faith in Central Mississippi," ibid. 59 (September 22, 1969): 15.

55. "Oak Cliff Church in Dallas Receives Negro as Member," *Presbyterian Outlook* 131 (May 23, 1949): 4; "W. Va. Session Votes to Receive First Negro Member," ibid. 142 (September 26, 1960): 3; "Kneel-Ins Bring Segregated Pews," ibid.; "Church's Open Policy Is Given Publicity," ibid. 145 (October 21, 1963): 11; Synod of Florida, Women of the Church, *Minutes*, 1949, p. 36.

56. PCUS, *Mins. 104th GA*, 1964, p. 79; G. Aiken Taylor, "The Assembly in Detail," *Presbyterian Journal* 23 (May 13, 1964): 19; "Open for All," *Presbyterian Outlook* 146 (May 11, 1964): 10–11; Synod of Alabama, *Minutes*, 1964, p. 20.

57. Shriver, *Unsilent South*, p. 45; Murray interview. This was not only a Presbyterian problem; see W. J. Cunningham, *Agony at Galloway* (Jackson: University Press of Mississippi, 1980).

58. St. Andrews Presbytery, *Minutes*, July 12, 1966, p. 24.

59. Synod of Alabama, *Minutes*, 1965, pp. 45–49, and 1966, p. 32.

60. Tuscaloosa Presbytery, *Minutes*, September 21, 1965, pp. 114–20.

61. *Presbyterian Survey* 54 (July 1964): 18; cf. ibid. (January 1964): 28.

62. *Presbyterian Survey* 60 (February 1970): 3–4.

63. Perry Biddle, Jr., to Editor, *Presbyterian Outlook* 146 (May 4, 1964): 2; "Negro, White Churches Unite in Dallas Plan," ibid. 150 (January 1, 1968): 10; Board of Church Extension, *Minutes*, July 1965, p. 169.

64. Bottoms interview; Thompson interview.

65. Reimers, *White Protestantism*, pp. 107–8; Thompson, *Presbyterians in the South*, 3:538; PCUS, *Mins. 90th GA*, 1950, p. 70.

66. See previous discussions in chapter 3.

67. *Presbyterian Outlook* 136 (October 4, 1954): 10; Synod of Arkansas, *Minutes*, 1954, p. 30; Synod of Mississippi, *Minutes of Adjourned Meeting*, November 4, 1954, pp. 446–49. The Synod of Mississippi adopted the minority report of the committee charged to respond to the 1954 General Assembly action, a report written and presented by Dr. G. T. Gillespie. See *Presbyterian Outlook* 136 (November 22, 1954): 5; Harmony Presbytery, *Minutes*, January 17, 1956, p. 16.

68. Synod of North Carolina, *Minutes*, 1954, p. 31, 1955, pp. 185–92.

69. Christian Action Conference (ca. 1964) Subject File, in Dabbs Papers; Synod of Virginia, *Minutes*, 1963, pp. 101–5; Synod of Texas, *Minutes*, 1962, pp. 472–74.

70. Second Presbyterian Church, Memphis, Tennessee, 1964, pp. 4–5,

and 1965, pp. 2–3, LCHP; G. Aiken Taylor, "The Assembly in Detail,"
Presbyterian Journal 23 (May 5, 1964): 10–11; "Carl Pritchett's Report,"
FOCUS: Newsletter of FOC, May 22, 1964, Office of Church and Society,
Board of Christian Education Records, DH, Montreat; Bethesda Presbyterian Church, Bethesda, Maryland, 1964, LCHP; "Bars Up at Memphis,
Second," *Presbyterian Outlook* 146 (May 11, 1964): 8.

71. "Memphis, 1965?" *Presbyterian Outlook* 146 (April 27, 1964): 8;
"Memphis, Second," ibid. (May 18, 1964): 8; John Leith, "The Church and
Race," ibid. (July 27, 1964): 6; Synod of North Carolina, *Minutes*, 1964, p.
49; Synod of Virginia, *Minutes*, 1964, pp. 89–90; Southwest Georgia Presbytery, *Minutes*, July 14, 1964, p. 21.

72. Memphis Presbytery, *Minutes*, January 26, 1964, pp. 16–18; Felix
Gear, "The 1965 General Assembly," *Presbyterian Outlook* 147 (February
8, 1965): 4; "Relocated Assembly," ibid., p. 8; Second Presbyterian
Church, Memphis, Tennessee, 1965, p. 4, LCHP.

73. "Petition Circulated at Memphis Second Church," *Presbyterian
Outlook* 147 (March 1, 1965): 3–4; Second Presbyterian Church, Memphis, Tennessee, 1965, pp. 4–6, LCHP.

74. Charles Conner Gillespie, *History of Second Presbyterian Church,
Memphis, 1844–1971* (Memphis, Tenn.: Second Presbyterian Church,
1971); *Presbyterian Outlook* 171 (May 29, 1989): 3–4; Presbyterian
Church (U.S.A.), *Minutes of the General Assembly*, 1989, part 2, p. 511.

5. The Civil Rights Movement and the Presbyterian Church, U.S., 1954–1973

1. PCUS, *Mins. 87th GA*, 1947, pp. 40–41, and *Mins. 90th GA*, 1950,
pp. 35–36; Synod of North Carolina, *Minutes*, 1950, p. 380; *Presbyterian
Outlook* 126 (September 24, 1945): 2.

2. Synod of North Carolina, *Minutes*, 1949, p. 244; *Presbyterian Outlook* 125 (December 10, 1945): 6–7; J. McDowell Richards, "Brothers in
Black," in *Change and the Changeless: Articles, Essays, and Sermons*
(Decatur, Ga.: Columbia Theological Seminary, 1972), p. 20. Richards's
title was not new to Southern religious leaders; see Sosna, *Silent South*,
pp. 7–8. His argument revolves around the idea that blacks are essentially
white people with black skin. See Anderson interview; James N. Murray
to Alexander R. Batchelor, March 12, 1950, DNW-CGS; "Brady's Alley
May Not Be Far from Your House," *Presbyterian Outlook* 132 (March 27,
1950): 4–5; "Housing in Your Town," ibid., pp. 8–9.

3. James McBride Dabbs to Olin Johnston, draft of letter, ca. 1946–52,
in Dabbs Collection, Southern Historical Collection; Mounger, "Racial
Attitudes" (B.D. thesis), pp. 132–33; Synod of Arkansas, Women of the
Church, *Minutes*, 1953, p. 23.

4. "Schools and Segregation," *Presbyterian Outlook* 135 (October 12,
1953): 8; "A Moral Issue," ibid. (December 7, 1953): 6–7; Morris, "Civil
Rights Movement and Its Black Power Structure," pp. 70–71.

5. Morris, "Civil Rights Movement and the Black Power Structure," pp. 78–80; "Desegregation and Economic Pressure," *Presbyterian Outlook* 137 (April 4, 1955): 8.

6. "Churches, Ministers Attacked," *Presbyterian Outlook* 136 (November 29, 1954): 3–4; "Thoughts at a Hearing," ibid. (December 6, 1954): 12; "Preachers Blamed for Desegregation Stand," ibid. 137 (June 13, 1955): 6; "For Schools and Constitution," ibid. (November 14, 1955): 8; Robbins L. Gates, *The Making of Massive Resistance: Virginia's Politics of Public School Desegregation, 1954–1956* (Chapel Hill: University of North Carolina Press, 1962), pp. 50–53, 80; Thompson interview; Synod of Virginia, *Minutes*, 1957, pp. 96–98; Bob Smith, *They Closed Their School: Prince Edward County, Virginia, 1951–1964* (Chapel Hill: University of North Carolina Press, 1965), pp. 113–15.

7. J. McDowell Richards, "A Call to Civil Obedience and Racial Goodwill," in *Change and the Changeless* (Decatur, Ga.: Columbia Theological Seminary, 1972), pp. 49–52; "U.S. Moderator in Support of Atlantans," *Presbyterian Outlook* 139 (December 2, 1957): 10; "Atlanta Climate," ibid. (December 9, 1957): 8; "On the South's Racial Crisis," ibid. 140 (December 8, 1958): 5–6.

8. Ernest Q. Campbell and Thomas F. Pettigrew, *Christians in Crisis: A Study of Little Rock's Ministry* (Washington, D.C.: Public Affairs Press, 1959), pp. 19–20; interview with Marion A. Boggs, Black Mountain, North Carolina, December 13, 1982; Ronald Schlundt, "Civil Rights Policies in the Eisenhower Years" (Ph.D. diss., Rice University, 1973), p. 144.

9. Marion Boggs, "A Time for Christian Citizenship," Boggs Biography File, DH, Montreat; Boggs interview; "Good Little Rock Leaders," *Presbyterian Outlook* 139 (October 14, 1957): 8.

10. "Two Elders Are Quoted on Segregation Items," *Presbyterian Outlook* 137 (May 23, 1955): 11; "With Troops and Tanks," *Southern Presbyterian Journal* 17 (September 24, 1958): 2–3.

11. Campbell and Pettigrew, *Christians in Crisis*, pp. 20–21, 70, 111; Thompson, *Presbyterians in the South*, 3:541.

12. Boggs interview; Resolution of Washburn Presbytery to Orval Faubus, *Presbyterian Outlook* 140 (September 29, 1958): 2.

13. "Using Churches for Schools," *Presbyterian Outlook* 140 (January 13, 1958): 5; "Christian Relations," ibid. (May 12, 1958): 9; "A Presbytery Said 'No,' " ibid. (October 13, 1958): 8; PCUS, *Mins. 98th GA*, 1958, pp. 37–38, 89; Synod of Arkansas, *Minutes*, 1959, p. 44.

14. Anderson interview; "Dallas Ministers Join in Desegregation Plea," *Presbyterian Outlook* 140 (May 19, 1958): 3–4.

15. "On Montgomery Buses," *Presbyterian Outlook* 138 (March 12, 1956): 8; "Lunch Counter Episodes," ibid. 142 (February 29, 1960): 8.

16. "On Picketing and Obedience," *Presbyterian Outlook* 142 (March 21, 1960): 4; Elligan interview.

17. "Davidson Students Find Church Closed to Sit-in Discussions," *Presbyterian Outlook* 142 (May 2, 1960): 4; "Not an Endorsement . . . ,"

ibid., p. 8; "Hats Off to Charlotte," ibid. (July 25, 1960): 8; "Carolina Demonstrations Have Presbyterian Help," ibid. 143 (February 27, 1961): 12; Sitkoff, *Struggle for Black Equality*, pp. 69–82.

18. Synod of Virginia, *Minutes*, 1960, p. 95; Synod of North Carolina, *Minutes*, 1961, pp. 178–80.

19. St. Andrews Presbytery, *Minutes*, October 16, 1962, pp. 20–21; "Oxford, Miss., Pastors Appeal to Repentance," *Presbyterian Outlook* 144 (October 22, 1962): 3; Shriver, *Unsilent South*, p. 74; Bailey, *Southern White Protestantism*, p. 149; Freundt interview; Murray interview.

20. Martin Luther King, Jr., *Letter from Birmingham Jail* (N.p.: American Friends Service Committee, 1963); First Presbyterian Church, Auburn, Alabama, *Minutes of Session*, February 3, 1963.

21. "Race Relations Body Named by Potomac," *Presbyterian Outlook* 145 (October 7, 1963): 12; Fayetteville Presbytery, *Minutes*, September 24, 1963, p. 48; Synod of Georgia, Women of the Church, *Minutes*, 1963, p. 16.

22. John Randolph Taylor, "Letter from Washington," *Presbyterian Outlook* 145 (September 9, 1963): 5–6; photograph of PCUS participants, ibid. (September 23, 1963): 3; *Presbyterian Survey* 53 (October 1963): 48; PCUS representatives to NCC to R. H. Edwin Espy, August 21, 1963; Espy to PCUS representatives to NCC, October 23, 1963; and John Randolph Taylor to PCUS representatives to NCC, August 26, 1963, all in NCCC: Commission on Religion and Race File, Evelyn Green Papers, DH, Montreat; Shriver, *Unsilent South*, pp. 102–5.

23. Rachel Henderlite, "The March to Selma," *Presbyterian Outlook* 147 (April 19, 1965): 5–6; "Alabama" (unsigned letter), ibid. (May 17, 1965): 2; *Presbyterian Survey* 55 (July 1965): 6, and (August 1965): 40; First Presbyterian Church, Auburn, Alabama, *Minutes of Session*, March 14, 1965.

24. PCUS, *Mins. 104th GA*, 1964, p. 154; Kenneth J. Foreman, Sr., "Law and Decency," *Presbyterian Outlook* 146 (May 6, 1964): 9; Thompson, *Presbyterians in the South*, 3:544–45.

25. "Fellowship Group Asks Senate Passage of Bill," *Presbyterian Journal* 23 (May 20, 1964): 5; Shriver interview; "FOCUS: Newsletter of FOC," December 1, 1965, and July 1966 and Education, Historical Foundation; F. Wellford Hobbie circular letter, May 24, 1966, Fellowship of Concern File, Office of Church and Society records, DH, Montreat.

26. "Suggestions from Chauncey for 'letter to members of FOC,' " Fellowship of Concern File, Office of Church and Society records; Shriver interview.

27. Unidentified clippings, Montreat Conference File, Office of Church and Society records; John B. Evans to John Doar, August 2, 1965, and Evans to Doar, August 30, 1965, ibid.; Mrs. Annie G. McKenzie to James McBride Dabbs, August 9, 1965, in Dabbs Papers, Southern Historical Collection; Elligan interview.

28. R. P. Bolton and D. T. Bryan to James Millard, July 10, 1965, and

C. Huiet Paul to Dr. Samuel J. Patterson, Jr., September 21, 1965, in Martin Luther King File, Office of Executive Secretary Case Files, Board of Christian Education, DH, Montreat (hereafter BCE Executive Secretary Case Files); Tuscaloosa Presbytery, *Minutes*, May 25, 1965, pp. 85–88; Pee Dee Presbytery, *Minutes*, June 22, 1965, p. 44; Harmony Presbytery, *Minutes*, September 21, 1965, pp. 24–26.

29. Memphis Presbytery, *Minutes*, July 20, 1965, pp. 31–32; V. Robert Jansen, "The Issue Is Freedom," *Presbyterian Outlook* 147 (May 10, 1965): 5.

30. Donald B. Patterson to Malcolm Calhoun, July 9, 1965; Charles A. Kimball to Board of Christian Education, July 13, 1965; Marshall C. Smith, Jr., to Marshall Dendy, with attachments, July 28, 1965; Dendy to Claude S. Betts, August 30, 1965; William F. S. Gresham to Dendy, September 14, 1965; Dendy to Men's Bible Class, Eau Claire Presbyterian Church, Columbia, South Carolina, August 11, 1965; Dendy to Session, Shenandoah Presbyterian Church, Miami, Florida, November 1, 1965; H. B. Rogers to Dendy, March 9, 1966, all in Martin Luther King File, BCE Executive Secretary Case Files.

31. Martin Luther King, Jr., "The Church on the Frontier of Racial Tension" (address at Christian Action Conference, Montreat, North Carolina, ca. August 12, 1965; audio tape at Martin Luther King, Jr., Library and Archives, Center for Non-violent Social Change, Atlanta, Georgia); "Martin Luther King at Montreat," *Presbyterian Outlook* 147 (September 6, 1965): 3.

32. Pratt, *Liberalization of American Protestantism*, pp. 160–63; L. E. Faulkner, "Reasons Why the Presbyterian Church (U.S.) Should Withdraw from the Federal Council of Churches of Christ in America," *Southern Presbyterian Journal* 6 (August 15, 1947): 13–17; "Findings of the Annual Meeting of the Continuing Church Committee," ibid. (September 1, 1947): 3; Faulkner, "Official Pronouncements of the Federal Council of Churches," ibid. (April 1, 1948): 18–19; L. Nelson Bell, "The National Council of Churches," ibid. 9 (December 13, 1950): 5–7; Blackwelder, "Fundamentalist Reactions," p. 336.

33. "They're Putting Pressure on Commissioners to the Assembly," *Presbyterian Outlook* 139 (April 22, 1957): 8; Mecklenberg Presbytery, *Minutes*, April 18, 1950, pp. 64–65; East Alabama Presbytery, *Minutes*, April 17, 1956, p. 31; Tuscaloosa Presbytery, *Minutes*, April 17, 1956, pp. 547–49; Florida Presbytery, *Minutes*, January 28, 1958, p. 12, and April 10, 1962, p. 28; Southwest Georgia Presbytery, *Minutes*, July 14, 1964, p. 22; Central Mississippi Presbytery, *Minutes*, October 15, 1964, pp. 24–25; Augusta-Macon Presbytery, *Minutes*, January 26, 1965, p. 13; PCUS, *Mins. 106th GA*, 1966, pp. 95–97; Synod of Arkansas, *Minutes*, 1961, pp. 94–99; Brazos Presbytery, *Minutes*, May 30, 1961, p. 22; Wallace M. Alston, Jr., to Clayton Bell, December 16, 1964, in First Presbyterian Church, Auburn, Alabama, *Minutes of Session*; Boggs interview; *Presbyterian Survey* 54 (June 1964): 8, and (August 1964): 8.

34. Pratt, *Liberalization of American Protestantism*, pp. 165–72; Alvis, "Rt. Rev. John M. Allin," pp. 89–90.

35. Summary Report of Commission to General Board, December 3–4, 1964, NCC Papers: Commission on Religion and Race in Delta Ministry Papers, King Library and Archives; Rt. Rev. Daniel Corrigan to Jon Reiger, October 10, 1964, and Reiger to Corrigan, October 28, 1964, NCC Papers: Commission Board Meeting Reports, in the Delta Ministry Papers at the King Library and Archives.

36. Memphis Presbytery, *Minutes*, December 14, 1965, pp. 10–16; East Alabama Presbytery, *Minutes*, January 25, 1966, pp. 25–26; Paul Tudor Jones, "God's Agents," in *The Unsilent South*, ed. Donald W. Shriver, Jr. (Richmond: John Knox Press, 1965), pp. 132–37.

37. Board of National Ministries, *Minutes*, February 1966, p. 202; February 1967, p. 3; and November 1967, p. 9; George Chauncy to Dr. Robert P. Douglass, November 17, 1966, Delta Ministry Subject File, Dabbs Papers, Southern Historical Collection; Chauncy to Jon Reiger, November 18, 1966, Norton Committee File, Office of Church and Society records.

38. Dr. Henry A. McCanna to James McBride Dabbs, March 2, 1967; Dabbs to John F. Anderson, June 30, 1968; Owen Brooks to Dabbs, August 21, 1969; John F. Anderson to Dabbs, September 8, 1969; Dabbs to Rev. J. R. Ballesteros, October 5, 1969, all in Delta Ministry Subject File, Dabbs Papers, Southern Historical Collection.

39. "Incident in Mississippi," *Presbyterian Journal* 24 (March 9, 1966): 12–13; *Presbyterian Survey* 54 (July 1964): 6; (September 1964): 8; and (October 1964): 6–7.

40. Bishop Edward J. Pendergrass, "Statement about the Delta Ministry," April 28, 1965 (?), Office of Church and Society records; Alvis, "Rt. Rev. John M. Allin," pp. 90–91.

41. Central Mississippi Presbytery, *Minutes*, April 16, 1964, pp. 5–6, 14; St. Andrews Presbytery, *Minutes*, October 18, 1966, pp. 35, 52.

42. Synod of Mississippi, *Minutes*, 1965, pp. 20–21; PCUS, *Mins. 106th GA*, 1966, pp. 177–78, and *Mins. 107th GA*, 1967, pp. 176–77; Lee M. Gentry to John F. Anderson, September 4, 1967, Executive Secretary Correspondence Files, 1953–73, Board of National Ministries, DH, Montreat. In 1967 the Board of Church Extension changed its name to the Board of National Ministries.

43. Minutes of the Delta Ministry Committee, July 14, 1967, Executive Secretary Correspondence Files, 1953–73; Synod of Mississippi, *Minutes*, 1967, pp. 136–41, and 1968, pp. 34–35, 68–70.

44. Synod of Mississippi, *Minutes*, 1969, pp. 82–83, and 1970, pp. 80–81.

45. Synod of Mississippi, *Minutes*, 1970, p. 81; 1971, pp. 64–66; and 1973, pp. 18, 53–54.

46. "Civil Rights Quandary," *Presbyterian Outlook* 148 (July 11, 1966): 8; "Presbyterians in the News: William Winter," ibid. (October 3, 1966): 8; *Presbyterian Survey* 55 (August 1965): 2–3; (October 1965): 6; and (December 1965): 6.

47. Thompson, *Presbyterians in the South*, 3:545; Blackwelder, "Fundamentalist Reactions" p. 336; Synod of North Carolina, *Minutes*, 1966, p. 183; 1967, p. 171; and 1968, pp. 168–69; Synod of Mississippi, *Minutes*, 1968, p. 28; William J. Fogelman, "Reality Sunday," February 12, 1967, Office of Church and Society records, DH, Montreat.

48. "A Declaration about the Crisis in American Society," October 20, 1967, BCE Executive Secretary Case Files.

49. Milton S. Carothers to Marshall C. Dendy, November 20, 1967; Fred P. Johnson to Dendy, November 29, 1967; Alan V. Shields to Dendy, December 19, 1967; Joint Resolution of the Edgefield Presbyterian Church, Edgefield, South Carolina, and Johnston Presbyterian Church, Johnston, South Carolina, to Marshall Dendy, December 6, 1967; William B. Kennedy to Samuel H. Zealy, December 6, 1967; Richard G. Glasgow to Dendy, January 11, 1968; Session of Hartness-Thornwell Presbyterian Church, Clinton, South Carolina, to Dendy, January 17, 1968; Session of First Presbyterian Church, Lake City, Florida, February 9, 1968, BCE Executive Secretary Case Files.

50. National Council of Churches, "Resolution on the Crisis in the Nation," September 4, 1967, SCLC—Washington Demonstration File, Office of Church and Society records; Margaret J. Thomas, *"The Crisis in the Nation": Presbyterian Church, U.S. Involvement* (Richmond: Board of Christian Education, 1968), pp. 37–40.

51. Thomas, *"Crisis in the Nation,"* pp. 5–6.

52. Pee Dee Presbytery, *Minutes*, January 23, 1968, p. 37; John F. Anderson, Jr., Evelyn Green, T. Watson Street, and Marshall Dendy to Presbyterian pastors, March 20, 1967; George Hutchins to Dendy, March 25, 1968; Session of First Presbyterian Church, Louisville, Mississippi, to Dendy, April 16, 1968; and Robert E. Burns III to William Kadel, July 1, 1968, all in Executive Secretary Case Files, Board of National Ministries.

53. Thomas, *"Crisis in the Nation,"* pp. 11–13, 33.

54. Board of Church Extension, *Minutes*, August 1967, Appendix B; "Adopt 'Project Equality'?" *Presbyterian Journal* 25 (March 15, 1967): 9–10; "Nashville Presbytery in Project Equality," *Presbyterian Outlook* 150 (June 10, 1968): 3.

55. George Chauncy to Southern Christian Leadership Conference, November 15, 1967, Office of Church and Society records; Marshall Dendy to Mrs. G. Herman Walker, October 31, 1967, SCLC File, BCE Executive Secretary Case Files.

56. William B. Kennedy to Session, Edgefield Presbyterian Church, Edgefield, South Carolina, December 19, 1967; Kennedy to Robert E. Shannon, December 20, 1967; and Marshall Dendy to Southern Christian Leadership Conference, April 5, 1968, all in BCE Executive Secretary Case Files; George Chauncy to Bernard Lee, August 30, 1965, SCLC File, Office of Church and Society records.

57. James O. Speed to William B. Kennedy, December 7, 1967; Kennedy to Speed, December 15, 1967; Charles O. Lee to Archie Smith, January 16, 1968; Charles Franklin Beall to Marshall Dendy, February 12,

1968; Rollin V. Wilson to Dendy, February 16, 1968, all in Resolution of Session of North Avenue Presbyterian Church, Atlanta, Georgia, March 11, 1968, SCLC File, BCE Executive Secretary Case Files; Harmony Presbytery, *Minutes*, January 23, 1968, pp. 43–44.

58. Marshall Dendy to Wade H. Sherrard, Jr., with attachments, March 20, 1968; J. Douglas Fry to Dendy, May 2, 1968; and William Kadel to William W. Peters, October 17, 1968, all in SCLC File, BCE Executive Secretary Case Files.

59. Board of National Ministries, *Minutes*, February 1968, pp. 5, 11; "PCUS Response," *Presbyterian Outlook* 150 (March 11, 1968): 3; Board of Church Extension, *Annual Report*, 1966, pp. 48–49; Board of National Ministries, *Minutes*, August 1967, p. 15, and February 1970, p. 12; Anderson interview.

60. Synod of Virginia, *Minutes*, 1966, p. 62, and 1967, pp. 44–45, 61, 72.

61. First Presbyterian Church, Auburn, Alabama, *Minutes of Session*, July 23 and September 26–27, 1968, January 30 and February 23, 1969.

62. Board of National Ministries, *Minutes*, August 1968, pp. 14ff.; Anderson interview; Ben L. Rose to Editor, *Presbyterian Outlook* 150 (April 29, 1968): 2.

63. Ben L. Rose to Editor; Board of National Ministries, *Minutes*, August 1968, Appendix A; C. Ray Dobbins to Ben L. Rose, *Presbyterian Outlook* 150 (May 27, 1968): 2.

64. Board of National Ministries, *Minutes*, August 1968, p. 15, Appendix A; "This Is Not the Way to 'Justice,' " *Presbyterian Journal* 26 (April 17, 1968): 12; "Love Shall Overcome," *Presbyterian Survey* 58 (June 1968): 3; Al Winn, "Can You Love Your Enemy?" ibid., pp. 8–9; Ben Hartley, "The Memphis Story," ibid., pp. 10–12, 42; Letters, ibid. (August 1968): 4–6; (September 1968): 5; and 59 (February 1969): 4.

65. Evelyn Green, T. Watson Street, John F. Anderson, Jr., and Marshall Dendy to local pastors; Women of the Church presidents and Presbytery Executive Secretaries, May 1, 1968; and Green to Lelia B. Thompson, all in Lelia B. Thompson Papers, DH, Montreat; PCUS, *Mins. 108th GA*, 1968, p. 101; "Three Minutes More," *Presbyterian Outlook* 150 (June 24, 1968): 16; "Henderlite Speech," ibid. (June 24, 1968): 15; Anderson interview.

66. Session, Weaverville Presbyterian Church, Weaverville, North Carolina, to Marshall Dendy, May 15, 1968, and T. Watson Street to Session, Weaverville Presbyterian Church, May 17, 1968, BCE Executive Secretary Case File.

67. Synod of Virginia, *Minutes*, 1968, p. 19; "Gift to March Is Criticized," *Presbyterian Outlook* 150 (June 10, 1968): 3.

68. Synod of Virginia, *Minutes*, 1969, pp. 31–32, 95–96.

69. Synod of Virginia, *Minutes*, 1971, p. 85, and 1972, pp. 91–93; Synod of North Carolina, *Minutes*, 1972, pp. 102–5; *Presbyterian Survey* 60 (March 1970): 13–14; (August 1970): 6; and 62 (August 1972): 41.

70. PCUS, *Mins. 110th GA*, 1970, p. 283; Board of National Ministries, *Minutes*, August 1969, Appendix D, and November 1969, Appendix C;

Anderson interview; Elligan interview; interview with Bridges Edwards, *Presbyterian Survey* 61 (February 1971): 2–5.

71. PCUS, *Mins. 110th GA*, 1970, p. 152, and *Mins. 112th GA*, 1972, pp. 321–22; Elligan interview.

72. PCUS, *Mins. 112th GA*, 1972, pp. 321–22.

73. PCUS, *Mins. 111th GA*, 1971, p. 162, and *Mins. 112th GA*, 1972, pp. 319–21.

74. Elligan interview; Bottoms interview.

75. "Response of the General Board of the National Council of Churches to the Black Manifesto," September 11, 1969, Black Manifesto—NCC Response File, Office of Church and Society records; Pratt, *Liberalization of American Protestantism*, pp. 189–93; Belle McMaster to George Chauncy, May 31, 1969; Evelyn Green to George Chauncy, June 2, 1969; Malcolm Calhoun to Division of Church and Society staff, June 3, 1969, all in CCS: Black Manifesto File, Office of Church and Society records; PCUS, *Mins. 110th GA*, 1970, pp. 212–13; Synod of Virginia, *Minutes*, 1971, pp. 80–81; Smith, *"How Is the Gold Become Dim,"* pp. 176–77; Elligan interview; Jeff Rogers, "The Meaning of Black Power for the Christian Church," *Presbyterian Survey* 58 (April 1968): 13–15; ibid. (June 1968): 39–41.

76. Edwards interview; *Presbyterian Survey* 61 (February 1971): 2–5; ibid. 63 (December 1973): 15.

6. Race, Schism, and Reunion

1. Interview with Kenneth Keyes, *Presbyterian Survey* 59 (November 1969): 6–8.

2. *Presbyterian Survey* 60 (September 1970): 8.

3. *Presbyterian Journal* 31 (June 21, 1972): 5, and (June 28, 1972): 8.

4. National Presbyterian Church in America, *Minutes of the First General Assembly*, 1973 (hereafter NPC, *Mins.*), pp. 40–42; PCUS, *Mins. 113th GA*, 1973, pp. 189–90.

5. Presbyterian Church in the Confederate States of America, *Minutes of the General Assembly of the Presbyterian Church in the Confederate States in America*, vol. 1 (Augusta, Ga.: Steam Power Press Chronicle and Sentinel, 1861), p. 56 (hereafter PCCSA, *Mins.*, 1861).

6. Ibid., pp. 59–60; NPC, *Mins.*, 1973, pp. 27–29; Farmer, *Metaphysical Confederacy*, pp. 285–89.

7. PCCSA, *Mins.*, 1861, pp. 54, 59–60; NPC, *Mins.*, 1973, p. 28.

8. Rick Nutt, "The Tie That No Longer Binds: The Origins of the Presbyterian Church in America," in *The Confessional Mosaic: Presbyterians and Twentieth-Century Theology*, ed. Milton J Coalter, John M. Mulder, and Louis B. Weeks, The Presbyterian Presence (Louisville: Westminster/John Knox Press, 1990), pp. 236–56; Longfield, *Presbyterian Controversy*, pp. 28–53.

9. Longfield, *Presbyterian Controversy*, pp. 31–53. The significance

of Machen's Southern upbringing is echoed in Marsden, *Understanding Fundamentalism and Evangelicalism*, pp. 194–97.

10. Longfield, *Presbyterian Controversy*, pp. 32–36; Holifield, *Gentlemen Theologians*, pp. 118–27; Nutt, "Tie That No Longer Binds," pp. 251–52.

11. Nutt, "Tie That No Longer Binds," pp. 252–54.

12. Ibid., pp. 243–48; Smith, *"How Is the Gold Become Dim,"* p. 153.

13. Nutt, "Tie That No Longer Binds," p. 245; Freundt interview; NPC, *Mins.*, 1973, p. 235.

14. *Presbyterian Journal* 33 (June 26, 1974): 5; *Presbyterian Outlook* 156 (July 8, 1974): 3; Smith, *"How Is the Gold Become Dim,"* p. 210.

15. Winn, Anderson, and Boggs interviews; Freundt, "Approach to Political Decision Making," pp. 5–7.

16. PCUS, *Mins. 112th GA*, 1972, p. 95, and *Mins. 113th GA*, 1973, p. 147. The General Assembly approved a restructure plan in 1972 which replaced the program boards of the PCUS—Women's Work, World Mission, National Ministries, and Christian Education—with one board known as the General Executive Board.

17. PCUS, *Mins. 113th GA*, 1973, p. 177; *Mins. 114th GA*, 1974, p. 177; *Mins. 115th GA*, 1975, p. 301; and *Mins. 116th GA*, 1976, p. 431.

18. *Presbyterian Survey* 68 (March 1978): 32.

19. Freundt, "Approach to Political Decision Making," p. 5; Anderson interview.

20. *Presbyterian Survey* 67 (January 1977): 22, 31.

21. Ibid. (June 1977): 57.

22. Ibid.

23. Ibid. 71 (October 1981): 15.

24. Ibid. 67 (January 1977): 20, and 71 (October 1981): 32.

25. Thompson, *Presbyterians in the South*, 3:7–8; John W. Kuykendall, "Presbyterians in the South Revisited—Critique," *Journal of Presbyterian History* 61 (Winter 1983): 445–59.

26. The Presbyterian Presence is a seven-volume series edited by Milton J Coalter, John M. Mulder, and Louis B. Weeks (Louisville: Westminster/John Knox Press, 1990–92). See especially *The Re-Forming Tradition: Presbyterians and Mainstream Protestantism* (Louisville: Westminster/John Knox Press, 1992) for a summary evaluation.

27. Marsden, *Understanding Fundamentalism and Evangelicalism*, pp. 197–201; John M. Mulder and Lee Wyatt, "The Predicament of Pluralism: The Study of Theology in Presbyterian Seminaries since the 1920s," in *The Pluralistic Vision: Presbyterians and Mainstream Protestant Education and Leadership*, ed. Milton J Coalter, John M. Mulder, and Louis B. Weeks, The Presbyterian Presence (Louisville: Westminster/John Knox Press, 1992), pp. 27–70.

28. Isaac Crosby, "From Conformity to Transformation," *Presbyterian Survey* 72 (May 1982): 35–36.

BIBLIOGRAPHY

Archival Series and Manuscript Collections

Atlanta, Georgia
  Martin Luther King, Jr., Center for Non-Violent Social Change
    Delta Ministry. Papers.
Auburn, Alabama
  Auburn University Archives
    First Presbyterian Church. *Minutes of Session*, 1950–68. Microfilm
    edition.
  First Presbyterian Church
    Minutes of Session, 1969–72.
Chapel Hill, North Carolina
  Southern Historical Collection, University of North Carolina Library
    Dabbs, James McBride. Papers.
Montreat, North Carolina
  Presbyterian Church (U.S.A.), Department of History
    Boggs, Marion. Biography File.
    Chapel Hill Presbyterian Church, Chapel Hill, North Carolina
    Davis, C. Grier. Papers.
    Green, Evelyn. Papers.
    Local Church History Program. History Manuscripts.
    Moore, Ansley C. Papers.
    Mountain Retreat Association. *Minutes*, 1950–65.
    Oral History Interviews conducted by Joel L. Alvis, Jr.
      Anderson, John F. December 8, 1983.
      Boggs, Marion A. December 13, 1982.
      Bottoms, Lawrence W. March 22, 1983.
      Elligan, Irvin, Jr. June 6, 1983.
      Freundt, Albert H., Jr. August 31, 1983.
      Murray, Spencer C. October 13, 1983.
      See, Ruth Douglas. January 27, 1983.
      Shriver, Donald W., Jr. June 6, 1983.
      Thompson, Ernest Trice. July 18, 1983.
      Walkup, Robert H. June 28, 1983.
      Winn, Albert Curry. June 2, 1983.
    Oral History Interview conducted by Florence F. Corley
      Hay, Samuel Burney. October 14 and 21, 1979.
    Presbyterian Church in the United States
      Assembly's Committee on Negro Work. *Minutes*, 1946–49.

Board of Christian Education
  Assembly's Youth Council Correspondence, 1945–53.
  Assembly's Youth Council *Minutes*, 1931–53.
  Office of Church and Society, Records, 1966–73.
  Office of Executive Secretary, Case Files, 1936–72.
Board of National Ministries
  Annual Report, 1945–72.
  Division of Negro Work. General Correspondence Series, 1951–
    56.
  Division of Negro Work. Subject Correspondence Series, 1952–58.
  Executive Secretary Case Files, 1953–73.
  Minutes, 1950–70.
Board of Women's Work
  Annual Report, 1921–72.
  Interracial Work Subject Files.
  Minutes, 1945–68.
Thompson, Lelia B. Papers.

Published Church Court Records

National Presbyterian Church. *Minutes of the First General Assembly,*
  1973.
Presbyterian Church in the Confederate States of America. *Minutes of the*
  General Assembly in the Confederate States of America. Vol. 1. Au-
  gusta, Ga.: Steam Power Press Chronicle and Sentinel, 1861.
Presbyterian Church in the United States. *Minutes of the General As-*
  sembly (with annual reports of boards, agencies, and committees),
  1933–76.
Presbyterian Church (U.S.A.). *Minutes of the General Assembly*, 1989.
Presbytery *Minutes*
  Augusta-Macon (Ga.), 1949–67.
  Birmingham (Ala.), 1952–65.
  Brazos (Tex.), 1945–63.
  Central Mississippi, 1955–72.
  East Alabama, 1953–71.
  East Hanover (Va.), 1948–57.
  Enoree (S.C.), 1958–65.
  Fayetteville (N.C.), 1950–68.
  Florida, 1954–69.
  Hanover (Va.), 1958–60.
  Harmony (S.C.), 1951–70.
  Louisiana, 1958–65.
  Mecklenburg (N.C.), 1947–65.
  Memphis (Tenn.), 1952–65.
  Pee Dee (S.C.), 1953–54, 1961–69.
  Red River (La.), 1947–63.

St. Andrews (Miss.), 1961–67.
Savannah (Ga.), 1950–64.
South Mississippi, 1964–68.
Southwest Georgia, 1948–67.
Tuscaloosa (Ala.), 1953–65.
Synod *Minutes*
  Alabama, 1944–73.
  Alabama, Women of the Church, 1946–68.
  Arkansas, 1948–68.
  Arkansas, Women of the Church, 1950–64.
  Arkansas-Oklahoma, 1969–72.
  Florida, 1947–69.
  Florida, Women of the Church, 1947–67.
  Georgia, 1948–62.
  Georgia, Women of the Church, 1950–67.
  Louisiana, 1947–63.
  Mississippi, 1945–73.
  Mississippi, Women of the Church, 1947–63.
  North Carolina, 1949–72.
  North Carolina, Women of the Church, 1948–69.
  Snedecor Memorial, 1946.
  South Carolina, 1947–71.
  South Carolina, Women of the Church, 1947–68.
  Texas, 1943–69.
  Texas, Women of the Church, 1948–56.
  Virginia, 1945–73.
  Virginia, Women of the Church, 1948–65.

Primary Sources

Books and Pamphlets

Batchelor, Alexander R. *Jacob's Ladder: Negro Work in the Presbyterian Church in the United States.* Atlanta: Board of Christian Education, 1953.

Boggs, Marion A. *What Does God Require—in Race Relations?* The Covenant Life Curriculum. Richmond: CLC Press, 1964.

Brown, Cecil Kenneth. *The Southern Position with Respect to the Bi-racial System.* Waco, Tex., n.d.

Dabbs, James McBride. *Who Speaks for the South?* New York: Funk and Wagnalls, 1964.

Gillespie, G. T. *A Christian View on Segregation.* Reprint of an Address Made before the Synod of Mississippi of the Presbyterian Church in the U.S., November 4, 1954. Greenwood, Miss.: Citizen's Council, n.d.

Gist, Margaret A., ed. *Presbyterian Women of South Carolina.* N.p.: Woman's Auxiliary of South Carolina, 1929.

Hallie Paxson Winnsborough. Atlanta: Committee on Woman's Work, 1941.

Johnson, Thomas Cary. *A History of the Presbyterian Church South*. American Church History Series, vol. 11. New York: Christian Literature, 1894.

Jones, Joseph S. *The Ku Klux Klan, the NAACP, and the Presbyterian Church*. Burlington, N.C. [ca. 1957].

King, Martin Luther, Jr. *Letter from Birmingham Jail*. N.p.: American Friends Service Committee, 1963.

McGill, Ralph. *The South and the Southerner*. Boston: Little, Brown, 1963.

McNeill, Robert B. *God Wills Us Free: The Ordeal of a Southern Minister*. New York: Hill and Wang, 1965.

Miller, Francis Pickens. *Man from the Valley of Virginia*. Chapel Hill: University of North Carolina Press, 1971.

Presbyterian Church in the United States. *Book of Church Order*. Rev. ed. N.p.: Board of Christian Education of the General Assembly of the Presbyterian Church in the United States, 1961.

————. *A Digest of the Acts and Proceedings of the General Assembly of the Presbyterian Church in the United States, 1861–1965*. Atlanta: Office of the General Assembly, 1966.

Richards, James McDowell. *Change and the Changeless: Articles, Essays, and Sermons*. Decatur, Ga.: Columbia Theological Seminary, 1972.

Rose, Ben Lacy. *Racial Segregation in the Church*. Richmond: Outlook Publishers, 1957.

Shriver, Donald W., Jr. *The Unsilent South: Prophetic Preaching in Racial Crisis*. Richmond: John Knox Press, 1965.

Smith, Morton H. *"How Is the Gold Become Dim" (Lamentations 4:1): The Decline of the Presbyterian Church, U.S., As Reflected in Its Assembly Actions*. 2d ed. Jackson, Miss.: Premier Printing, 1973.

Thomas, Margaret J. *"The Crisis in the Nation": Presbyterian Church, U.S. Involvement*. Richmond: Board of Christian Education, 1968.

Thompson, Ernest Trice. *The Spirituality of the Church*. Richmond: John Knox Press, 1961.

Winnsborough, Hallie Paxson. *The Woman's Auxiliary—Presbyterian Church, U.S.* Richmond: Committee of Publication, 1927.

————. *Yesteryears*. Atlanta: Assembly's Committee on Woman's Work, 1937.

Articles and Sermons

"The Agony of the Church." *Christian Century* 79 (October 10, 1962): 1215–16.

Boggs, Marion A. "Lessons for Pastors Arising out of the Little Rock Crisis." Chapel talk, Columbia Theological Seminary, Decatur, Georgia, ca. fall 1961.

Central Mississippi Presbytery. "The Re-examination of the Reverend A. M. Hart." Transcript, 1964.

Crosby, Isaac. "From Conformity to Transformation." *Presbyterian Survey* 72 (May 1982): 35–36.

Iverson, William T. "It Can Happen Anywhere!" *Presbyterian Survey* 43 (June 1953): 24–26.

King, Martin Luther, Jr. "The Church on the Frontier of Racial Tension." Address at the Christian Action Conference, Montreat, North Carolina, ca. August 12, 1965. Audio tape at the Martin Luther King, Jr., Center for Non-Violent Social Change, Archives and Library, Atlanta.

Lee, Robert. "Social Sources of the Radical Right." *Christian Century* 79 (May 9, 1962): 595–97.

Lingle, Walter L. "What Would Jesus Do?" *Christian Observer* 138 (March 29, 1950): 2–3.

Richards, J. McDowell. "Brothers in Black." In *Change and the Changeless: Articles, Essays, and Sermons.* Decatur, Ga.: Columbia Theological Seminary, 1972.

Smith, Morton H. "The Racial Problem Facing America." *Presbyterian Guardian* 33 (October 1964): 125–68.

Periodicals

Presbyterian in the South 117 (June 10, 1942): 3, 15.

Presbyterian Journal 18–26 (1959–68).

Presbyterian Outlook 126–50 (1946–68).

Presbyterian Survey 52–72 (1962–82).

Southern Presbyterian Journal 1–18 (1942–59).

Secondary Sources

Books

Ahlstrom, Sydney. *A Religious History of the American People.* New Haven: Yale University Press, 1972.

Bailey, Kenneth K. *Southern White Protestantism in the Twentieth Century.* New York: Harper and Row, 1964.

Bartley, Numan V. *The Rise of Massive Resistance: Race and Politics in the South during the 1950's.* Baton Rouge: Louisiana State University Press, 1969.

Brackenridge, R. Douglas, and Francisco O. Garcia-Treto. *Iglesia Presbiteriana: A History of Mexican-Americans in the Southwest.* San Antonio, Tex.: Trinity University Press, 1974.

Campbell, Ernest Q., and Thomas F. Pettigrew. *Christians in Racial Crisis: A Study of Little Rock's Ministry.* Washington, D.C.: Public Affairs Press, 1959.

Carter, Paul. *The Decline and Revival of the Social Gospel: Social and Political Liberalism in American Protestant Churches, 1920–1940.* Ithaca, N.Y.: Cornell University Press, 1954.

Clarke, Erskine. *Wrestlin' Jacob.* Atlanta: John Knox Press, 1978.

Coalter, Milton J, John M. Mulder, and Louis B. Weeks, *The Re-Forming*

Tradition: Presbyterians and Mainstream Protestantism. The Presbyterian Presence. Louisville: Westminster/John Knox Press, 1992.

Cunningham, W. J. _Agony at Galloway._ Jackson: University Press of Mississippi, 1980.

Earle, John R., Dean D. Knudsen, and Donald W. Shriver, Jr. _Spindles and Spires: A Re-Study of Religion and Social Change in Gastonia._ Atlanta: John Knox Press, 1976.

Ely, James W., Jr. _The Crisis of Conservative Virginia: The Byrd Organization and the Politics of Massive Resistance._ Knoxville: University of Tennessee Press, 1976.

Farmer, James Oscar, Jr. _The Metaphysical Confederacy: James Henley Thornwell and the Synthesis of Southern Values._ Macon, Ga.: Mercer University Press, 1986.

Gates, Robbins L. _The Making of Massive Resistance: Virginia's Politics of Public School Desegregation, 1954–1956._ Chapel Hill: University of North Carolina Press, 1962.

Gillespie, Charles Conner. _History of Second Presbyterian Church, Memphis, 1844–1971._ Memphis, Tenn.: Second Presbyterian Church, 1971.

Hadden, Jeffery K. _The Gathering Storm in the Churches._ Garden City, N.Y.: Doubleday, 1969.

Hall, Jacquelyn Dowd. _Revolt against Chivalry: Jessie Daniel Ames and the Women's Campaign against Lynching._ New York: Columbia University Press, 1979.

Hill, Samuel S., Jr. _Southern Churches in Crisis._ New York: Holt, Rinehart and Winston, 1967.

Holifield, Brooks. _The Gentlemen Theologians: American Theology in Southern Culture, 1795–1860._ Durham, N.C.: Duke University Press, 1978.

Kluger, Richard. _Simple Justice: The History of Brown v. Board of Education and Black America's Struggle for Equality._ New York: Alfred A. Knopf, 1976.

Lingle, Walter L., and John W. Kuykendall. _Presbyterians: Their History and Beliefs._ 4th ed. Atlanta: John Knox Press, 1978.

Loescher, Frank S. _The Protestant Church and the Negro._ New York: Association Press, 1948.

Longfield, Bradley J. _The Presbyterian Controversy: Fundamentalists, Modernists, and Moderates._ New York: Oxford University Press, 1991.

McDowell, John P. _The Social Gospel in the South: The Woman's Home Missionary Movement in the Methodist Episcopal Church, South, 1886–1939._ Baton Rouge: Louisiana State University Press, 1982.

Mars, Florence. _Witness at Philadelphia._ Baton Rouge: Louisiana State University Press, 1977.

Marsden, George M. _The Evangelical Mind and the New School Experience._ New Haven: Yale University Press, 1970.

———. _Fundamentalism and American Culture: The Shaping of Twentieth-Century Evangelicalism._ New York: Oxford University Press, 1980.

————. *Understanding Fundamentalism and Evangelicalism.* Grand Rapids, Mich.: William B. Eerdmans Publishing, 1991.

Miller, Robert Moats. *American Protestantism and Social Issues.* Chapel Hill: University of North Carolina Press, 1958.

Morris, Aldon D. *The Origins of the Civil Rights Movement: Black Communities Organizing for Change.* New York: Free Press, 1984.

Murray, Andrew E. *Presbyterians and the Negro—A History.* Philadelphia: Presbyterian Historical Society, 1966.

Muse, Benjamin. *The American Negro Revolution: From Nonviolence to Black Power, 1963–1967.* Bloomington: Indiana University Press, 1968.

Myrdal, Gunnar. *An American Dilemma: The Negro Problem and Modern Democracy.* 2 vols. New York: Pantheon Books, 1972.

Niebuhr, H. Richard. *The Social Sources of Denominationalism.* New York: New American Library, 1975.

Pratt, Henry J. *The Liberalization of American Protestantism: A Case Study in Complex Organization.* Detroit: Wayne State University Press, 1972.

Reimers, David M. *White Protestantism and the Negro.* New York: Oxford University Press, 1965.

Scott, E. C. *Ministerial Directory of the Presbyterian Church, U.S., 1861–1941; Revised and Supplemented, 1942–1950.* Atlanta: Hubbard Printing, 1950.

Shaloff, Stanley. *Reform in Leopold's Congo.* Richmond: John Knox Press, 1970.

Sitkoff, Harvard. *The Struggle for Black Equality, 1954–1980.* New York: Hill and Wang, 1981.

Smith, Frank Joseph. *The History of the Presbyterian Church in America: The Continuing Church Movement.* Manassas, Va.: Reformed Education Foundation, 1985.

Smith, Robert Collins. *They Closed Their Schools: Prince Edward County, Virginia, 1951–1964.* Chapel Hill: University of North Carolina Press, 1965.

Sosna, Morton. *In Search of the Silent South: Southern Liberals and the Race Issue.* New York: Columbia University Press, 1977.

Sprinkle, Patricia Houck. *The Birthday Book: First Fifty Years.* Atlanta: Board of Women's Work, Presbyterian Church in the United States, 1972.

Terry, Paul W., and Tennent Lee. *A Study of Stillman Institute: A Junior College for Negroes.* University: University of Alabama Press, 1946.

Thompson, Ernest Trice. *Presbyterian Missions in the Southern United States.* Richmond: Presbyterian Committee on Publication, 1934.

————. *Presbyterians in the South.* 3 vols. Richmond: John Knox Press, 1963–73.

Tindall, George Brown. *The Emergence of the New South, 1913–1945.* A History of the South, vol. 10. Baton Rouge: Louisiana State University Press, Louisiana Paperbacks, 1970.

Weatherford, Willis D. *American Churches and the Negro: An Historical Study from Earliest Slave Days to Present*. Boston: Christopher Publishing House, 1957.

Wilmore, Gayraud S. *Black and Presbyterian: The Heritage and the Hope*. Philadelphia: Geneva Press, 1983.

Woodward, C. Vann. *The Origins of the New South*. A History of the South, vol. 9. Baton Rouge: Louisiana State University Press, Louisiana Paperbacks, 1971.

———. *The Strange Career of Jim Crow*. 3d rev. ed. New York: Oxford University Press, 1974.

Wuthnow, Robert. *The Restructuring of American Religion: Society and Faith since World War II*. Princeton: Princeton University Press, 1988.

Articles

Alvis, Joel L., Jr. "Racial Turmoil and Religious Reaction: The Rt. Rev. John M. Allin." *Historical Magazine of the Protestant Episcopal Church* 50 (March 1981): 83–96.

Bailey, Kenneth K. "The Post–Civil War Racial Separations in Southern Protestantism: Another Look." *Church History* 46 (December 1977): 453–73.

Blackwelder, Julia Kirk. "Southern White Fundamentalism and the Civil Rights Movement." *Phylon* 40 (December 1979): 334–41.

Dornbusch, Sanford M., and Roger D. Irle. "The Failure of Presbyterian Union." *American Journal of Sociology* 64 (January 1959): 352–55.

Flynt, J. Wayne. "Dissent in Zion: Alabama Baptists and Social Issues, 1900–1914." *Journal of Southern History* 35 (November 1969): 523–42.

———. "Feeding the Hungry and Ministering to the Broken-Hearted: The Presbyterian Church in the United States and the Social Gospel, 1900–1920." In *Religion in the South*, ed. Charles Reagan Wilson, pp. 83–138. Jackson: University Press of Mississippi, 1985.

———. "One in the Spirit, Many in the Flesh: Southern Evangelicals." In *Varieties of Southern Evangelicalism*, ed. Edwin Harrell, pp. 21–44. Macon, Ga.: Mercer University Press, 1981.

Furlow, Frances. "Gentleman from South Carolina." *Presbyterian Survey* 56 (October 1966): 20–23.

Hadden, Jeffery K. "Clergy Involvement in Civil Rights." *Annals of the American Academy of Political and Social Science* 387 (January 1970): 118–27.

Hobson, Fred. "James McBride Dabbs: Isaac McCaslin in South Carolina." *Virginia Quarterly Review* 53 (Autumn 1977): 640–59.

Kuykendall, John W. "Presbyterians in the South Revisited—A Critique." *Journal of Presbyterian History* 61 (Winter 1983): 445–59.

Leith, John Haddon. "Ernest Trice Thompson . . . Churchman." In *Ernest Trice Thompson: An Appreciation*. Richmond: Union Theological Seminary, n.d.

Maddex, Jack P. "From Theocracy to Spirituality: The Southern Presbyterian Reversal on Church and State." *Journal of Presbyterian History* 54 (Winter 1976): 438–58.

Mathews, Donald. "Charles Colcock Jones and the Southern Evangelical Crusade to Form a Biracial Community." *Journal of Southern History* 41 (August 1975): 299–320.

Miller, Robert Moats. "The Attitude of American Protestantism toward the Negro, 1919–1939." In *The Negro in Depression and War: Prelude to Revolution*, ed. Bernard Sternsher, pp. 106–26. Chicago: Quadrangle Books, 1969.

———. "Southern White Protestantism and the Negro, 1865–1965." In *The Negro in the South since 1865: Selected Essays in American History*, ed. Charles E. Wynes. Southern Historical Publication no. 10. University: University of Alabama Press, 1965.

Mounger, Dwyn M. "Racial Attitudes in the Presbyterian Church in the United States." *Journal of Presbyterian History* 48 (Winter 1970): 38–58.

Mulder, John M., and Lee A. Wyatt. "The Predicament of Pluralism: A Study of Theology in Presbyterian Seminaries since the 1920s." In *The Pluralistic Vision: Presbyterians and Mainstream Protestant Education and Leadership*, ed. Milton J Coalter, John M. Mulder, and Louis B. Weeks, pp. 37–70. The Presbyterian Presence. Louisville: Westminster/John Knox Press, 1992.

Nutt, Rick. "The Tie That No Longer Binds: The Origins of the Presbyterian Church in America." In *The Confessional Mosaic: Presbyterians and Twentieth Century Theology*, ed. Milton J Coalter, John M. Mulder, and Louis B. Weeks, pp. 236–56. The Presbyterian Presence. Louisville: Westminster/John Knox Press, 1990.

Orser, W. Edward. "Racial Attitudes in Wartime: The Protestant Churches during the Second World War." *Church History* 41 (September 1972): 337–53.

Pratt, Henry J. "The Growth of Political Activism in the National Council of Churches." *Review of Politics* 34 (July 1972): 323–41.

Reimers, David M. "The Race Problem and Presbyterian Union." *Church History* 31 (June 1962): 203–15.

Smylie, James H. "The Bible, Race, and the Changing South." *Journal of Presbyterian History* 59 (Summer 1981): 197–217.

Staiger, C. Bruce. "Abolitionism and the Presbyterian Schism of 1837–1838." *Mississippi Valley Historical Review* 36 (December 1950): 395–414.

Thompson, Ernest Trice. "Black Presbyterians: Education and Evangelism after the Civil War." *Journal of Presbyterian History* 51 (Summer 1973): 174–98.

Wilmore, Gayraud S., Jr. "Identity and Integration: Black Presbyterians and Their Allies in the Twentieth Century." In *The Presbyterian Predica-*

ment: Six Perspectives, ed. Milton J Coalter, John M. Mulder, and Louis B. Weeks, pp. 109–33. The Presbyterian Presence. Louisville: Westminster/John Knox Press, 1990.

———. "The 'New Negro' and the Protestant Churches." In *Freedom Now: The Civil Rights Struggle in America,* ed. Alan F. Westin, pp. 302–6. New York: Basic Books, 1964.

Wuthnow, Robert. "The Restructuring of American Presbyterianism: Turmoil in One Denomination." In *The Presbyterian Predicament: Six Perspectives,* ed. Milton J Coalter, John M. Mulder, and Louis B. Weeks, pp. 27–48. The Presbyterian Presence. Louisville: Westminster/John Knox Press, 1990.

Unpublished Sources

Alston, Wallace McPherson. "A History of Young People's Work in the Presbyterian Church in the United States (1861–1938)." Th.D. diss., Union Theological Seminary in Virginia, 1943.

Barry, Sara. "The Role of the Presbyterian Church in the United States in a Segregated Society." M.R.E. thesis, Biblical Seminary in New York, 1955.

Blackwelder, Julia Kirk. "Fundamentalist Reactions to the Civil Rights Movement to 1969." Ph.D. diss., Emory University, 1972.

Boles, John. "Religion in the South: Recent Historiography." Paper given at the Southern Historical Association, Memphis, Tennessee, November 6, 1982.

Ellis, Ann Wells. "The Commission on Interracial Cooperation, 1919–1944: Its Activities and Results." Ph.D. diss., Georgia State University, 1975.

Freundt, Albert H., Jr. "An Approach to Open and Honest Political Decision Making in the Presbytery of Central Mississippi in Connection with the Vote on Presbyterian Reunion." D.Min. major project, McCormick Theological Seminary, 1984.

Howard, Victor B. "The Anti-Slavery Movement in the Presbyterian Church, 1835–1861." Ph.D. diss., Ohio State University, 1961.

Johnson, Thomas Lindeman. "James McBride Dabbs—a Life Story." Ph.D. diss., University of South Carolina, 1980.

Mellin, Willard C. "Theological and Non-theological Factors in the Development of Policy and Action of the United Presbyterian Church Regarding the Negro, 1900–1965." Ph.D. diss., Union Theological Seminary, New York, 1975.

Moore, Kathleen L. "John Haddon Leith: The Auburn Years." Paper for Dr. W. David Lewis, Auburn University, May 30, 1980. Copy in the author's possession.

Morris, Aldon D. "The Rise of the Civil Rights Movement and the Movement's Black Power Structure, 1953–1963." Ph.D. diss., State University of New York at Stony Brook, 1979.

Mounger, Dwight Mecklin. "Racial Attitudes in the Presbyterian Church, U.S., 1944–1954." B.D. thesis, Princeton Theological Seminary, 1965.

Schlundt, Ronald. "Civil Rights Policies in the Eisenhower Years." Ph.D. diss., Rice University, 1973.

Sherman, Billy Don. "The Ideology of American Segregationism." Th.D. diss., Southwestern Baptist Theological Seminary, 1966.

Sikes, William Marion. "The Historical Development of Stillman Institute." M.A. thesis, University of Alabama, 1930.

Smith, Donald B. "Black Ministers, Presbyterian Church, U.S., with an Update on Black Churches." Tuscaloosa, Ala., Stillman College Office of Institutional Planning, November 5, 1975.

Spence, Thomas Hugh, Jr. "The Southern Presbyterian Church and the Spirituality of the Church." S.T.D. thesis, Biblical Seminary in New York, 1929.

Taylor, Charlotte A. "A Study of the Contribution of the Presbyterian Church in the United States to the Life of the Negro Woman of the South." M.R.E. thesis, Biblical Seminary in New York, 1938.

INDEX

Afro-American Presbyterian Church, 14–15
Alabama, Synod of, 23, 32, 57–58, 89, 91–93, 98, 122
Alabama Experiment, 80
Alabama Polytechnic Institute, 88–89
Alexander, James J., 26–27
Anderson, John, 125, 127, 128, 139
Anderson, Robert C., 84
Appalachia, Synod of, 122
Assembly Training School, 33
Association of Southern Women for the Prevention of Lynching, 7, 80
Atlanta, Georgia, 104, 105, 106; North Avenue Presbyterian Church, 123–24
Atlanta Manifesto, 106–107
Auburn, Alabama, 43, 58, 59, 88–89; First Presbyterian Church, 58, 89, 124
Auburn Affirmation, 61
Augusta, Georgia: 1861 General Assembly, 133
Augusta-Macon Presbytery (Georgia), 93

Bainbridge, Georgia: First Presbyterian Church, 114
Baltimore, Maryland: Franklin Street Presbyterian Church, 135
Baptists, 5–6, 13, 37
Barfield, Emmett, 98
Barker, Frank, 132
Barth, Karl, 144
Batchelor, Alexander R., 17, 19–22, 27–28
Baton Rouge, Louisiana: 1953 bus boycott, 8–9
Beaumont, Texas: Pioneer Presbyterian Church, 34
Belhaven College, 90–91, 150 (n. 33)
Bell, L. Nelson, 51–53, 132, 161 (n. 19)
Biblical references:
—Genesis (9:18–27), 53; (11:1–9), 53; (27:46–28:4), 54
—Deuteronomy (7:2–3), 54
—Isaiah (2:2–4), 55
—Micah (4:1–4), 55
—Matthew (ch. 25), 125
—Acts (ch. 5), 118; (ch. 10), 55, 161–62 n. 27, (17:22–31), 2, 54
Billy Graham Evangelistic Association, 98
Birmingham, Alabama, 75, 80–81, 110–11; Westminster Presbyterian Church, 36; South Highland Presbyterian Church, 57–58; First Presbyterian Church, 64; Briarwood Presbyterian Church, 133
Birmingham Presbytery (Alabama), 36, 89, 93
Birthday Offering: and Stillman College, 43
Black Manifesto, 130
Black Power, 123
Black Presbyterian Leadership Caucus, 128–30, 137–39
Blake, Eugene Carson, 72
Blue, Mary M., 81
Boggs, Marion, 64, 69, 107
Bottoms, Lawrence W., 17, 25–28, 36, 86, 99, 137
Bouchelion, William, 1
Boyce, J. H. M., 91
Brazos Presbytery (Texas), 33, 89, 91
Breckenridge, Robert J., 4
Brown v. Board of Education, 8–9, 19, 21, 44, 54, 57, 59, 63, 91, 100, 105
Broyles, Vernon, 86

Calhoun, Malcolm, 113
Campbell, Ernest Q., 109
Central Alabama Presbyterial, 82
Central Alabama Presbytery, 14–15, 23, 36, 91
Central Louisiana Presbytery, 1
Central Mississippi Presbytery, 36, 63, 66–68, 89–90, 93, 96, 137, 164 (n. 58), 165 (n. 62)
Chapel Hill, North Carolina, 64–65
Charleston, South Carolina: First Scots Presbyterian Church, 114
Charlotte, North Carolina, 109–10, 128
Chauncey, George, 123
Chester, South Carolina, 14
Christian Action, Division of, 113
Christian Century, 12, 59
Christian Education, Board of, 38, 74, 91, 93, 109, 115
Christian Relations: Committee on, 104; Division of, 105
Church Extension, Board of, 25, 27, 34, 38, 43, 91, 99, 118, 119
church union, 60–63, 148 (n. 15). *See also* reunion
civil disobedience, 70–72
Civil Rights Act of 1964, the, 9, 71, 120

About the Author

Joel L. Alvis, Jr., is Pastor of the St. Pauls Presbyterian Church, St. Pauls, North Carolina. He received the M.Div. from Louisville Presbyterian Theological Seminary and the Ph.D. in American History from Auburn University. A former staff member of the Presbyterian Church (U.S.A.), Department of History, he participated in the Presbyterian Presence study conducted through Louisville Seminary.